SOME ACCOUNT

OF THE

WRITINGS AND OPINIONS

OF

JUSTIN MARTYR.

SOME ACCOUNT

OF THE

WRITINGS AND OPINIONS

OF

JUSTIN MARTYR.

BY

JOHN, BISHOP OF LINCOLN.

SECOND EDITION, REVISED.

WIPF & STOCK · Eugene, Oregon

Wipf and Stock Publishers
199 W 8th Ave, Suite 3
Eugene, OR 97401

Some Account of the Writings and Opinions
of Justin Martyr; Second Edition, Revised
By Kaye, John
Softcover ISBN-13: 978-1-6667-0499-0
Hardcover ISBN-13: 978-1-6667-0500-3
eBook ISBN-13: 978-1-6667-0501-0
Publication date 3/9/2021
Previously published by J. G. & F. Rivingtons, 1836

This edition is a scanned facsimile
of the original edition published in 1836.

ADVERTISEMENT

TO THE SECOND EDITION

BESIDES other additions, the Reader will find in this Edition, at page 20, note 3, an Examination of Wetstein's objections to the genuineness of the Dialogue with Trypho: and at page 184, note 2, Remarks on Beausobre's Comment on a remarkable passage of Tatian.

CONTENTS.

CHAPTER I.
On the Writings of Justin Martyr .... PAGE 1

CHAPTER II.
The Opinions of Justin respecting the Λόγος, and the Trinity 46

CHAPTER III.
Justin's opinions respecting original sin, the freedom of the will, grace, justification, predestination 75

CHAPTER IV.
Justin's opinions respecting Baptism and the Eucharist, with a particular reference to a passage in the first Apology 84

CHAPTER V.
The immortality of the soul—the resurrection of the body—the Millennium—future judgment—angels—dæmons .. 99

CHAPTER VI.
The condition of the Christians in the time of Justin; and the causes of the rapid diffusion of Christianity 112

CHAPTER VII.

The heresies mentioned by Justin—Miscellaneous observations... 125

CHAPTER VIII.

An examination of the question, whether Justin quoted the Gospels which we now have?..................... 132

CHAPTER IX.

Containing illustrations of the preceding Chapters from the writings of Tatian, Athenagoras, and Theophilus of Antioch, with additional remarks..................... 153

The following Pages contain the substance of part of a Course of Lectures, delivered at Cambridge, in the Lent Term of 1821.

SOME ACCOUNT OF THE WRITINGS

OF

JUSTIN MARTYR.

CHAPTER I.

ON THE WRITINGS OF JUSTIN MARTYR.

How strenuous soever men may be in maintaining that no regard ought to be paid to authority in the determination of disputed points, and that our conclusions ought to rest solely on the convictions of our own reason, few, even of those who are loudest in asserting the unlimited liberty of private judgment, are found to possess such undoubting confidence in the correctness of their own decisions, as not gladly to avail themselves of every opportunity of showing, that the same opinions have previously received the sanction of others. With respect to questions which have long occupied the attention of mankind, and of which it is consequently reasonable to suppose that they have already been viewed in all their bearings, we cannot but feel that the novelty of an opinion is *primâ facie* a presumption against its truth. That, if at all deserving of attention, it should never have occurred to the minds of former inquirers is improbable: the fair inference, therefore, is, that they knew, but rejected it, because they were satisfied of its unsoundness. On the subject of Religion, there appears to be a peculiar propriety in appealing to the opinions of past ages. In human science we find a regular advance from less to greater degrees of knowledge. Truth is elicited by the labours of successive inquirers; each adds something to the stock of facts which have been previously accumulated; and, as new discoveries are continually made, the crude notions of those who first engaged in the pursuit are discarded for more matured and more enlarged views. The most recent opinions are those which are most likely to be correct. But, in the case of a Divine Revelation, this tentative process can have no place. They, to whom is committed the trust of communicating it to others, are thoroughly instructed in its nature and its objects—and possess a knowledge which no inquiries of subsequent ages can improve. What they deliver is the truth itself; which cannot be rendered more pure, though it may, and too probably will be adulterated in its transmission to succeeding generations. The greater the distance from the fountain-head, the greater the chance that the stream will be polluted. On these considerations is founded the persuasion which has generally prevailed, that, in order to ascertain what was the doctrine taught by the Apostles, and what is the true interpretation of their writings, we ought to have recourse to the authority of those who lived nearest to their times. In all the controversies which have taken place on the subject of Religion, we find each party anxious to show that Christian antiquity is on its side; and so long as this anxiety subsists, the writings of the early Fathers will continue to be read with attention and interest.

Among the Fathers, Justin Martyr is the earliest, of whose works we possess any considerable remains. He marks the commencement of what may be termed the Ecclesiastical, in contradistinction from the Apostolic period. Hence, the care with which his opinions have been examined, and the importance which has been attached to them. One party appeals to him as expressing the sentiments of the primitive Christians, on some of the fundamental Articles of our Faith; while another regards him as having exerted a most fatal influence over the interests of Religion, by introducing into the Church a confused medley of Christianity and Platonism, to the exclusion of the pure and simple truths of the Gospel. The object of the present work is to enable the Theological Student to pronounce between these contradictory representations, by laying before him an accurate account of Justin's opinions.

It is not my intention to engage in the discussion of the different hypotheses which have been framed respecting the Chronology of Justin's life. The data are too few and too uncertain to justify us in coming to any decided conclusion. We know [1] from himself that he was born at Flavia Neapolis, in Samaria, [2] of Gentile parents; and we are told by [3] Eusebius, who refers to Tatian, Justin's scholar, that he suffered martyrdom at Rome, in the [4] reign of Marcus Antoninus. One important circumstance, from its connexion with the history of his opinions, is, that [5] he had carefully studied the

---

[1] Apol. I. sub initio. See also Apol. II. p. 52 A. Dial. p. 349 C. Ed. Paris. 1636. to which the references in this work will be made.

[2] ἑαυτοὺς ἡμᾶς ὁρῶντες πλείονάς τε καὶ ἀληθεστέρους τοὺς ἐξ ἐθνῶν τῶν ἀπὸ Ἰουδαίων καὶ Σαμαρέων Χριστιανοὺς (εἰδότες). Apol. I. p. 88 B. See also Dial. p. 226 A. 245 C. 348 C. 351 D.

[3] Eccl. Hist. L. iv. c. 16. Tatian, Oratio ad Græcos, p. 157 D. Ed. Par. 1636.

[4] See also Jerome in Catalogo. Dodwell, Diss. iii. in Irenæum, §. 19. Diss. iv. §. 34. supposes him to have suffered martyrdom in the year 149, at the age of thirty; this inference he draws from an account, manifestly erroneous, given by Epiphanius, Hær. 26 or 46.

[5] See the commencement of the Dialogue with Trypho; and with respect to the Platonists, Apol. II. p. 50 A.

tenets of the different philosophical Sects; having successively attached himself to the Stoics, the Peripatetics, the Pythagoreans, and the Platonists. To the last he manifestly gave the preference; but, not deriving from any of them the entire satisfaction which he had expected, he was induced to examine, and, having examined, to embrace Christianity; finding it, as he himself states, [1] the only sound and useful philosophy. He appears, however, after his conversion, to have retained a fondness for his former pursuits, which he evinced [2] by continuing to wear the philosophic habit.

Of the works printed in the Paris edition, it is now generally admitted, that the Confutation of certain Tenets of Aristotle, the Christian Questions to the Greeks, the Greek Questions to the Christians, the Answers to the Orthodox, the Exposition of the True Faith respecting the Trinity, the Epistle to Diognetus, and the Epistle to Zenas and Serenus, were not composed by Justin. The following circumstances induce me also to entertain

---

[1] ταύτην μόνην εὕρισκον φιλοσοφίαν ἀσφαλῆ τε καὶ σύμφορον. p. 225 C. Justin gives an interesting account of the manner in which he was induced to study the Prophetic Writings, by the arguments of an aged man, whom he accidentally met on the sea-shore, p. 219 E. and to whom he appears to allude, p. 241 B. κηρύξω ἐγὼ θεῖον λόγον, ὃν παρ᾽ ἐκείνου ἤκουσα τοῦ ἀνδρός.

[2] Dialog. cum Tryph. p. 217 B. C.

doubts respecting the genuineness of the Hortatory Address to the Greeks. In p. 20 B [1], where the Author is endeavouring to show that Plato, having met with the writings of Moses in Egypt, had embraced the doctrine of the Divine Unity, but was deterred from openly declaring his sentiments, by dread of encountering the same fate which befel Socrates, he mentions the appearance of God to Moses out of the burning bush, and speaks as if God had himself appeared; whereas Justin, not only in his Dialogue with Trypho, where he might be supposed to hold a different language from that in which he addressed the Gentiles, but in [2] his first Apology, maintains that it was Christ, who, on that occasion, appeared to Moses. The account also of the origin of Polytheism, which is given in p. 19 D, does not correspond with the statement in the second Apology. In the [3] former passage, we are told that the Serpent,

---

[1] εἰδὼς τοίνυν ὁ Θεὸς τὴν τῆς πολυθεότητος μὴ ἀληθῆ δόξαν ὥσπερ τινὰ νόσον τῇ τῶν ἀνθρώπων ἐνοχλοῦσαν ψυχῇ, ἀνελεῖν καὶ ἀνατρέψαι βουλόμενος, πρῶτον μὲν τῷ Μωσῇ φανεὶς, ἔφη πρὸς αὐτὸν, ἐγώ εἰμι ὁ ὤν. ἔδει γὰρ, οἶμαι, τὸν ἄρχοντα καὶ στρατηγὸν τοῦ τῶν Ἑβραίων γένους ἔσεσθαι μέλλοντα πρῶτον ἁπάντων τὸν ὄντα γιγνώσκειν Θεόν. διὸ καὶ τούτῳ πρώτῳ φανεὶς, ὡς ἦν δυνατὸν ἀνθρώπῳ φανῆναι Θεὸν, ἔφη πρὸς αὐτὸν, ἐγώ εἰμι ὁ ὤν.

[2] p. 96 B.

[3] See also p. 34 C. 36 C. In p. 32 B, the Author says, that the Heathen were induced to represent their Gods under human forms, by the statement in the Book of Genesis, that God made

when he assured our first Parents that if they ate of the fruit of the tree of knowledge, they should be as Gods, impressed them with the persuasion that there were other Gods besides the Creator of heaven and earth; and that they, retaining this persuasion after their expulsion from Paradise, transmitted it to their posterity. But in [1] the latter passage the statement is, that the Angels, to whom God had committed the superintendence of this lower world, transgressing his commands, became connected with women; and that from this intercourse sprang Dæmons, who were the authors of Idolatry and Polytheism. The accounts of the Septuagint translation in p. 13 D. and in the first Apology p. 72 C. do not appear to me to have proceeded from the same pen; and in [2] p. 21 C. the author of

man in his own likeness after his image, from which they inferred that man is in form like unto God; τῆς γὰρ Μωσέως ἱστορίας ἐκ προσώπου τοῦ Θεοῦ λεγούσης, ποιήσωμεν ἄνθρωπον κατ' εἰκόνα κ. τ. ἑ. See also p. 36 C. Compare this with the mode in which the same text is applied in the Dialogue with Trypho, p. 285 A. In the Fragment of the Tract on the Resurrection, ascribed to Justin, the Author applies this Text to the fleshly man, ἦ γὰρ οὐ φησὶν ὁ λόγος· ποιήσωμεν ἄνθρωπον κατ' εἰκόνα ἡμετέραν, καὶ καθ' ὁμοίωσιν; ποῖον; δηλονότι σαρκικὸν λέγει ἄνθρωπον. Grabe Spicil. T. II. p. 187.

[1] p. 44 A. Compare Apol. I. p. 55 E. 67 D. 69 C.

[2] καίτοι πολλῆς διαφορᾶς ἐν τούτοις οὔσης, κατὰ τὴν αὐτοῦ Πλάτωνος δόξαν. ὁ μὲν γὰρ ποιητὴς, οὐδενὸς ἑτέρου προσδεόμενος, ἐκ τῆς ἑαυτοῦ δυνάμεως καὶ ἐξουσίας ποιεῖ τὸ ποιούμενον· ὁ δὲ δημιουργὸς, τὴν τῆς δημιουργίας δύναμιν ἐκ τῆς ὕλης εἰληφὼς, κατασκευάζει τὸ γιγνόμενον.

the Hortatory Address makes after Plato a distinction between ποιητὴς and δημιουργὸς—words which Justin uses[1] indiscriminately. To evade the inference drawn from these discrepancies, it may be said that Bishop Bull (Def. Fid. Nic. Sect. 3. C. 2.) has pointed out a coincidence of sentiment in this work and in the second Apology. The Author of the [2] former says of Plato, that "having heard in Egypt that God, when he sent Moses to the Hebrews, said ἐγώ εἰμι ὁ ὤν, he (Plato) knew that God had not declared his proper name; since no proper name can be assigned to God. For names are given for the purpose of describing and distinguishing things, inasmuch as they are many and various. But no one existed before God, who could give him a name; nor did he deem it right to give himself a name,

[1] Thus Apol. I. p. 57 A. μετὰ Θεοῦ τοῦ πάντων πατρὸς καὶ δημιουργοῦ. And p. 66 C. τὸν πάντων ποιητὴν Θεόν. See also p. 60 C. 66 E. 70 A. B. 92 A.

[2] ἀκηκοὼς γὰρ ἐν Αἰγύπτῳ τὸν Θεὸν τῷ Μωσῇ εἰρηκέναι, ἐγώ ιμι ὁ ὤν, ὁπηνίκα πρὸς τοὺς Ἑβραίους αὐτὸν ἀποστέλλειν ἔμελλεν, ἔγνω ὅτι οὐ κύριον ὄνομα ἑαυτοῦ ὁ Θεὸς πρὸς αὐτὸν ἔφη· οὐδὲν γὰρ ὄνομα ἐπὶ Θεοῦ κυριολογεῖσθαι δυνατόν. τὰ γὰρ ὀνόματα εἰς δήλωσιν καὶ διάγνωσιν τῶν ὑποκειμένων κεῖται πραγμάτων, πολλῶν καὶ διαφόρων ὄντων· Θεῷ δὲ οὔτε ὁ τιθεὶς ὄνομα προυπῆρχεν, οὔτε αὐτὸς ἑαυτὸν ὀνομάζειν ᾠήθη δεῖν, εἷς καὶ μόνος ὑπάρχων, ὡς αὐτὸς διὰ τῶν ἑαυτοῦ προφητῶν μαρτυρεῖ λέγων, ἐγὼ Θεὸς πρῶτος καὶ ἐγὼ μετὰ ταῦτα, καὶ πλὴν ἐμοῦ Θεὸς ἕτερος οὐκ ἔστι. διὰ τοῦτο τοίνυν, ὡς καὶ πρότερον ἔφην, οὐδὲ ὀνόματός τινος ὁ Θεὸς ἀποστέλλων πρὸς τοὺς Ἑβραίους τὸν Μωσέα μέμνηται, ἀλλὰ διά τινος μετοχῆς ἕνα καὶ μόνον Θεὸν ἑαυτὸν εἶναι μυστικῶς διδάσκει, ἐγὼ γάρ, φησίν, εἰμι ὁ ὤν. p. 19 B.

inasmuch as he is one and alone; as he himself testifies through his Prophets, saying, I God am the first, and I am the last, and besides me is no other God. (Is. xliv. 6.) On this account, therefore, as I said before, God, when he sent Moses to the Hebrews, did not mention any name; but mystically declared himself to be the one and only God, by means of a participle, ἐγὼ γάρ, φησίν, εἰμι ὁ ὤν." With this passage Bull compares one in the [1] second Apology, to which reference will hereafter be made, and which is as follows: " But no name has been given to the Father of all things, inasmuch as he is unbegotten; for by whatever name any one is called, he must be posterior to him who gave the name: and Father, God, Creator, Lord, Master, are not names, but appellations given from his benefits and works. But his Son, who alone is properly called Son, the Word, who was with him before the Creation, and begotten when in the beginning he created and adorned all

---

[1] ὄνομα δὲ τῷ πάντων πατρὶ θετὸν, ἀγεννήτῳ ὄντι, οὐκ ἔστιν· ᾧ γὰρ ἂν καὶ ὀνόματι (f. ὀνόματί τις) προσαγορεύηται, πρεσβύτερον ἔχει τὸν θέμενον τὸ ὄνομα· τὸ δὲ Πατὴρ, καὶ Θεὸς, καὶ Κτίστης, καὶ Κύριος, καὶ Δεσπότης, οὐκ ὀνόματά ἐστιν, ἀλλ' ἐκ τῶν εὐποιιῶν καὶ τῶν ἔργων προσρήσεις. ὁ δὲ υἱὸς ἐκείνου, ὁ μόνος λεγόμενος κυρίως υἱὸς, ὁ λόγος πρὸ τῶν ποιημάτων καὶ συνὼν καὶ γεννώμενος, ὅτε τὴν ἀρχὴν δι' αὐτοῦ πάντα ἔκτισε καὶ ἐκόσμησε, Χριστὸς μὲν, κατὰ τὸ κεχρίσθαι καὶ κοσμῆσαι τὰ πάντα δι' αὐτοῦ τὸν Θεὸν, λέγεται, ὄνομα καὶ αὐτὸ περιέχον ἄγνωστον σημασίαν. ὃν τρόπον καὶ τὸ Θεὸς προσαγόρευμα οὐκ ὄνομά ἐστιν, ἀλλὰ πράγματος δυσεξηγήτου ἔμφυτος τῇ φύσει τῶν ἀνθρώπων δόξα. p. 44 D. Compare Apol. I. p. 58 B. 94 D.

things by him, is called Christ, because he was anointed, and because God adorned all things by him; a name which also contains in itself an unknown signification: like as the appellation Θεὸς is not a name, but the notion of an ineffable thing, implanted in the nature of men." Between these passages there is undoubtedly one point of coincidence; in both it is said, that no name could be given to God; because no one existed before God to give the name. But here the coincidence ends. We have already observed the discrepancy respecting the Divine Person who appeared to Moses. We may add, that the word κυριολογεῖσθαι is used in the former passage in a sense totally different from that in which Justin uses it [1] in the Dialogue with Trypho, where it signifies *to apply the title κύριος to Christ*. These circumstances, though minute, appear to me to confirm the suspicions respecting the spuriousness of the work which [2] Dupin seems to have

[1] P. 277 B. ὅτι καὶ παρὰ τὸν νοούμενον ποιητὴν τῶν ὅλων ἄλλος τὶς κυριολογεῖται ὑπὸ τοῦ ἁγίου πνεύματος. Compare also the use of the word θεολογεῖν in the Hortatory Address, p. 20 E, where it signifies *to discourse on divine things, to play the Theologian*, and in the Dialogue with Trypho, p. 277 C, where it signifies to apply the title Θεὸς to Christ, εἰ οὖν καὶ ἄλλον τινὰ θεολογεῖν καὶ κυριολογεῖν τὸ πνεῦμα τὸ ἅγιον φατὲ ὑμεῖς. It is used, however, in the former sense, p. 340 B. ἀλλὰ διὰ τί μὲν ἐν ἄλφα πρώτῳ προσετέθη τῷ Ἀβραὰμ ὀνόματι θεολογεῖς.

[2] Bibliothèque, Tom. I. p. 58. Casimir Oudin also expressed doubts respecting the genuineness of the work. De Script. Eccl.

formed from the difference between the style and that of Justin's acknowledged writings. I shall, therefore, in the following pages, confine my references to the two Apologies and to the Dialogue with Trypho; the Fragment of the Treatise περὶ μοναρχίας, and the Address to the Greeks, whether genuine or not, affording nothing which can assist me in the prosecution of my present design.

The first Apology, which stands second in the Paris edition, was addressed to Antoninus Pius, Marcus Antoninus, Lucius Verus, the Senate, and the People of Rome. Authors differ respecting the date. Justin, in the course of the work, speaks of Christ as having been born [1] one hundred and fifty years before, evidently using round numbers. There are allusions to the [2] death and deification of Antinous, as to events which had recently occurred; as well as to the [3] revolt of Barchochebas and the [4] decree of Adrian, by which the Jews were forbidden to set foot in Jerusalem under pain of death. These notices, however, will not assist us in determining the precise year in which the Treatise was

---

Tom. I. p. 187. His arguments are stated by the Benedictine Editors in their Preface, where the reader will also find their reasons for believing the work to be the same as that mentioned by Eusebius under the title of ἔλεγχος.

[1] p. 83 B.   [2] p. 72 A.
[3] p. 72 E.   [4] p. 84 B.

composed.[1] Dodwell supposed it to have been written in the very commencement of the reign of Antoninus Pius, before Marcus Antoninus received the appellation of Cæsar, because he is not designated by that title in the Introduction; but many Critics, among them the Benedictine editors, place it as late as 150.—The Treatise itself highly deserves our attention, as the earliest specimen which has reached our times of the mode in which the Christians defended the cause of their Religion. It is not remarkable for the lucid arrangement of the materials of which it is composed; its contents, however, may be reduced to the following heads. I. [2]Appeals to the justice of the ruling powers, and expostulations with them on the unfairness of the proceedings against the Christians, who were condemned without any previous investigation into their lives or opinions, merely because they were Christians; and were denied the liberty allowed to all the other subjects of the Roman Empire, of worshipping the God whom they themselves preferred.

---

[1] Diss. III. in Irenæum, § 14. See the Prolegomena to the Bibliotheca Veterum Patrum; Venice, 1775. Tom. I. c. 17. Sect. 1.

[2] Sub in. 54 D. 56 E. 68 D. Justin plays upon the words Χριστὸς and χρηστὸς, p. 55 A. He contends that the evil lives of some professing themselves Christians ought not to be urged as an argument against Christianity itself: inasmuch as the same argument might be urged with still greater force against Philosophy. 55 B. 56 C

II. ¹ Refutations of the charges of Atheism, Immorality, Disaffection towards the Emperor, which were brought against the Christians; these charges Justin refutes by appealing to the purity of the Gospel-precepts, and to the amelioration produced in the conduct of those who embraced Christianity; and by stating that the kingdom, to which Christians looked forward, was not of this world, but a heavenly kingdom. III. Direct arguments in proof of the truth of Christianity, drawn from Miracles and Prophecy. ² With respect to the former, Justin principally occupies himself in refuting the objection, that the Miracles of Christ were performed by Magical Arts. With respect to the latter, he states in ³ forcible terms the general nature of the argument from Prophecy, and shows the accomplishment of many particular ⁴Prophecies in the person of

¹ p. 56 B. 70 B. 58 E. 59 A. 60 C. 61 B. 64 C. 78 B. Apol. II. p. 51 B. In the second passage Justin seems to insinuate that the charges of gross sensuality and cruelty, which were falsely alleged against the orthodox, might possibly be truly alleged against the heretics. See Dodwell, Diss. in Iren. IV. § 26.

² p. 72 A.

³ p. 88 A. τίνι γὰρ ἂν λόγῳ ἀνθρώπῳ σταυρωθέντι ἐπειθόμεθα, ὅτι πρωτότοκος τῷ ἀγεννήτῳ Θεῷ ἐστι, καὶ αὐτὸς τὴν κρίσιν τοῦ παντὸς ἀνθρωπείου γένους ποιήσεται, εἰ μὴ μαρτύρια, πρὶν ἢ ἐλθεῖν αὐτὸν ἄνθρωπον γενόμενον, κεκηρυγμένα περὶ αὐτοῦ εὕρομεν; κ. τ. ἑ. See p. 60 A. 72 B. and some remarks on the interpretation of Prophecy, 76 D. Dial. cum. Tryph. p. 341 C.

⁴ Among the Prophecies specified are Genesis c. xlix. Psalm i. iii. xix. xxii. xcvi. cx. Isaiah i. ii. vii. ix. xi. xxxv. l. liii. lxiv. lxv. Micah v. Zechariah ix. See from page 73 to 87.

Jesus: [1] inferring, from their accomplishment, the reasonableness of entertaining a firm persuasion that the Prophecies, yet unfulfilled—that, for instance, respecting Christ's second Advent—will in due time be accomplished. IV. [2] Justin does not confine himself to defending Christianity, but occasionally becomes the assailant, and exposes with success the absurdities of the Gentile Polytheism and Idolatry. In further confirmation of the innocuous, or rather beneficial character of Christianity, [3] Justin concludes the Treatise with a description of the mode in which Proselytes were admitted into the Church, of its other rites and customs, and of the habits and manner of life of the primitive Christians. At the end of this Treatise, in the Paris edition, is found a rescript of Adrian in favour of the Christians, as translated by [4] Eusebius, from the Latin. Justin alludes to such a document towards the conclusion of the Apology, and its genuineness is generally admitted. There is moreover an [5] Edict, addressed by Antoninus Pius to the Com-

---

[1] p. 87 A.

[2] p. 57 C, where Justin speaks of the immoral lives of the Artisans who were employed in making Idols. 58 A. 67 A. In p. 93 D. Justin observes that the most unlearned Christians were well instructed in the knowledge of divine things.

[3] p. 93 D.

[4] Eccl. Hist. L. iv. c. 9

[5] See Lardner's Heathen Testimonies, c. 14. He defends its genuineness.

mon Council of Asia, respecting which doubts are entertained; and a letter of Marcus Antoninus to the Senate of Rome, ascribing his victory during the German War to the prayers of the Christian soldiers in his army. This letter is manifestly spurious.

According to [1] Eusebius, the second Apology was presented to Marcus Antoninus; but Pearson, and after him Thirlby, thought that it was addressed, as well as the former, to Antoninus Pius, relying on the passage in p. 43 B. οὐ πρέποντα εὐσεβεῖ αὐτοκράτορι οὐδὲ φιλοσόφου Καίσαρος παιδὶ, οὐδὲ τῇ ἱερᾷ συγκλήτῳ κρίνεις. In the Title it is said to be addressed to the Roman Senate; in the beginning of the Treatise, as it at present stands, we find the words ὦ 'Ρωμαῖοι, and, subsequently, the expressions [2]φανερὸν ὑμῖν ἐστὶν, εἰδέναι ὑμᾶς βούλομαι. But we also find [3] σοὶ τῷ αὐτοκράτορι, from which we might be induced to suppose that it was addressed to the Emperor. It has been inferred, from the expectation expressed by Justin, p. 46 E. that he should

---

[1] L. iv. c. 16. See the Note of Valesius on c. 17. and the Prolegomena to the Bibliotheca Veterum Patrum, Tom. I. c. 17. §. 3. We find in p. 46 C. the expression Μουσώνιον δὲ ἐν τοῖς καθ' ἡμᾶς, but it affords no clue to the date.
[2] p. 47 C. B.
[3] p. 42 C. See also p. 47 B. βασιλικὸν δ' ἂν καὶ τοῦτο ἔργον εἴη.

become the victim of the artifices and calumnies of the Philosopher Crescens, that he composed this Treatise not long before his martyrdom. This is the statement of Eusebius L. iv. c. 16. Lardner supposes that the beginning is lost; and it appears to be in other respects imperfect [1]. It was occasioned by the punishment inflicted on three persons at Rome, whom Urbicus, the Prefect of the city, had put to death merely because they were Christians. After exposing the gross injustice of this proceeding, Justin replies to two objections which the enemies of the Gospel were accustomed to urge. [2] The first was, "Why, if the Christians were certain of being received into Heaven, they did not destroy themselves, and save the Roman Governors the trouble of putting them to death?" Justin's answer is, that if they were so to act, they would contravene the designs of God, by diminishing the number of believers, preventing the diffusion of true Religion, and, as far as depended upon them, extinguishing the human race. The [3] second objection was, "Why, if they were regarded by God with an eye of favour, He suffered them to be exposed to injury and oppression?" Justin replies, that

---

[1] The words προέφημεν, ὡς προέφημεν occur p. 43 D. 45 A. 46 C. 47 E. Pearson supposes the references to be to the first Apology, p. 58 B. 96 A. (perhaps rather to 68 C. or 75 A.) 83 C. 71 C.

[2] p. 43 C.   [3] p. 43 E.

the persecutions with which they then were, and with which many virtuous men among the Heathens had before been visited, originated in the malignant artifices of Dæmons, the offspring of the Apostate Angels, who were permitted to exercise their power until the designs of the Almighty were finally accomplished. Another [1] objection, of a different kind, appears to have been urged against the Christians: that in exhorting men to live virtuously, they insisted, not upon the beauty of virtue, but upon the eternal rewards and punishments which await the virtuous and wicked. Justin replies that these are topics on which every believer in the existence of God must insist; since in that belief is involved the further belief, that he will reward the good, and punish the bad. [2] With respect to direct arguments to prove the divine origin of Christianity, that which Justin principally urges is drawn from the fact, that no man ever consented to die in attestation of the truth of any philosophical tenets; whereas men, even from the lowest ranks of life, braved danger and death in the cause of the Gospel. [3] Towards the conclusion of the Tract, Justin states that he

---

[1] p. 47 D Some appear also to have urged the different notions of right and wrong entertained by different nations, in confirmation of the belief, that all actions are indifferent, and that there will be neither rewards nor punishments after death. p. 48 A.

[2] p. 48 E. Compare Dict. p. 350 A.

[3] p. 50 A. Compare Tertullian's Apology, sub. fin.

was himself induced to embrace Christianity, by observing the courage and constancy with which its professors encountered all the terrors of persecution.

The Dialogue with Trypho was posterior to the first Apology, to which it contains a [1] reference; but with respect to the precise date, there is the same difference of opinion among the Critics, as in the case of the other treatises. Trypho says [2] of himself, that he resided principally at Corinth, having been obliged to quit Judæa by the war which had just taken place; in which passage he is usually supposed to allude to the revolt of Barchochebas; though [3] Dodwell thinks that the allusion is to a revolt mentioned by Julius Capitolinus in his [4] life of Antoninus Pius. Scaliger inferred, from the words τὸν νῦν γενόμενον πόλεμον, that the Dialogue was composed during the reign of Adrian. But even if we interpret the word νῦν strictly, the fair inference is, that the Dialogue then took place, not that it was then [5] committed to writing; which

---

[1] p. 349 C. οὐδὲ γὰρ ἀπὸ τοῦ γένους τοῦ ἐμοῦ, λέγω δὲ τῶν Σαμαρέων, τινὸς φροντίδα ποιούμενος, ἐγγράφως Καίσαρι προσομιλῶν, εἶπον πλανᾶσθαι αὐτοὺς πειθομένους τῷ ἐν τῷ γένει αὐτῶν μάγῳ Σίμωνι, ὃν Θεὸν ὑπεράνω πάσης ἀρχῆς καὶ ἐξουσίας καὶ δυνάμεως εἶναι λέγουσι. See Apol. I. p. 69 D. Compare also Apol. II. p. 52 A.

[2] p. 217 D. Compare p. 227 A.

[3] Diss. Iren. III § 14. IV. § 42. See the Bibliotheca Veterum Patrum. Tom. I. c. 17. Sect. 2. [4] c. 5.

[5] Justin mentions in p. 306 D. his intention of committing the

was done some time afterwards, for the information of Justin's friend, [1] Marcus Pompeius. The revolt of Barchochebas, however, must have been finally suppressed before the Dialogue took place; since there [2] is a reference to the Decree of Adrian, by which the Jews were prevented from going up to Jerusalem, and they are said no longer to have possessed the power of persecuting the Christians. The word νῦν must consequently be interpreted with some degree of latitude. Some critics have suspected that Justin's Jew is a fictitious personage, or at least that no such Dialogue actually took place; nor are there wanting circumstances which give countenance to the suspicion. The introduction looks like an imitation of the introductions to Plato's Dialogues, and to the philosophical Dialogues of Cicero. It is difficult, also to conceive that Justin would have ventured, in a real Dialogue, [3] upon

conversation to writing, in order to convince the Jews that he really entertained the sentiments which he had expressed: and that he did not put them forth merely for the purpose of making converts of Trypho and his friends. From more than one passage it appears that Justin did not put down all that was actually said. See p. 229 A. 278 B. 356 B. 357 E.

[1] p. 371 B. Who this Marcus Pompeius was, is unknown. Thirlby, not without reason, ridicules Grabe's conjecture, that he was a bishop of Jerusalem.

[2] p. 234 A. C.

[3] I allude particularly to his derivation of the words Israel, p. 354 D. and Satan, p. 331 B. Jones, however, infers from the latter derivation, that Justin was acquainted with the Syriac.

the interpretations of Hebrew words which sometimes occur; or if he had so ventured, that his opponents would have allowed them to pass uncontradicted. The suspicion, however, had never occurred to [1] Eusebius, who assigns Ephesus as the scene of the Dialogue; and Le Nourry thinks that he discovers in the interruptions, digressions, &c. proofs of its reality. Whether it was real or not, is immaterial to our purpose; which is only to ascertain what were Justin's opinions. If it was real, it occupied two days; on the latter of which [2] some Jews were present, who did not hear the former day's disputation, and on whose account Justin repeats several arguments which he had before urged. The part containing the end of the first and the beginning of the second day's disputation is lost; as is proved by the [3] references, found in

On the Canon, Part I. c. 16, Thirlby contends that Justin was acquainted with the Hebrew, or rather that these derivations do not prove the contrary. Note on p. 331 B.

[1] Hist. Eccl. L. iv. c. 18. See p. 237 C.

[2] See p. 304 A. 311 D. 320 B. 322 B. 346 D. 351 A. 352 E. The name of one of those who were present only on the second day was Mnaseas, p. 312 B.

[3] See p. 306 A. D. 333 A. 364 A. See, however, p. 288 E. 291. D. and Grabe's remark, Spicil. Tom. II. p. 162. The Benedictine editors deny that there is any thing wanting; and account for these appearances by saying that, as Justin wrote down his conversation with Trypho from memory, he sometimes forgot to insert passages to which he afterwards referred, supposing that he had inserted them.

It has been remarked to me, that I was, in the former Edition

the latter part of the Dialogue, to arguments and quotations which no longer appear.

of this work, guilty of an omission in taking no notice of the doubt cast upon the genuineness of the Dialogue with Trypho, by Wetstein, in the Prolegomena to his Edition of the Greek Testament. I will now, therefore, supply that omission. Wetstein's words are—" Ego vero cuperem mihi eximi scrupulum de hujus Dialogi auctore ex diligenti ejus lectione injectum, nimirum, quod non utatur in Veteris Testamenti locis citandis Versione τῶν ο', sed magis accedat ad Origenis Editionem Hexaplarem ; quum quæ Origenes obelis jugulavit omittat, quibusque asteriscos apposuit addat etiam : quum idem in Daniele aliâ Versione, nescio an Symmachi, utatur. Si Justinus mortuus est, antequam Symmachi atque Theodotionis Versio ederetur, et si integro sæculo præcessit Origenem, quomodo potuit istius opere uti ? aut si non usus est, quomodo potuit accidere ut prorsus eadem verba iisdem in locis adderet vel demeret, ubi ille vel asteriscis quid vel obelis significaverit ? Quare de hoc auctore quid statuendum sit, doctiores viderint ; mihi rem compertam proposuisse sat est." In the eighth Chapter of this work I have shown that Justin frequently quoted from memory. No inference, therefore, unfavourable to the genuineness of the Dialogue, could be drawn from the want of agreement between his quotations and the present Text of the Septuagint Version; even if that Text accurately represented the Text as it stood in his day. But that is not the case. It is admitted on all hands that we possess no *pure* copy of that Version, as it existed before the time of Origen. Although, therefore, Justin's quotations differ from the present Text, they may have agreed with the Text of the Edition of the Septuagint Version (ἡ κοινή) generally used in his time. The same remark applies to the Hexaplar Edition, as corrected by Origen : we possess no *pure* copy of that Edition, and cannot infer from the agreement of Justin's quotations with the present Hexaplar Text, that they agreed with that Text, as framed by Origen. On the supposition, then, that Wetstein's statements were correct, they would afford very slight ground for questioning the genuineness of the Dialogue ;

The remark which was made upon the first Apology applies equally to this work: it is not perspi-

ascribed, as it is, expressly to Justin by Eusebius, and containing, as it does, many internal marks of genuineness.

But M. Krom, Minister of the Church, and Professor of Ecclesiastical History in the College, of Middleburgh, in a Tract published in 1778 (for the use of which I am indebted to the kindness of Professor Jeremie, of the East India College) denies the correctness of Wetstein's statements. He examines several of Justin's quotations, particularly a very long one from Isaiah cc. 52, 53, 54, and shows that they agree in general with the present Text of the Septuagint Version, even in places in which it differs widely from the Versions of Symmachus and Theodotion; and that neither are the words, marked with asterisks in the Hexaplar Edition, generally inserted, nor those marked with obeli omitted. Thus that which Wetstein denominates *res comperta* proves, on a more accurate examination, to be contrary to fact.

M. Krom, however, admits that Justin's quotations do occasionally differ from the present Text of the Septuagint, and assigns several causes from which the difference may have arisen. Justin may have either quoted from memory, or satisfied with representing the sense of the passage, may have been careless about the words; or, as I have already suggested, the Text of the Septuagint Version which he used may have differed from the present Text. One remarkable instance of such a difference occurs p. 348 E, where Justin affirms, that in the Greek Version used by the Jews the reading of Genesis xlix. 10. was ἕως ἂν ἔλθῃ τὰ ἀποκείμενα αὐτῷ, whereas the reading of the Septuagint was ἕως ἂν ἔλθῃ ᾧ ἀπόκειται. In our present Text, however, the reading is not ᾧ ἀπόκειται, but τὰ ἀποκείμενα αὐτῷ. The passage is twice quoted in the first Apology, and in both instances the reading is ὃ (manifestly an error of the Transcriber) ἀπόκειται. Another consideration, which ought to render us diffident in drawing conclusions from Justin's quotations is, that in his writings, as well as in those of the other Fathers, the Transcribers appear frequently to have corrected his quota-

cuously written, and we have difficulty in discovering the train of the Author's reasoning. After an [1] Introduction, in which Justin gives an account of the manner of his conversion to Christianity, and earnestly exhorts Trypho to follow his example, tions by the Text of the Septuagint Version which they used. This circumstance will account for the instances in which words marked with asterisks, in the Hexaplar Edition, are inserted, or words marked with obeli omitted.

With respect to Justin's quotations from Daniel, if (as we suppose) he quoted the Edition of the Septuagint then generally used, his quotations could not but differ from our present Text, which is not the Text of the Septuagint, but of Theodotion. M. Krom, however, denies the existence of that close resemblance between Justin's quotations and the Version of Symmachus, which Wetstein professes to have found; and states, that they approach more nearly to the readings of the Version which was published, under the title *Daniel secundum Septuaginta ex Tetraplis Origenis*, from the Codex Chisianus. Justin more than once refers to a Greek Version used by the Jews, p. 353 C. 360 C. 367 A, and supposed by some to be the Version of Aquila. In some instances he probably adopted its readings: Symmachus, in framing his Version, may have done the same; and we may thus account for any occasional agreement which may be found between Justin's quotations and the Version of Symmachus. The conclusion, therefore, at which we arrive is, that Wetstein's statements are incorrect; and that, even if they were correct, they would furnish very slight grounds for questioning the genuineness of the Dialogue with Trypho.

Wetstein appears, on nearly similar grounds, to have cast doubts on the genuineness of nearly the whole of Philo's works. He was answered by Wesseling in an Epistle to Herman Venema *de Aquilæ in scriptis Philonis Judæi fragmentis*, published in 1748, which has not fallen in my way.

The Editor of the Bibliotheca Veterum Patrum has also examined Wetstein's objections in his Prolegomena.

[1] From the beginning to p. 225 D.

Trypho [1] replies to the exhortation, by saying that Justin would have acted more wisely in adhering to any one of the Philosophical Sects to which he had formerly been attached, than in leaving God, and placing all his reliance upon a man. In the former case, if he lived virtuously, he might hope to obtain salvation : in the latter he could have no hope. His only safe course, therefore, was to be circumcised, and comply with the other requisitions of the Mosaic Law. Justin answers that [2] the Christians had not deserted God, though they no longer observed the Ceremonial Law. They worshipped the God who brought the forefathers of the Jews out of the land of Egypt, and gave the Law, but who had plainly declared by the Prophets that he should give a new Law—a Law appointing a [3] new mode of purification from sin, by the baptism of repentance and of the knowledge of God — and requiring a spiritual, not a [4] carnal circumcision.

[1] p. 225 D Trypho admits that he did not believe the horrible charges brought against the Christians ; and says, that the Morality of the Gospel was of a character so sublime, that no man could live up to it. p. 227 B.

[2] p. 227 E. One objection urged against the Christians was, that they drank hot drinks on the Sabbath. See Thirlby's Note, p. 246 E.

[3] p 229 D. See p. 251 C. 287 C. 292 B. 351 B.

[4] p. 229 C. 233 D. 235 E 236 C 245 D. 261 D 341 A. 342 A. 366 D. Justin states that one design of the rite of circumcision was to distinguish the Jews from other people ; particularly in the latter times, when they were to suffer the punishment decreed against them for crucifying the Messiah, p. 234 A

[1] The Ceremonial Law was in truth given to the Jews on account of the hardness of their hearts; as a mark of God's displeasure at their apostacy, when they made the golden calf in Horeb. All its ordinances, its sacrifices, its sabbath, the prohibition of certain kinds of foods, were designed to counteract the inveterate tendency of the Jews to fall into idolatry. If, [2] says Justin, we contend that the Ceremonial Law is of universal and perpetual obligation, we run the hazard of charging God with inconsistency, as if he had appointed different modes of justification at different times; since they who lived before Abraham were not circumcised, and they who lived before Moses neither observed the [3] sabbath, nor offered sacrifices, although God bore

236 B. 238 A, where he quotes Ezech. xx. 19. p. 366 E. Christians had the true circumcision, that of the heart. p. 320 A. The Jews affixed a carnal meaning to all the ordinances of the Law. p. 231 D.

[1] p. 235 E. 237 A. 244 C. E 263 E. 265 B. 291 D. In p. 247 A. Justin seems to contend that the reasonableness of the Ceremonial Law can only be maintained on this supposition. In p. 263 A. he says that some parts of the Law were designed to enforce piety and justice; others referred mystically to Christ; others were directed against the hardness of heart of the Jews. In 263 E. he distinguishes between the authority of the Natural and Ritual Law, in p. 292 C. between that which is of perpetual and universal obligation (τὰς αἰωνίας καὶ φύσει δικαιοπραξίας καὶ εὐσεβείας. p. 266 B. τὰ αἰώνια δικαιώματα. p. 264 D. see also p. 320 D.), and that which was merely directed against the perverseness of the Jewish people. In p. 320 E. he refers to the φυσικαὶ ἔννοιαι, the sense of right and wrong implanted in our nature. See Ap. 2. p. 52 A.

[2] p. 240 E. See also p. 236 C. 245 B. 261 C. 265 A. 292 A. 319 C. 320 B.

[3] It has been inferred, as it appears to me erroneously, from

testimony to them that they were righteous. Having, as he thinks, satisfactorily proved that the Ceremonial Law is no longer binding, Justin replies to an argument urged by Trypho—that the Prophecy of Daniel vii. 9. taught the Jews to expect that the Messiah would be great and glorious; whereas the Messiah of the Christians was unhonoured and inglorious, and fell under the extreme curse of the Law; for he was crucified. ² Justin's answer is, that the Scriptures of the Old Testament speak of two Advents of the Messiah; one in humiliation, the other in glory: though the Jews, blinded by their prejudices, looked only to those passages which foretold the latter. He then proceeds to ³ quote

Justin's reasoning in this passage, that he believed the first institution of the Sabbath and of the rite of sacrifice to have taken place during the sojourning of the Israelites in the wilderness. I conceive him to have alluded to the peculiar sacrifices of the Mosaic Law, and to the peculiar mode in which the Jews kept the Sabbath. In p. 236 he speaks of the sacrifices offered by Abel.

² p. 249 C. See also p. 232 D. 245 D. 247 E. 268 B. Ap. I. p. 87 A. Justin refers, in proof of the two-fold Advent, to Psalm cx. which the Jews interpreted of Hezekiah, p. 250 D. 309 B; to Psalm lxxii. which they interpreted of Solomon, p. 251 D. 288 D; to Genesis xlix. p. 271 C. 272 C; Micah iv. p. 336 A, which the Jews themselves applied to the Messiah. Justin speaks of the personal appearance of Christ as mean—an opinion derived from the literal interpretation of Isaiah liii. 2, 3. p. 255 C. 326 E. 316 C. 311 A. The two goats mentioned in Leviticus xvi. 7. were also types of the two Advents, p. 259 D. 338 A.

³ He refers to Psalm xxiv. p. 310 E. which the Jews applied to Solomon, p. 254 E. or to Hezekiah, Psalm xlvii. and Psalm xcix. p. 255 D. E. Psalm xlv. p. 256 E. Justin also founds an argument on the fulfilment of the predictions of Christ

passages of the Old Testament, in which the Messiah is called God, and Lord of Hosts. In this part of the Dialogue Justin extracts from the Old Testament several texts in which he finds allusions to the Gospel history. Thus [1] the Paschal Lamb was a type of Christ's crucifixion : the [2] offering of fine flour, for those who were cleansed from the leprosy, was a type of the bread in the Eucharist ; the [3] twelve bells attached to the robe of the high priest, of the twelve Apostles.

Justin [4] next undertakes to prove that the various prophecies respecting the Messiah were fulfilled in Jesus. [5] But having quoted Isai. vii. to prove that the Messiah was to be born of a Virgin, he first runs into a digression caused by an [6] inquiry from Trypho, whether Jews, who led holy lives, like Job, Enoch, and Noah, but observed the Mosaic law, could be saved; and afterwards into a second di-

himself respecting the false Prophets, who would come in his name. p. 253 B.
  [1] p. 259 B. [2] p. 259 E.
  [3] p. 260 D. Exodus xxxix. 25. The number of bells is not mentioned.
  [4] Trypho had called upon Justin to give this proof, p. 254 C. 258 E. It was impossible, he contended, that a crucified man should have conversed with Moses and Aaron, p. 256 C.
  [5] p. 262 A. The Jews contended that the word translated παρθένος ought to be translated νεᾶνις, and applied the prediction to Hezekiah, p. 291 A. 294 A. 297 D. See also p. 310 C. where Justin contends that the mere fact of a young woman giving birth to a son could not be deemed a sign.
  [6] p. 263 C.

gression, occasioned by a remark of Trypho ¹ that

---

¹ p. 267 B. Trypho here expressly asserts that the Jews expected in their Messiah a mere man whom Elias was to anoint, καὶ γὰρ πάντες ἡμεῖς τὸν Χριστὸν ἄνθρωπον ἐξ ἀνθρώπων προσδοκῶμεν γενήσεσθαι, καὶ τὸν Ἠλίαν χρίσαι αὐτὸν ἐλθόντα, p. 268 A. Allix, in his Judgment of the Jewish Church, c. 25. sub in had remarked that this was Justin's representation of the expectation of the Jews in his day *A greater objection*, he says, *than all these may be very naturally made by a judicious reader, concerning what I said of the testimonies of the Jews before Christ, about the distinction of the Divine Persons and the Divinity of the* Λόγος. *On the one side may he say, you own that the Jews after Christ have opposed the doctrine, as being contrary to the unity of God, there are plain proofs of it, even in the second century. And it is certain that Trypho did not believe that the Messias was to be any other than a mere man, and so did the Jews believe, as it is witnessed by Origen, Lib. u. contr. Cels.* p. 79. Burgh also had spoken of Trypho as arguing in the very spirit of modern Unitarianism, Vol. I p. 86 Yet I find in Dr. Burton's "Testimonies of the Ante-Nicene Fathers," p. 41, (2d ed. p. 47,) the following statement. "Justin. Dial. cum Trypho. c. lxviii. p. 166. Ed. Bened. The next passage is important, as showing the opinion which the Jews entertained concerning their Messiah. Justin's words are these *As to the Scriptures which we quote to them (the Jews) which expressly prove that Christ was to suffer and to be worshipped, and that he is God, they are compelled to allow that these were spoken concerning Christ, but they have the presumption to say that this (Jesus) is not the Christ; but they acknowledge that he was to come, and to suffer, and to be a King, and to be worshipped as God.*"

"According to the opinion of the Jews, therefore, who ought to be the best interpreters of their own prophecies, the human nature, and the humble condition of Jesus were not the obstacles to their believing him to be the Messiah : and it was their belief, as it is that of Christians, that the Messiah, who was to come, was God. Dr. Priestley was, therefore, entirely at variance with Justin Martyr when he said, *that the Jews expected that their Messiah would be a mere man, and even be born as other men are.* If Justin reported the opinion of the Jews fairly, the Christian doctrine respecting the pre-existence and Divinity of Christ, and his subsequent their expectations concerning the Messiah were directly opposite to these." (In his second edition the learned Author adds, " And a remarkable expression of Philo-Judæus may be quoted in this place, who, when he is speaking of the repugnance felt by the Jews to pay divine honours to Caligula, observes, that they would more easily believe that God would change into man, than a man into God.") " Origen, however, certainly says that all the Jews did not expect their Messiah to come as God or Son of God. We may observe also, that in this and other places already quoted, (See No. 25. p. 37, 2d ed. p. 42.) Justin expressly says that Christ is *to be worshipped* as God ; and yet he as plainly says in many places, that there is *only one God* "

" Justin's arguments in this Chapter arise from the following remark of Trypho, who said to him, *You are attempting to demonstrate a thing which is incredible and almost impossible, that God submitted to be born, and to become Man.* Justin, however, acknowledges the proposition, and proceeds to demonstrate it."

In the above statement there are several particulars in which I must be permitted to dissent from the learned author. I cannot allow that the Jews *ought to be the best interpreters of their own prophecies* if so, we Christians are sadly in error. But perhaps the learned author meant to say that the Jews *ought to be the best interpreters of the meaning which they themselves affixed to their own prophecies*. Again, I cannot allow that, according to Justin's representation of the opinions of the Jews in his day, *the humble condition of Jesus was not an obstacle to their believing him to be the Messiah* In p. 249 B. is the following passage. Καὶ ὁ Τρύφων, παυσαμένου μου, εἶπεν, ὦ ἄνθρωπε, αὗται ἡμᾶς αἱ γραφαὶ καὶ τοιαῦται ἔνδοξον καὶ μέγαν ἀναμένειν, τὸν παρὰ τοῦ παλαιοῦ τῶν ἡμερῶν ὡς υἱὸν ἀνθρώπου παραλαμβάνοντα τὴν αἰώνιον βασιλείαν, ἀναγκάζουσιν· οὗτος δὲ ὁ ὑμέτερος λεγόμενος Χριστὸς ἄτιμος καὶ ἄδοξος γέγονεν, ὡς καὶ τῇ ἐσχάτῃ κατάρᾳ τῇ ἐν τῷ νόμῳ τοῦ Θεοῦ περιπεσεῖν· ἐσταυρώθη γάρ. *And Trypho, when I concluded, said, these and similar passages of Scripture, compel us to look for a glorious*

assumption of humanity, was monstrous and absurd.

and great personage, who, as the Son of Man, is to receive an eternal kingdom from the Ancient of days : whereas he whom you call Christ was unhonoured and inglorious, so as even to fall under the extreme curse of the Law ; for he was crucified. Justin, in answer to this objection, proceeds to show at considerable length that the Prophets speak of two Advents of the Messiah ; the one in humiliation, the other in glory. Surely he might have spared himself this trouble, if he had not supposed that the humble condition of Jesus was an obstacle to his being received by the Jews as their Messiah.

Lastly, notwithstanding the learned author's statement, I must still adhere to the opinion expressed by Allix, *that Trypho*, whom Justin brings forward as representing the Jews of his day, *did not believe that the Messias was to be any other than a mere man.* I observe that Justin takes considerable pains to prove that the ancient Prophets have applied the titles of God and Lord of Hosts to the future Messiah. (See p. 254 E. et sequ.) This was surely an unnecessary waste of time and labour, if the prevalent belief of the Jews of his day was, *that the Messiah, who was to come, was God.* To what purpose does Trypho quote Isaiah xlii. 8. (p. 289 B.), but in order to prove the absolute unity of God, in opposition to Justin's assertions respecting the Divinity of the Messiah ? But to remove all doubt on the subject, let us consider the whole passage, from which the sentence at the commencement of this Note is an extract. Trypho thus addresses Justin, ἀναλαβὼν οὖν κ. τ. ἑ. p. 267 A. *Finish your argument, taking it up from the point where you left off ; for to me it appears strange and wholly incapable of proof.* (May I suggest to the learned author, on whose remark I am commenting, the propriety of reconsidering the translation of this sentence in p. 39 N. 27. ? I observe that it is allowed in his second edition, p. 45.) *For that you should say that this Christ existed, being God, before all ages, and then submitted to be born and to become a man, and that he was not a man born of man, appears to me not only strange, but foolish.* Justin replies, *I know that this doctrine appears strange, and especially to those*

One [1] argument urged by Trypho, in order to prove that Jesus was not the Messiah, is that *of your race, who, as God himself exclaims, were never willing either to understand or do what God prescribes, but listen only to your own teachers. But, even if I cannot show that this Jesus pre-existed, being God, the Son of the Maker of the Universe, and became man born of the Virgin; even then it does not follow that he is not the Christ of God. But as I have shown that he, whoever he may be, is the Christ of God, though I may not have shown that he pre-existed and submitted, in compliance with the will of his Father, to be born a man, subject to like passions with us, and having flesh, you ought to say that I am mistaken only in this* (latter) *respect, but ought not to deny that he is the Christ,* (even) *if he appears as a man born of men, and is proved to be elected to the office of the Messiah.* If Justin thought that he was addressing men who believed that *the Messiah, who was to come, was God,* he must be allowed to be most unfortunate in the selection of his arguments. Then follows a passage, which has furnished ample matter for discussion; containing an admission on the part of Justin that there were persons in his day, who confessed that Jesus was the Messiah, but said that he was a mere man. To this reasoning of Justin Trypho replies in the following manner, ἐμοὶ μὲν δοκοῦσιν οἱ λέγοντες ἄνθρωπον γεγονέναι αὐτὸν, καὶ κατ' ἐκλογὴν κεχρίσθαι, καὶ Χριστὸν γεγονέναι, πιθανώτερον ὑμῶν λέγειν, τῶν ταῦτα ἄπερ φῇς λεγόντων· καὶ γὰρ πάντες ἡμεῖς τὸν Χριστὸν ἄνθρωπον ἐξ ἀνθρώπων προσδοκῶμεν γενήσεσθαι, καὶ τὸν Ἠλίαν χρίσαι αὐτὸν ἐλθόντα· ἐὰν δὲ οὗτος φαίνηται ὦν ὁ Χριστὸς, ἄνθρωπον μὲν ἐξ ἀνθρώπων γενόμενον ἐκ παντὸς ἐπίστασθαι δεῖ· ἐκ δὲ τοῦ μηδὲ Ἠλίαν ἐληλυθέναι οὐδὲ τοῦτον ἀποφαίνομαι εἶναι. *What they say, who affirm that he was born a man, and was selected to be anointed, and thus became Christ, appears to me more credible, than what is said by them who talk as you do. For we all expect that the Christ will be born a man from human parents, and that Elias will come and anoint him. If, therefore, this* (Jesus) *appears to be the Christ, be assured that he was a man born of men; but as*

---

[1] p. 268 A. Justin's answer to Trypho's inquiry, "How the spirit of Elias could be in John," deserves notice, p. 269 A.

Elias, who, according to the Prophets, was to be the precursor of the Messiah, had not appeared.

Elias has not yet come, I affirm that he was not the Christ We must either say that Trypho does not express the opinion of the Jews of his day ; or that their belief was not *that the Messiah, who was to come, was God* But what are we to say to the passage produced by Dr. Burton ? Let us examine it in connexion with the context. As Dr. Burton observes, Trypho had said to Justin, *You are attempting to demonstrate a thing, which is incredible and almost impossible, that God submitted to be born and became man.* p. 292 D. Justin answers that, if he had endeavoured to establish this point by appealing to human authority, Trypho might have justly been indignant ; but he had rested the proof entirely on the authority of Scripture. Justin subsequently asks Trypho, *Do you understand that in the Sacred Scriptures any other person is proposed as an object of worship, and is called Lord and God, besides him who made this Universe, and Christ, who has been proved by so many quotations from Scripture to have been born a man ?* Trypho rejoins, *How can we admit it, when this lengthened discussion has turned upon the inquiry, whether there is another (God) besides the Father only ?* Justin then quotes Isaiah liii. 8. *Who shall declare his generation ?* to prove that the Messiah was not to be the seed of the race of man. *How then*, replies Trypho, *was it said to David, that God should take to himself a Son out of his (David's) loins, &c. ?* Justin endeavours to explain this seeming contradiction ; and then proceeds to charge the Jewish teachers firstly, with saying that those passages in the Septuagint Translation, which were directly opposed to their own opinions, were not extant in the original ; secondly, with affirming that those predictions which could in any way be accommodated to events in the time of Solomon, Hezekiah, &c. were intended to refer to those monarchs, and not to the Messiah , and thirdly, when they were compelled to confess that there were passages in Scripture which clearly spoke of the Messiah as suffering, and as an object of worship, and as God, with taking refuge in the cavil, that this (Jesus) was not the Messiah . though they

Justin answers, that the Prophecies concerning Elias had, with respect to Christ's first coming, been accomplished in John the Baptist: and that before Christ's second Advent, Elias would himself appear. Justin [1] further contends that the Messiah admitted that the Messiah was to come, and to suffer, and to reign, and to be worshipped as God. ἃς δ' ἂν λέγωμεν αὐτοῖς γραφὰς αἳ διαρρήδην τὸν Χριστὸν καὶ παθητὸν καὶ προσκυνητὸν καὶ Θεὸν ἀποδεικνύουσιν, ἃς καὶ προανιστόρησα ὑμῖν, ταύτας εἰς Χριστὸν μὲν εἰρῆσθαι ἀναγκαζόμενοι συντίθενται, τοῦτον δὲ μὴ εἶναι τὸν Χριστὸν τολμῶσι λέγειν. ἐλεύσεσθαι δὲ καὶ παθεῖν, καὶ βασιλεῦσαι, καὶ προσκυνητὸν γενέσθαι Θεὸν ὁμολογοῦσιν, ὅπερ γελοῖον καὶ ἀνόητον, ὃ ὁμοίως ἀποδείξω. (p. 294 C. the passage translated by Dr. Burton.) This passage, therefore, taken in connexion with the context, far from proving the belief of the Jews in Justin's time to have been *that the Messiah, who was to come, was God*, proves on the contrary that Trypho and his companions entered upon the inquiry, not only not entertaining such a belief, but most unwilling to entertain it; and that it was only by compulsion, as it were, ἀναγκαζόμενοι—because they could not elude the force of the express declarations of Scripture—that they admitted the prophetic descriptions of the Messiah to imply that he was God. In confirmation of this interpretation, I would refer the reader to the admission made by Trypho, p. 302 C. which Allix has noticed.

If any reliance can be placed on Justin's authority, the Jews of his day, as Allix expresses himself, did not believe that the Messias was to be any other than a mere man, who was to be selected from the rest of his countrymen on account of his strict observance of the Mosaic Law. p. 291 B. E 267 D. They suspected that the time fixed for his coming by the Prophets had passed; but affirmed that he was living in a state of obscurity, and would remain ignorant of his high character and destination, until he should be anointed and made manifest by Elias. p. 226 B. 336 D.

[1] p. 270 E. In p. 314 A, Justin says that the spiritual gifts, formerly conferred singly upon the Jewish kings and

must have already come, because, after John the Baptist, no Prophet had arisen among the Jews: and [1] they had lost their national independence agreeably to the prediction of Jacob. [2] Trypho now calls upon Justin to show, that in the Old Testament mention is ever made of another God, strictly so called, besides the Creator of the Universe. Justin answers that, whenever in Scripture God is said to appear to man, we must understand the appearance to be of the Son, not of the Father; as when God appeared [3] to Abraham at the oak of

prophets, were all united in Christ, agreeably to Isaiah xi. on which Trypho had founded an argument against Christ's Divinity.

[1] p. 271 E. Genesis xlix. 10. According to Justin, Gen. xlix. 11. and Zechariah ix. 9. were prophetic of the calling of the Gentiles, p. 272 C. D. 273 A. But Gen. xlix. 11. contained other predictions. The words "he washed his garments in wine, and his clothes in the blood of the grape," were prophetic of the washing of the sins of mankind by Christ's blood, inasmuch as true believers are his garments. Since, also, the blood of the grape is the gift of God, not the produce of human labour, this verse predicted that Christ was to have blood, but not blood derived from a human source, p. 273 E. 286 D. 301 C. See Apol. I. p. 74 B.

[2] p. 274 B. Trypho admits that the word God is often used in a lower signification, as when God is called the "God of Gods." See also p. 269 B. 293 C.

[3] p. 275 A. Gen. xviii. 340 D. 356 A. According to Trypho, the Jews understood that God the Father appeared in the first instance, and then three angels in human form, two of whom were sent to destroy Sodom, the third to announce to Sarah that she would have a son. See p. 342 A.

Mamre, to [1] Lot, [2] to Jacob, to [3] Moses, out of the burning bush, and to [4] Joshua. Justin also appeals to Psalm cx. and xlv. to show that David speaks of another Lord and God, besides the Creator of the Universe; and quotes [5] Proverbs viii. and Genesis i. 26. iii. 22. to prove the pre-existence of Christ.

After these digressions, Justin resumes his proof that the Messiah was to be born of a Virgin, and quotes [6] Isaiah liii. 8. Psalm xlv. 7. [7] Trypho however interrupts him, and says, that although Jesus might be recognized as the Lord, and Messiah, and God, by the Gentiles, the Jews who were the worshippers of God, who made him as well as them, were not bound to recognize or worship him. Justin, in answer, quotes Psalm xcix. and lxxii. to show that, even among the Jews, they who obtained salvation, obtained it only through

---

[1] p. 236 D. 277 A. Genesis xix.

[2] p 280 D. Genesis xxviii. xxxii. xxxv. p. 313 A. 354 D. 355 E.

[3] p. 282 C. 340 D. 357 E. Exodus iii. 2. Trypho says that an angel appeared to Moses, though God the Father conversed with him. See Apol. I. p. 95 B. 96 C.

[4] p. 286 A.

[5] p. 285 A. In Genesis i. 26. the Jews contended that God addressed the words "Let us make man," &c. either to himself or to the elements.

[6] p. 286 C. 301 B.

[7] p. 287 C.

Christ. But [1] what, rejoins Trypho, are we to say to the words which the prophet Isaiah speaks in the name of God himself, "I am the Lord God, that is my name, I will not give my glory to another?" Justin replies, that Scripture cannot contradict itself. If we are unable to reconcile, entirely to our satisfaction, those passages in which God declares his absolute Unity with those in which he speaks of Christ as God, we ought to rest assured that they are reconcileable, though our imperfect faculties may be unequal to the task. In this case, however, the context plainly shows that God meant to say, that he would give his glory only to him who was to be the light of the Gentiles, that is, to Christ.

Justin [2] now returns once more to Isaiah vii. and to the proof that the Messiah was to be born of a Virgin; but is interrupted by Trypho, who tells him that he ought to be ashamed of narrating stories respecting the birth of Christ, which could only be compared to the [3] fables, current among

---

[1] Isaiah xlii. 8. p. 289 B.   [2] p. 290 D

[3] 291 B. 297 B. Justin contends that this fable, and others of a similar nature, as the stories of Bacchus, Hercules, Æsculapius, were mere corruptions of the predictions of the Old Testament respecting the Messiah, put forth by the devil, for the purpose of deluding mankind. He makes the same observation respecting certain ceremonies introduced into the mysteries of Mithras, p. 294 E. 296 B. 304 B.

the Heathen, respecting the birth of Perseus from Danae, and the descent of Jupiter, under the appearance of a shower of gold. It would be better at once to say that the Messiah was a mere man, elected to the office on account of his exact compliance with the Mosaic Law, than to [1] hazard the incredible assertion, that God himself submitted to be born and to become a man. Justin, in answer, again [2] quotes Isaiah liii. 8. in order to prove that the Messiah was not to be born after the ordinary manner of men; and asserts, that when Isaiah, vii. 14. said, "A Virgin shall conceive," &c. he intended to interpret the promise made mystically to David, in Psalm cxxxii. 11. which had been alleged by Trypho to show that the Messiah was to descend, in the natural course of generation, from David. In this part of the Dialogue, Justin observes, that in some instances, the Jews denied the genuineness of the passages which directly confuted their opinions; in others, applied passages, manifestly prophetic of the events of the Messiah's life, to the actions of mere men: and when they were obliged to confess that a passage did apply to the Messiah, they took refuge in the assertion that Jesus was not that Messiah; but that the Messiah was still to come, and to suffer, and to reign, and to be adored as

[1] p 291 C.   [2] p. 293 D. 301 B.

God. Justin [1] quotes also Isaiah xxxv. to show that the Messiah was to effect miraculous cures. After [2] charging the Jewish teachers with having expunged from the Septuagint version several passages clearly prophetic of the Messiah, and quoting portions of Scripture, some of which he had before alleged, to prove that the Messiah was not to be born after the ordinary manner of men, he [3] proceeds to show that Isaiah vii. could not apply to Hezekiah, but was fulfilled in Jesus.

Trypho [4] now inquires of Justin whether he really believed that Jerusalem would be rebuilt, and all the Gentiles, as well as the Jews and Proselytes, collected there under the government of the Messiah; or whether he merely professed such a belief, in order to conciliate the Jews. Justin, in answer, admits that this belief was not universal among the orthodox Christians; but that he himself maintained that the dead would rise again in the body, and live for a thousand years in Jerusalem, which would be

---

[1] p. 295 E. In p. 308 C. Justin contends that Jesus was the Messiah, because the predictions which he delivered respecting the rise of heresies after his ascension, and the sufferings which his followers would undergo, had been exactly fulfilled. See p. 254 A. 271 B.

[2] p. 297 E.   [3] p. 302 C.

[4] p. 306 B. See also p. 312 C. 368 A. 369 A. In p. 346 B. Justin says that the sacrifices which will then be offered to God will be the spiritual sacrifices of prayer and praise.

rebuilt, and beautified, and enlarged: he appeals in support of his opinion to Isaiah, and to the Apocalypse, which he ascribes to John, one of Christ's Apostles.

[1] Justin having produced several passages from the Old Testament, in which he finds allusions, sufficiently fanciful, to the particular mode of the Messiah's death, and to the Cross, Trypho rejoins, "The whole Jewish nation expects the Messiah. I also admit that the passages of Scripture which you have quoted apply to him; and the name of Jesus or Joshua, given to the son of Nun, inclines me somewhat to the opinion that your Jesus is the Messiah. The Scriptures moreover manifestly predict a suffering Messiah: but that he should suffer death upon the Cross, the death of those who are pronounced accursed by the Law, fills me with perplexity." Justin answers, [2] that the curse applied only to those who were crucified on account of their transgressions: whereas Christ was sinless, and submitted to this ignominious death, in obedience to the will of his Father, in order that he might rescue the human race from the penalty due to their sins.

---

[1] p. 312 E. 316 E. 259 C. 338 B. The Jews seem to have been at a loss to understand why Moses, who forbade them to make any likeness of any creature, set up the brazen serpent, p. 322 B. 339 A. Compare Ap. I. p. 90 B.

[2] Compare p. 338 B.

After quoting Psalm iii. 5, Isaiah lxv. 2, and liii. 9, as prophetic of the Messiah's crucifixion and resurrection, Justin shows at considerable length that Psalm [1] xxii. is descriptive of the perfect humanity, of the sufferings, death, and resurrection of the Messiah.

[2] Justin comes at last to speak of the conversion of the Gentiles; and contends that the Christians are the true people of God, inasmuch as they fulfil the spiritual meaning of the law, and do not merely conform, like the Jews, to the letter. They [3] have the true circumcision of the heart; [4] they are the true race of priests dedicated to God, and typified by Jesus the High Priest in [5] the prophecy of Zechariah; they offer the true spiritual sacrifices which are pleasing to God, agreeably to the [6] prophecy of

[1] p. 324 C. The Jews denied that this Psalm was prophetic of the Messiah. The mode, in which Justin explains an expression in the Psalm, from which it might be inferred that Christ was ignorant of his own fate, is worthy of attention. p. 326 B.

[2] p. 335 E. The Jews appear to have applied some of the passages, which predict the conversion of the Gentiles, to the proselytes, as Isaiah xlix. 6. p. 350 C

[3] p. 342 A.

[4] ἀρχιερατικὸν τὸ ἀληθινὸν γένος ἐσμὲν τοῦ Θεοῦ. p. 344 C. Ἰσραηλιτικὸν γὰρ τὸ ἀληθινὸν πνευματικόν. κ. τ. ἑ. p. 228 E. λαὸς ἅγιός ἐσμεν. p. 347 B. 365 D. 353 B and 366 A.

[5] iii. 1. p. 342 C. 344 C.

[6] i. 10. The meaning affixed to this prediction by the Jews was that God rejected the sacrifices offered by those who *then*

41

Malachi: they are the [1] seed promised to Abraham, because they are actuated by the same principle of faith which actuated Abraham; they [2] are, in a word, the true Israel.

[3] Justin concludes with enumerating the benefits conferred upon the Jews by God, and reproaching them with their ingratitude. They had at last filled up the measure of their iniquities, by crucifying his only-begotten Son: and they still persecuted his disciples, although it was evident that the [4] capture of Jerusalem, and the destruction of their temple by the Romans, was a punishment inflicted on them for their rejection of Jesus, and for that only; since they were no longer addicted to the idolatrous practices which had drawn down the vengeance of the Almighty on their forefathers. Their only hope, therefore, of safety lay in repenting of their transgressions, renouncing the errors of their teachers, and cordially embracing Christianity.

Although I am far from wishing to deny that there are in this Treatise many weak and incon-

---

inhabited Jerusalem, but accepted, as sacrifices, the prayers of the Jews who were dispersed by the Captivity. p. 344 E.

[1] p. 347 C.
[2] p. 349 E. 352 E. 355 B. 359 D.
[3] p. 360 D. *ad fin.*
[4] The application of the prophecy of Noah to the Jews and Romans deserves attention. p. 368 B.

clusive arguments, many trifling applications and erroneous interpretations of Scripture, many attempts to extract meanings which never entered into the mind of the Sacred writer, yet I cannot think it deserving of the contempt with which some later critics have spoken of it. It proves at least that the state of the controversy was not essentially different in the days of Justin from its present state; that after the lapse of seventeen hundred years, the difficulties to be encountered in disputing with the Jews, the objections to be answered, the prejudices to be overcome, are nearly the same. It supplies us also incidentally with some curious facts, illustrative of the spirit by which the Jews and Christians were mutually actuated towards each other. With respect to the sentiments entertained by the Christians towards the Jews, we find Trypho, p. 263 C. inquiring whether they who lived according to the Mosaic Law would be saved. Justin answers, that, as the Mosaic Law comprehended the unchangeable and fundamental principles of morality, they who had lived up to it before the coming of Christ would be saved through him; and after his coming they also would be saved who observed the whole Law, both Moral and Ceremonial, provided that they believed the crucified Jesus to be the Christ of God, and did not attempt to force the observance of the ritual Law upon others. He admits, however, that many thought otherwise, and contended that the observance of the Mosaic rites was incompatible with the profession of Christianity. Thus the Gentile converts in Justin's age, and the Jewish in the Apostolic times, appear to have been equally ready to act on the principle of exclusion. [1] On the other hand we learn [2] that the Rabbis forbade their hearers to hold any intercourse with the Christians; that they pronounced [3] curses against them in the synagogues; and that [4] they sent persons into every part of the civilized world with directions to denounce Christianity as a pestilent heresy, and to misrepresent the conduct and morals of its professors. Justin speaks of the [5] proselytes as animated by a more bitter spirit of hostility than the Jews themselves. He ridicules the [6] trivial questions on which the Jews wasted their time and labour, and [7] censures their cavilling temper. He [8] charges them with denying Christ through fear of

---

[1] See Wilson's Illustration, &c c. xi
[2] p. 256 C. 339 D.
[3] p. 234 B. 266 E. 321 D. 323 D. 345 A. 363 D. 366 E. From the last passage it appears that the curse was pronounced after the conclusion of the prayers. See Jerome in Esaiam v. 18. xlix. 7. lii. 4. and in Amos i. 11. where he says that the Jews cursed the Christians under the name of Nazarenes. See Ap. I. p. 77 A.
[4] p. 234 E. 335 C. where the charges against the Christians are mentioned more in detail.
[5] p. 350 E.
[6] p. 339 D. 340 B.
[7] p. 343 C.
[8] p. 258 C. 262 E.

persecution, with [1] entertaining low and unworthy notions of God, and with [2] corrupting the Septuagint Version. With respect, however, to the last charge, the [3] Christians appear to have been more

[1] p. 341 E. Justin accuses them of Anthropomorphism. See p. 364 A

[2] p. 297 C. 349 A. See also 343 D. Justin's specific charges against the Jews were,

I. That they had suppressed a passage in Ezra, in which the passover was represented as a type of the Redeemer: but this passage is not now extant in any either of the Greek or Hebrew copies. Lactantius quotes it. Institut. iv. 18.

II. That they had suppressed a passage in Jeremiah, which, however, is now extant in every copy, both Greek and Hebrew, xi. 19. Justin admits that in his day it was found in some of the copies used in the synagogues.

III. That they had suppressed another passage in Jeremiah, which is not now found in any copy, either Greek or Hebrew. This passage is cited more than once by Irenæus, who in one instance ascribes it to Isaiah. L. iii. c. 23. L. iv. c. 39 56. 66. L. v. c. 31

IV. That they have suppressed the words ἀπὸ τοῦ ξύλου in the ninety-sixth Psalm, v. 10. In the Epistle of Barnabas, c. viii. we find the following passage: ὅτι ἡ βασιλεία τοῦ Ἰησοῦ ἐπὶ τῷ ξύλῳ, from which we may infer that the author had ἀπὸ τοῦ ξύλου in his copy, but there is nothing corresponding to the passage in the old Latin Version. The reading was known to Tertullian, and many of the Fathers; and Le Nourry says that it is found in some manuscript Psalters of great antiquity. See Ap. I. p. 80 B. and Dr. Bernard's Note on Cotelerii Patr. Apostol.

Justin further charges the Jews with having erased a passage containing an account of the mode of Isaiah's death, p. 349 B

[3] Some writers have thought that Justin himself was the guilty party. See Thirlby's note on p. 297 B. and Pearson on the Creed, Article v. p. 242. 5th Ed. The Jews asserted that the

justly liable to it than the Jews. Justin [1] further affirms that the Jews were allowed by their Rabbis to have a plurality of wives, and that the polygamy of the Patriarchs was alleged in defence of the practice.

There is in p. 307 A. an enumeration of Jewish sects, in which the names of the Genistæ, Meristæ, and Helleniani occur; of the former two, Isidorus, Origin. viii. 4. p. 63, has given some, though not a satisfactory account; of the Helleniani, no trace, I believe, is to be found in any other writer.

Without meaning to lay any particular stress upon the authority of Justin in such matters, I will observe that he appears not to have recognised any other than *circumcised* Proselytes.[2]

Version of the Septuagint was in some places incorrect. p. 294 B.

[1] p. 363 E. According to Justin a great mystery was concealed under the polygamy of the Patriarchs, καὶ ἡ μία δὲ αὕτη τῆς παραπτώσεως τοῦ Δαβὶδ πρὸς τὴν τοῦ Οὐρίου γυναῖκα πρᾶξις, ὦ ἄνδρες, ἔφην, δείκνυσιν ὅτι οὐχ ὡς πορνεύοντες πολλὰς ἔσχον γυναῖκας οἱ πατριάρχαι, ἀλλ' οἰκονομία τὶς, καὶ μυστήρια πάντα δι' αὐτῶν ἀπετελεῖτο p. 371 A. See p. 364 B.

[2] p 351 D.

CHAPTER II.

THE OPINIONS OF JUSTIN RESPECTING THE ΛΟΓΟΣ AND THE TRINITY.

HAVING given the above short account of the genuine works of Justin, which have descended to our times, we will proceed to the examination of his opinions; and will in the first place consider what he has delivered respecting the Λόγος, and the doctrine of the Trinity. That he asserted the divinity of the Λόγος, and a real Trinity, is admitted even by those who are most anxious to prove that the early Christians were Unitarians: but they endeavour to invalidate his testimony by contending that he was the first who openly maintained these doctrines, which were suggested to him by the writings of Plato—in other words, that he was the first who corrupted the Gospel, by endeavouring to engraft the notions of Gentile philosophy upon its sublime but simple truths. That Justin had studied and admired the Platonic philosophy, we know from himself; but that he was indebted to it for the doctrines of the Divinity of the Λόγος, and of the Trinity, is a position to which we cannot yield our assent; because, in the first place, no sufficient proof has yet been produced, that even the germ of those doctrines exists in the writings of Plato; and because, in the next place, his own references to those writings are wholly at variance with the position.

The design of his two Apologies is to give an accurate description of the faith of the Christians, and to remove the prejudices which existed against them in the minds of the heathen. One of these prejudices was, that they ¹ worshipped a crucified man. Not so, he replies; the object of our worship is the Divine Λόγος, who was content to become incarnate, and to die on the cross for the sake of mankind. Now as Justin's wish was to render the doctrines of Christianity ² as acceptable as possible to the Gentiles, by pointing out features of resemblance between them and the tenets of the philosophers, it is reasonable to suppose that he would not fail to allege those passages of Plato's writings, which he conceived to afford the strongest confir-

¹ ἐνταῦθα γὰρ μανίαν ἡμῶν καταφαίνονται, δευτέραν χώραν, μετὰ τὸν ἄτρεπτον καὶ ἀεὶ ὄντα Θεὸν καὶ γεννήτορα τῶν ἁπάντων, ἀνθρώπῳ σταυρωθέντι διδόναι ἡμᾶς λέγοντες, ἀγνοοῦντες τὸ ἐν τούτῳ μυστήριον ᾧ προσέχειν ὑμᾶς, ἐξηγουμένων ἡμῶν, προτρεπόμεθα. p. 61 A. Compare p. 68 A. 90 B.

² οὐχ ὅτι ἀλλότριά ἐστι τὰ Πλάτωνος διδάγματα τοῦ Χριστοῦ, ἀλλ' ὅτι οὐκ ἔστι πάντη ὅμοια, ὥσπερ οὐδὲ τὰ τῶν ἄλλων, Στωικῶν τε, καὶ ποιητῶν, καὶ συγγραφέων. p. 51 B. Compare 66 C.

mation of his opinions respecting the Λόγος and the Trinity. What, then, are the passages which he produces? One[1] from the Timæus, to prove that when Plato, speaking of the Person who is second to the Supreme God, said, ἐχίασεν αὐτὸν ἐν τῷ παντὶ, he alluded to the brazen serpent set up by Moses in the wilderness, but did not understand that the serpent was typical of the cross of Christ. Another[2] passage quoted by Justin is from the second

---

[1] The passage in Justin runs thus, καὶ τὸ ἐν τῷ παρὰ Πλάτωνι Τιμαίῳ φυσιολογούμενον περὶ τοῦ υἱοῦ τοῦ Θεοῦ, ὅτε λέγει, ἐχίασεν αὐτὸν ἐν τῷ παντὶ, παρὰ Μωσέως λαβὼν ὁμοίως εἶπεν. p. 92 E. But Plato in the place alluded to is speaking of the creation of the soul of the universe. ταύτην οὖν τὴν ξύστασιν πᾶσαν διπλῆν κατὰ μῆκος σχίσας, μέσην πρὸς μέσην ἑκατέραν ἀλλήλαις, οἷον χ, προσβαλὼν, κατέκαμψεν εἰς κύκλον. p. 36. Tom. III. Ed. Serr.

[2] καὶ τὸ εἰπεῖν αὐτὸν τρίτον, ἐπειδὴ, ὡς προείπομεν, ἐπάνω τῶν ὑδάτων ἀνέγνω ὑπὸ Μωσέως εἰρημένον ἐπιφέρεσθαι τὸ τοῦ Θεοῦ πνεῦμα. δευτέραν μὲν γαρ χώραν τῷ παρὰ Θεοῦ λόγῳ, ὃν κεχιάσθαι ἐν τῷ παντὶ ἔφη, δίδωσι· τὴν δὲ τρίτην τῷ λεχθέντι ἐπιφέρεσθαι τῷ ὕδατι πνεύματι, εἰπὼν, τὰ δὲ τρίτα περὶ τὸν τρίτον. p. 93 B. The passage in Pluto runs thus, περὶ τὸν πάντων βασιλέα πάντ᾿ ἐστὶ, καὶ ἐκείνου ἕνεκα πάντα· καὶ ἐκεῖνο αἴτιον ἁπάντων τῶν καλῶν. δεύτερον δὲ περὶ, τὰ δεύτερα· καὶ τρίτον περὶ, τὰ τρίτα p. 312. Tom. III. Comp. Dial. p. 220 C. καὶ τοῦτο μέγιστον καὶ τιμιώτατον ἔργον ἡγεῖσθαι, τὰ δὲ λοιπὰ δεύτερα καὶ τρίτα. If the hortatory address to the Greeks was the composition of Justin, the argument acquires still greater force; for though the author of that work mentions many of Plato's opinions respecting the nature of God, the creation of the world, &c., which he supposes to have been borrowed from the writers of the Old Testament; yet he is wholly silent concerning the Λόγος Indeed Justin's repeated assertion, that Plato was indebted to the writings of Moses and the prophets for whatever right

Epistle, where he endeavours to discover an allusion to the Trinity in the words τὰ δὲ τρίτα περὶ τὸν τρίτον, in which he supposes Plato to have referred to the description of the Spirit moving on the face of the waters, in the first chapter of Genesis. It is utterly impossible that passages like these should have been the sources from which Justin originally drew his notions respecting the Λόγος and the Trinity.

If we turn to the Dialogue with Trypho, we learn that the Jews, as well as the Gentiles, objected against the Christians the divine honours paid by them to a crucified man. How does Justin answer the objection? By alleging passages from the Old Testament; from which he proves that Christ, who preached and was crucified under the Emperor Tiberius, was the Λόγος, made flesh, who had before conversed with the Patriarchs; and whom, together with the Holy Spirit, the Father addressed when he created man. Are we, therefore, to conclude that he was indebted solely to those passages for his knowledge of the doctrines of the Divinity of the Λόγος and the Trinity? Yet this surely is as reasonable a conclusion as to infer, from the passages before cited, that he borrowed them from

notions he possessed on the subject of religion, is incompatible with the supposition that he would himself borrow doctrines from Plato.

Plato. In both instances he used arguments which he deemed most likely to have weight with the persons whom he was addressing. He was anxious to persuade both the Gentiles and the Jews, that the writings which they respectively esteemed of the highest authority contained intimations, however obscure, of those sublime doctrines; but the sources from which he himself derived the knowledge of them were the rule of faith, handed down in the Church, and the writings of the New Testament. I mean not to affirm that the notions which he imbibed in the schools of heathen philosophy have not affected his language in speaking of the doctrines: I say only that he did not derive the doctrines themselves from that source.

Another circumstance well deserving consideration is the manner in which Justin mentions these doctrines. He uniformly speaks of them as held not by himself alone, or the more enlightened few, but by all the members of the Christian community. Had he been conscious that he was broaching opinions either utterly unknown, or not generally received, in the Church, he would surely have deemed it necessary to allude to the fact; and to anticipate the charge, to which he obviously exposed himself, of misrepresenting the tenets of the Christians. He has indeed been accused of betraying this consciousness, in a [1] passage in the Dialogue with Trypho; where he admits, if we may believe

[1] Justin had been contending that, even if it could not be proved that Christ was God, the Son of the Ruler of the universe, and born of a Virgin, yet it did not, therefore, follow that the Jews were justified in rejecting him; since, though a man born of men, he might have been elected to be the Messiah. He then goes on, καὶ γάρ εἰσί τινες, ὦ φίλοι, ἔλεγον, ἀπὸ τοῦ ἡμετέρου γένους ὁμολογοῦντες αὐτὸν Χριστὸν εἶναι, ἄνθρωπον δὲ ἐξ ἀνθρώπων γενόμενον ἀποφαινόμενοι· οἷς οὐ συντίθεμαι. οὐδ᾽ ἂν πλεῖστοι ταῦτά μοι δοξάσαντες εἴποιεν, ἐπειδὴ οὐκ ἀνθρωπείοις διδάγμασι κεκελεύσμεθα ὑπ᾽ αὐτοῦ τοῦ Χριστοῦ πείθεσθαι, ἀλλὰ τοῖς διὰ τῶν μακαρίων προφητῶν κηρυχθεῖσι, καὶ δι᾽ αὐτοῦ διδαχθεῖσι. p. 267 E. This passage has exercised the ingenuity of the Commentators. The Latin translation in Thirlby's edition is as follows. Sunt enim nonnulli, o amici, dixi, ex genere nostro profitentes ipsum Christum esse, sed hominem ex hominibus genitum esse affirmant. Quibus non assentior; neque id sane multi qui in eâdem mecum sententiâ sunt (though ταῦτα is in the text, the translator appears to have read ταύτα) dixerint. Siquidem jussi sumus, &c. Bull, instead of ἡμετέρου, would read ὑμετέρου, and understand the expression ὑμετέρου γένους of the Jewish Christians: this correction derives support from the expressions ἀπὸ τοῦ γένους τοῦ ὑμετέρου, ἀπὸ τοῦ γένους ὑμῶν, which are frequently applied by Justin to the Jews. I am inclined, however, to retain ἡμετέρου, and to translate thus. " For there are some, my friends, of our race (Christians, as opposed to Jews, ὑμέτερον γένος) who confess that he was the Christ, but affirm that he was a man born of human parents; with whom I do not agree; nor should I, even if very many of those who think as I do were to say so; since we are commanded by Christ to attend, not to the doctrines of men, but to that which was proclaimed by the blessed prophets, and taught by himself;" where I understand the words πλεῖστοι ταῦτα μοι δοξάσαντες to mean those who agreed with Justin in professing Christianity. But, whether this translation is correct or not, the word τινὲς, opposed as it is to πλεῖστοι, is alone sufficient to prove that the doctrine of the mere humanity of Christ was the

the Unitarian writers, that the majority of Christians in his day regarded Christ as a mere man, born after the manner of men. The passage is not without difficulty; but the sense put upon it by the Unitarians is at variance with every sound principle of Interpretation. The fact, moreover, that, among the other charges urged against the early Christians, they were accused of *worshipping* a crucified man, is scarcely compatible with the supposition that the doctrine of the mere humanity of Christ was the prevalent opinion among them. In a word, the whole tenor of Justin's language is irreconcileable with the theory, that he invented, or at least first published, the doctrines of the Divinity of the Λόγος and of the Trinity.

Some writers, in order to remove from the early Fathers the charge of borrowing their doctrine respecting the Λόγος from Plato, point out the Apocryphal Books of the Old Testament, the works of Philo, and the traditional Interpretations of Scripture current among the Jews of our Saviour's time, and preserved in the Chaldee Paraphrases, as the

opinion of the minority, and that a small minority, in the time of Justin. Wilson, Illustration, &c. p. 152. translates the passage nearly as I do. "There *are some* of our race who acknowledge him to be Christ; yet maintain that he was a man born of human parents: with whom I do not agree: nor should I, if very many, who entertains the same opinions with myself, were to declare" for this doctrine.

sources from which the language of the early Fathers respecting it was derived; but they are not, as it appears to me, borne out in their opinion by the works of Justin Martyr. A large portion of his Dialogue with Trypho is occupied in proving that, whenever God is said in the Old Testament to have appeared to the Patriarchs, it was, in fact, the Λόγος who appeared. How greatly would he have added to the force of his arguments, if he had shown that this interpretation of the passages in Scripture to which he appealed was in strict conformity with the tradition of the Jewish Church! But neither he, nor his opponent, seems to have entertained the slightest suspicion that any such traditional interpretations existed. I mean not to allege Justin's silence as a proof that they did not exist; but that, even if they did exist, it is most improbable that he derived his own opinions from them.

Having, as we think, satisfactorily replied to the charge which has been brought against Justin, of corrupting the Gospel by an admixture of philosophical notions derived from the writings of Plato, we will proceed to consider what he has actually delivered respecting the Λόγος and the Trinity.

In [1] the first Apology, Justin, when defending

[1] p. 60 C. τὸν δημιουργὸν τοῦδε τοῦ παντὸς σεβόμενοι—τὸν διδάσκαλόν τε τούτων γενόμενον ἡμῖν καὶ εἰς τοῦτο γεννηθέντα

the Christians against the charge of Atheism, says that they worshipped the Creator of the Universe, and placed next to him his Son, and honoured in the third place the Prophetic Spirit. In [1] another Ἰησοῦν Χριστὸν, τὸν σταυρωθέντα ἐπὶ Ποντίου Πιλάτου τοῦ γενομένου ἐν Ἰουδαίᾳ ἐπὶ χρόνοις Τιβερίου Καίσαρος ἐπιτρόπου, υἱὸν αὐτὸν τοῦ ὄντως Θεοῦ μαθόντες καὶ ἐν δευτέρᾳ χώρᾳ ἔχοντες, πνεῦμά τε προφητικὸν ἐν τρίτῃ τάξει—τιμῶμεν. See, with reference to the Λόγος, p. 59 E, Apol. II. p. 51 D.

[1] ἀλλ' ἐκεῖνόν τε, καὶ τὸν παρ' αὐτοῦ υἱὸν ἐλθόντα καὶ διδάξαντα ἡμᾶς ταῦτα καὶ τὸν τῶν ἄλλων ἑπομένων καὶ ἐξομοιουμένων ἀγαθῶν ἀγγέλων στρατὸν, πνεῦμά τε τὸ προφητικὸν σεβόμεθα καὶ προσκυνοῦμεν. p. 56 C. This passage has been alleged by the Roman Catholics to prove that, in the earliest times of the Christian Church, worship was paid to angels To get rid of the inference, Protestant writers have had recourse to various expedients. Grabe connects καὶ τὸν—στρατὸν with ἡμᾶς, and supposes Justin to have meant that "the Son of God communicated the truths (of which Justin was speaking) to us (men) and to the host of good angels." This interpretation he supports by referring to Ephes. iii. 10. ἵνα γνωρισθῇ νῦν ταῖς ἀρχαῖς καὶ ταῖς ἐξουσίαις ἐν τοῖς ἐπουρανίοις διὰ τῆς ἐκκλησίας ἡ πολυποίκιλος σοφία τοῦ Θεοῦ. And to Irenæus, Lib. ii. c. 55. Semper co-existens Filius Patri olim et ab initio, semper revelat Patrem et Angelis, et Archangelis, et Potestatibus, et Virtutibus, et omnibus quibus vult revelare Deus. Others, and among them Le Nourry, though a Benedictine, connect καὶ τὸν—στρατὸν with ταῦτα, and suppose Justin to mean that the Son of God communicated to us these truths (viz. that the dæmons were not Gods) and also the knowledge of the existence of a host of good angels (We find διδάξαντος ταῦτα. Apol. II. p. 49 A. ἐδίδαξε ταῦτα. Apol. I. p. 99 B.) Others, instead of στρατὸν, would read στρατηγὸν, and construct for Justin a sentence, which, careless as he is, we believe him to have been incapable of writing. One thing is certain—that Justin, who expressly states that there were three objects of Christian worship, the Creator of the universe, his Son, and the Prophetic Spirit, could not intend to represent the angelic host as a distinct object of worship. I have sometimes

place the same statement is made with reference to the same charge. Again, speaking of the opinions of Plato, Justin says[1] δευτέραν μὲν γὰρ χώραν τῷ παρὰ Θεοῦ λόγῳ, ὃν κεχιάσθαι ἐν τῷ παντὶ ἔφη, δίδωσι· τὴν δὲ τρίτην τῷ λεχθέντι ἐπιφέρεσθαι τῷ ὕδατι πνεύματι, εἰπών· τὰ δὲ τρίτα, περὶ τὸν τρίτον. And with reference to the rite of Baptism[2], ἐπ' ὀνόματος γὰρ τοῦ πατρὸς τῶν ὅλων καὶ δεσπότου Θεοῦ, καὶ τοῦ σωτῆρος ἡμῶν Ἰησοῦ Χριστοῦ, καὶ πνεύματος ἁγίου, τὸ ἐν τῷ ὕδατι τότε λουτρὸν ποιοῦνται. And again,[3] ἐπὶ πᾶσί τε οἷς προσφερόμεθα εὐλογοῦμεν τὸν ποιητὴν τῶν πάντων, διὰ τοῦ υἱοῦ αὐτοῦ Ἰησοῦ Χριστοῦ, καὶ διὰ πνεύματος τοῦ ἁγίου.

When we proceed further to enquire into the manner in which Justin distinguishes between the

thought that in this passage καὶ τὸν—στρατὸν is equivalent to μετὰ τοῦ—στρατοῦ, and that Justin had in his mind the glorified state of Christ, when he should come to judge the world, surrounded by the host of heaven. Compare the Dialogue with Trypho, p. 247 E. ὡς υἱὸς γὰρ ἀνθρώπου ἐπάνω νεφελῶν ἐλεύσεται, ὡς Δανιὴλ ἐμήνυσεν, ἀγγέλων σὺν αὐτῷ ἀφικνουμένων· Apol. I. p. 87 B. ὅταν μετὰ δόξης ἐξ οὐρανῶν μετὰ τῆς ἀγγελικῆς αὐτοῦ στρατιᾶς κ. τ. ἑ. So p. 71 B. Justin, speaking of Satan, says, ὃν εἰς τὸ πῦρ πεμφθήσεσθαι μετὰ τῆς αὐτοῦ στρατιᾶς καὶ τῶν ἑπομένων ἀνθρώπων, κολασθησομένους τὸν ἀπέραντον αἰῶνα, προεμήνυσεν ὁ Χριστός. In the Dialogue, p. 264 A. we find ἵνα διὰ τῆς οἰκονομίας ταύτης ὁ πονηρευσάμενος τὴν ἀρχὴν ὄφις καὶ οἱ ἐξομοιωθέντες αὐτῷ ἄγγελοι καταλυθῶσι. See also p. 327 D. 360 D. and 284 B. where Christ is said to have called himself the Leader of the Heavenly Host. Compare p. 286 A.

[1] Apol. I. p. 93 B. [2] Apol. p. 94 A. [3] Ib. p. 98 C.

persons of the Trinity, we find that there are certain epithets and expressions which he applies to the first Person alone; such as [1] Unbegotten, Ineffable, the Maker and [2] Creator of all things. He says [3] also, that the Father never descended on

[1] So I translate ἀγέννητος Waterland, in all these passages, would substitute ἀγένητος for ἀγέννητος, Vol. III. p. 248. Ed. Oxon. 1823. ὅτι πρωτότοκος τῷ ἀγεννήτῳ Θεῷ ἐστι. Apol. I. p. 88 A. τὸν γὰρ ἀπὸ ἀγεννήτου καὶ ἀρρήτου Θεοῦ λόγον μετὰ τὸν Θεὸν προσκυνοῦμεν καὶ ἀγαπῶμεν. Apol. II. p. 51 D. See also p. 50 C. ὁ γὰρ ἄρρητος πατὴρ καὶ κύριος τῶν πάντων οὔτε ποι ἀφῖκται οὔτε περιπατεῖ, οὔτε καθεύδει, οὔτε ἀνίσταται, ἀλλ' ἐν τῇ αὐτοῦ χώρᾳ ὅπου ποτὲ μένει, κ. τ. ἑ. Dial. p. 356 E. τοῦ μόνου καὶ ἀγεννήτου καὶ ἀρρήτου Θεοῦ υἱόν. p. 355 D. τῷ ἀγεννήτῳ Θεῷ δια τοῦ Χριστοῦ. Apol. I. p. 85 B. μετὰ τὸν ἄτρεπτον καὶ ἀεὶ ὄντα Θεόν. p. 61 A. Θεῷ δὲ μόνῳ τῷ ἀγεννήτῳ διὰ τοῦ υἱοῦ ἐπομεθα. p. 61 B. Justin, as we have already seen, says that God has no proper name, no name expressive of his Essence : the names which we apply to him are expressive only of his Attributes. Thus Apol. I. p. 94 D. ὄνομα γὰρ τῷ ἀρρήτῳ Θεῷ οὐδεὶς ἔχει εἰπεῖν. p. 95 C. τὸν ἀνωνόμαστον Θεὸν λελαληκέναι τῷ Μωσεῖ. Apol. II. p. 44 D. See p. 9. n. 1. ὄνομα δὲ τῷ πάντων πατρὶ θετὸν, ἀγεννήτῳ ὄντι, οὐκ ἔστιν. Dial p. 277 B. παρὰ τὸν νοούμενον ποιητὴν τῶν ὅλων. A doubt, however, may arise whether in some cases Justin does not use the word *God* absolutely ; not with reference to the Father, as distinct from the Son and Holy Spirit.

[2] Thus he is called ὁ πάντων πατὴρ καὶ δημιουργός. Apol. I. p. 57 A. ὁ ποιητὴς τοῦδε τοῦ παντός. p. 70 B ὁ δημιουργὸς τοῦδε τοῦ παντός. p. 60 C. 92 A ὁ δεσπότης πάντων καὶ πατὴρ Θεός. p. 76 E. 81 C. 83 D. ὁ ποιητὴς τῶν ὅλων Θεὸς καὶ πατήρ. Dial. p. 225 A. ὁ παντοκράτωρ καὶ ποιητὴς τῶν ὅλων Θεός. p. 234 B. 310 A. ὁ πατὴρ τῶν ὅλων καὶ ἀγέννητος Θεός. p. 342 A.

[3] ὑπὸ ἄλλου τοῦ ἐν τοῖς ὑπερουρανίοις ἀεὶ μένοντος, καὶ οὐδενὶ ὀφθέντος, ἢ ὁμιλήσαντος δι' ἑαυτοῦ ποτε, ὃν ποιητὴν τοῦ ὅλου καὶ πατέρα νοοῦμεν. Dial. p. 275 A. οὐ τὸν ποιητὴν τῶν ὅλων καὶ πατέρα, καταλιπόντα τὰ ὑπὲρ οὐρανὸν ἅπαντα, ἐν ὀλίγῳ γῆς

earth or appeared to man, but remained always in the highest heaven.

With respect to the second Person in the Trinity, Justin says, that [1] in the beginning before all created things, God begat from himself a certain Rational Power, who is called by the Holy Spirit the Glory of the Lord, sometimes the Son, sometimes the Wisdom; and he illustrates the mode of generation by a comparison borrowed from a fire, which does not diminish the fire from which it is lighted. So this Rational Power was generated without any abscission or division of the Essence or Substance of the Father. Sometimes instead of the word generation, Justin uses [2] emission or

μορίῳ πεφάνθαι πᾶς ὁστισοῦν, κᾶν μικρὸν νοῦν ἔχων, τολμήσει εἰπεῖν. p. 283 B. See also p. 356 E. quoted in Note 1. p. 56. 357 B.

[1] ἀρχὴν πρὸ πάντων τῶν κτισμάτων ὁ Θεὸς γεγέννηκε δύναμίν τινα ἐξ ἑαυτοῦ λογικὴν, ἥτις καὶ δόξα Κυρίου ὑπὸ τοῦ πνεύματος τοῦ ἁγίου καλεῖται, ποτε δὲ υἱὸς, ποτὲ δὲ σοφία—καὶ ὁποῖον ἐπὶ πυρὸς ὁρῶμεν ἄλλο γιγνόμενον, οὐκ ἐλαττουμένου ἐκείνου ἐξ οὗ ἡ ἄνοψις γέγονεν, ἀλλὰ τοῦ αὐτοῦ μένοντος. Dial p. 284 A. εἰπὼν τὴν δύναμιν ταύτην γεγεννῆσθαι ἀπὸ τοῦ πατρὸς δυνάμει καὶ βουλῇ αὐτοῦ, ἀλλ' οὐ κατὰ ἀποτομὴν, ὡς ἀπομεριζομένης τῆς τοῦ πατρὸς οὐσίας, ὁποῖα τὰ ἄλλα πάντα μεριζόμενα καὶ τεμνόμενα οὐ τὰ αὐτά ἐστιν ἃ καὶ πρὶν τμηθῆναι· καὶ παραδείγματος χάριν παρειλήφειν τὰ ὡς (f. ὡς τὰ) ἀπὸ πυρὸς ἀναπτόμενα πυρὰ ἕτερα ὁρῶμεν, οὐδὲν ἐλαττουμένου ἐκείνου, ἐξ οὗ ἀναφθῆναι πολλὰ δύνανται, ἀλλὰ ταὐτοῦ μένοντος. p. 358 D.

[2] ἀλλὰ τοῦτο τὸ τῷ ὄντι ἀπὸ τοῦ πατρὸς προβληθὲν γέννημα, πρὸ πάντων τῶν ποιημάτων συνῆν τῷ πατρί. καὶ τούτῳ ὁ πατὴρ προσομιλεῖ f. προσωμίλει. p. 285 E. νενοήκαμεν ὄντα καὶ πρὸ

prolation. The general opinion of the Ante-Nicene Fathers appears to have been that, previously to this generation or emission, the Logos subsisted from eternity in a state of most intimate union with the Father, though personally distinct from him; being his Intelligence and his Counsellor, in devising the plan of Creation. But though we find in Justin's writings nothing decidedly at variance with this opinion, he no where expresses it in clear and explicit terms. For most of the passages, quoted by [1] Bull and Grabe, in order to prove that

πάντων ποιημάτων, ἀπὸ τοῦ πατρὸς δυνάμει αὐτοῦ καὶ βουλῇ προελθόντα. p. 327 B. ὅτι οὐκ ἔστιν ἀνθρώπινον ἔργον, ἀλλὰ τῆς βουλῆς τοῦ προβάλλοντος αὐτὸν πατρὸς τῶν ὅλων Θεοῦ. p. 301 B.

[1] ὄνομα δὲ τῷ πάντων πατρὶ θετὸν, ἀγεννήτῳ ὄντι, οὐκ ἔστιν. ᾧ γὰρ ἂν καὶ ὀνόματι (f. ὀνόματί τις) προσαγορεύηται, πρεσβύτερον ἔχει τὸν θέμενον τὸ ὄνομα. τὸ δὲ πατὴρ, καὶ Θεὸς, καὶ κτιστὴς, καὶ Κύριος, καὶ δεσπότης οὐκ ὀνόματά ἐστιν, ἀλλ' ἐκ τῶν εὐποιιῶν καὶ τῶν ἔργων προσρήσεις. ὁ δὲ υἱὸς ἐκείνου, ὁ μόνος λεγόμενος κυρίως υἱὸς, ὁ Λόγος πρὸ τῶν ποιημάτων καὶ συνὼν καὶ γεννώμενος, ὅτε τὴν ἀρχὴν δι' αὐτοῦ πάντα ἔκτισε καὶ ἐκόσμησε, Χριστὸς μὲν κατὰ τὸ κεχρίσθαι καὶ κοσμῆσαι τὰ πάντα δι' αὐτοῦ τὸν Θεὸν, λέγεται· ὄνομα καὶ αὐτὸ περιέχον ἄγνωστον σημασίαν· ὃν τρόπον καὶ τὸ Θεὸς προσαγόρευμα, οὐκ ὄνομά ἐστιν, ἀλλὰ πράγματος δυσεξηγήτου ἔμφυτος τῇ φύσει τῶν ἀνθρώπων δόξα. Apol. II. p. 44 D. translated in p. 9. of this work. On this passage Bull remarks, In his verbis docet Justinus Deo Patri et Filio nullum propriè nomen competere, sed tantùm appellationes quasdam, ab ipsorum beneficiis et operibus petitas, ipsis a nobis tribui. Hujus autem assertionis rationem hanc affert: quod Deus Pater ingenitus atque æternus sit; Filius vero ut Verbum ejus ipsi coexistat; ac proinde uterque neminem habeat se antiquiorem, qui ipsi nomen imponeret. Quin et Christi nomen ejus Divinitati tribuit Justinus, quasi scilicet ὁ Λόγος et Filius Dei Deo Patri coexistens et ex ipso *ab æterno* nascens (tanquam

Justin held the doctrine of the co-eternity of the Logos with the Father, are capable of a different interpretation, and may be understood merely of an scilicet æternæ lucis æternus splendor) tum Christi nomen sortitus fuerit, quum Pater per ipsum cuncta conformaverit ornaveritque. Def. Fid. Nic. Sect. III. c. 2. sub. in. With respect to this comment, we may observe in the first place, that Justin does not assert that no name can properly and essentially be given to the Son, but to the Father of all things, an appellation uniformly applied by him to the Father, as distinct from the Son; in the next place, that Justin does not say that the Son existed together with the Father *from eternity*, but before all created things, πρὸ τῶν ποιημάτων; and thirdly, that Justin does not say that the Son received the name of Christ, when the Father made all things by him. Grabe accordingly seems not to have been satisfied with Bull's Interpretation, though he contends that the word συνὼν *implies* the eternal existence of the Son with the Father; referring in support of his opinion to the Dialogue with Trypho, p. 267 B. προυπάρχειν Θεὸν ὄντα πρὸ αἰώνων τοῦτον Χριστόν. p. 276 D. τὸν καὶ πρὸ ποιήσεως κόσμου ὄντα Θεόν. and to p. 285 E. quoted in note 2. p. 57, of which passages, as well as of p. 264 A. ὃς καὶ πρὸ ἑωσφόρου καὶ σελήνης ἦν, it may still be said that they are not decisive; for Arius appears to have been willing to call Christ, τὸν ἐκ πατρὸς πρὸ πάντων τῶν αἰώνων γεγενημένον, Θεὸν λόγον. Socrates, Hist. Eccl. L. I. c. 26. Waterland also classes Justin among the writers who make the generation of the Son *temporary*, Vol. I. p. 104. Observe too what he says respecting Bishop Bull in p. 105. There is in p. 302 B. a very remarkable passage, καὶ Δαβὶδ δὲ πρὸ ἡλίου καὶ σελήνης ἐκ γαστρὸς γεννηθήσεσθαι αὐτὸν κατὰ τὴν τοῦ πατρὸς βουλὴν ἐκήρυξε. The reference is to Psalm cx. 3. ἐν ταῖς λαμπρότησι τῶν ἁγίων σου, ἐκ γαστρὸς πρὸ ἑωσφόρου ἐγέννησά σε. Commentators generally understand this verse of the generation of the Son to create the universe : but in p. 286 E. Justin refers it to his birth from the Virgin. See p. 82 E. 250 C. 310 A. In p. 309 C. the words ἐκ γαστρὸς are omitted.

existence prior to the creation of all things. The expression which is in appearance most opposed to the doctrine of the co-eternity of the Son with the Father, is in a passage of the Dialogue with Trypho, p. 358 E. where Justin quotes Genesis xix. 24. to prove that the Old Testament recognizes two distinct Lords; one who descended on earth to hear the cry of Sodom ; the other who remained in heaven, *who*, Justin goes on to say, *is the Lord of the Lord on earth, as being Father and God, and is the cause of his (the Lord on earth) being both powerful, and Lord, and God*. ὃς καὶ τοῦ ἐπὶ γῆς Κυρίου Κύριός ἐστιν, ὡς πατὴρ καὶ Θεὸς, αἴτιός τε αὐτῷ τοῦ εἶναι καὶ δυνατῷ, καὶ Κυρίῳ, καὶ Θεῷ. See Bull's remarks on this passage, Sect iv. c. 1. Def. Fid. Nic. Again, p. 311, B Justin says, ὅς ἐστι Κύριος τῶν δυνάμεων διὰ τὸ θέλημα τοῦ δόντος αὐτῷ πατρός. *Who is the Lord of Hosts by the will of the Father who gave him the dominion*. When, however, we find it expressly stated that it was Christ who appeared to Moses, and described himself as the Necessarily Existing [1]ἐγώ εἰμι ὁ ὤν, we must conceive Justin to have maintained the perfect Divinity of Christ, and consequently his co-eternity with the Father.

This rational power, according to Justin, was begotten or emitted, that he might be the [2]Minis-

---

[1] Apol. I. p. 95 E.
[2] μετὰ τοῦ φαινομένου μὲν, ἐκ τοῦ τῇ τοῦ πατρὸς βουλῇ

ter of the Father in [1] creating the universe, and conducting what the Fathers term the [2] Œconomy.

[1] ὑπηρετεῖν· Θεοῦ δὲ, ἐκ τοῦ εἶναι τέκνον πρωτότοκον τῶν ὅλων κτισμάτων. Dial. p. 354 D. Compare p. 279 A. 280 D. 283 B. 284 A. 356 C. 357 C.
ἀλλ' ἐπειδὴ ἐννοηθέντα τὸν Θεὸν διὰ λόγου τὸν κόσμον ποιῆσαι ἔγνωσαν. Apol. I. p. 97 B. ὥστε λόγῳ Θεοῦ ἐκ τῶν ὑποκειμένων καὶ προδηλωθέντων διὰ Μωσέως γεγενῆσθαι τὸν πάντα κόσμον καὶ Πλάτων, καὶ οἱ ταῦτα λέγοντες, καὶ ἡμεῖς ἐμάθομεν. p. 92 D. ὥσπερ τἄλλα πάντα ζῶα λόγῳ Θεοῦ τὴν ἀρχὴν ἐγεννήθη. Dial. p. 310 C. It has been already observed that Justin applies the expressions, Maker and Creator of all things, to the Father exclusively: the Λόγος was Ministerial. Justin speaks of the world as created out of matter without form: ὕλην ἄμορφον οὖσαν στρέψαντα (1 τρέψαντα) τὸν Θεὸν κόσμον ποιῆσαι. Apol. I. p. 92 C. Compare p. 58 B. 99 A. We must not, however, thence infer that he maintained the eternity of Matter.

[2] By the word οἰκονομία, I understand that Dispensation which commenced with the generation of the Son for the purpose of creating the universe, and will end when "he shall deliver up the kingdom to God, even the Father." 1 Cor. xv. 24. This is the meaning of the word in its fullest acceptation. but it is also applied to any particular event or epoch in that Dispensation. Thus to the Passion of Christ, καὶ τῇ τοῦ γενομένου πάθους αὐτοῦ οἰκονομίᾳ. Dial. p. 247 D. 331 A; to his assumption of our nature p. 264 A; to his compliance with the Mosaic ordinances p. 291 E; to his Ministry on earth p. 315 A; to his birth from the Virgin p. 348 B. Sometimes the word appears to be equivalent to mystery, and to signify that some hidden meaning is couched under any action or event, for instance, under the polygamy of the Patriarchs. p. 364 A. 371 A. So we find p. 334 E. with reference to Jonah's gourd, διὰ τῆς οἰκονομίας τοῦ ἐκ τῆς γῆς ἀνατεῖλαι αὐτῷ σικυῶνα. Mosheim Cent. II. p. 2. c. 3. § 8. speaks of a mode of disputing κατ' οἰκονομίαν; but there is no vestige of this use of the word in Justin or the earlier Fathers. In my work on Clement of Alexandria, p. 398, I have gone fully into this question.

Hence we find him present at [1] the creation of man; he it was who appeared [2] to Abraham, who [3] wrestled with Jacob, who [4] conversed with Moses from the burning bush, who [5] announced the approaching fall of Jericho to Joshua, who [6] inspired the prophets, who [7] in the fulness of time condescended to be born of the Virgin, to assume the human form, and to suffer death on the Cross; who rose again from the dead, ascended into heaven, and shall come again [8] to judge mankind.

Of the titles applied by Justin to the second Person in the Trinity, some have reference to his

[1] Dial. p. 285 B.
[2] ὅτι ὁ ὀφθεὶς τῷ 'Αβραὰμ πρὸς τῇ δρυὶ τῇ Μαμβρῇ Θεός. Dial. p. 275 A. 276 E. 281 E. See p. 34. n. 3.
[3] Dial. p. 281 E. See p. 35. n. 2.
[4] ἐν ἰδέᾳ πυρὸς ἐκ βάτου προσωμίλησεν αὐτῷ (τῷ Μωσεῖ) ὁ ἡμέτερος Χριστός. Apol. I. p. 95 B. Dial. p. 282 D. 340 D. See p. 35 n. 3.
[5] Dial. p. 286 A.
[6] λόγος γὰρ ἦν καί ἐστιν ὁ ἐν παντὶ ὤν, καὶ διὰ τῶν προφητῶν προειπὼν τὰ μέλλοντα γίγνεσθαι. Apol. II. p. 49 A.
[7] λοιπὸν οὖν καὶ ὅτι οὗτος διὰ τῆς παρθένου ἄνθρωπος γεννηθῆναι κατὰ τὴν τοῦ πατρὸς αὐτοῦ βούλησιν ὑπέμεινεν, ἀπόδειξον, καὶ σταυρωθῆναι, καὶ ἀποθανεῖν· δῆλον (f. δηλοῦ) δὲ καὶ ὅτι μετὰ ταῦτα ἀναστὰς ἀνελήλυθεν εἰς τὸν οὐρανόν. Dial. p. 286 C. ἀλλ' εἰς ἀπόδειξιν γεγόνασιν οἵδε οἱ λόγοι, ὅτι υἱὸς Θεοῦ καὶ ἀπόστολος Ἰησοῦς ὁ Χριστός ἐστι, πρότερον λόγος ὢν καὶ ἐν ἰδέᾳ πυρός ποτε φανείς· ποτὲ δὲ καὶ ἐν εἰκόνι ἀσωμάτων· νῦν δὲ διὰ θελήματος Θεοῦ ὑπὲρ τοῦ ἀνθρωπείου γένους ἄνθρωπος γενόμενος, ὑπέμεινε καὶ παθεῖν κ. τ. έ. Apol. I. p. 96. A.
[8] καὶ αὐτὸς τὴν κρίσιν τοῦ πάντος ἀνθρωπίνου γένους ποιήσεται. Apol. I. p. 88 A. See p. 57 B.

nature; some to the relation in which he stands to the Father; some to the part which he bears in the Gospel Œconomy. In the first respect he is repeatedly called [1] God, and [2] said to be the object of worship.

In the second respect he is called the [3] Son of God in a peculiar sense, or his only-begotten Son,

---

[1] ὃς καὶ λόγος (f. supplend. καὶ) πρωτότοκος ὢν τοῦ Θεοῦ, καὶ Θεὸς ὑπάρχει. Apol. I. p. 96 D. Dial. p. 267 B. 276 D. quoted in Note 1. p. 58. 314 B. οὗτος αὐτὸς Θεὸς ὢν σημαίνει τῷ Μωσεῖ. p. 282 E. καὶ ἄγγελος καλούμενος καὶ Θεὸς ὑπάρχων. p. 283 D. μαρτυρήσει δέ μοι ὁ Λόγος τῆς σοφίας, αὐτὸς ὢν οὗτος ὁ Θεὸς ἀπὸ τοῦ πατρὸς τῶν ὅλων γεννηθείς, p. 284 C. ἵνα καὶ Θεὸν ἄνωθεν προελθόντα, καὶ ἄνθρωπον ἐν ἀνθρώποις γενόμενον, γνωρίσητε. p. 288 E. ὁ μὲν γὰρ (Μωσῆς) πρόσκαιρον ἔδωκεν αὐτοῖς τὴν κληρονομίαν, ἅτε οὐ Χριστὸς ὁ Θεὸς ὤν, οὐδὲ υἱὸς Θεοῦ. p. 340 D. 354 A. τῶν ὑπὸ τοῦ ἡμετέρου ἱερέως, καὶ Θεοῦ, καὶ Χριστοῦ, υἱοῦ τοῦ πατρὸς τῶν ὅλων, γίγνεσθαι μελλόντων. p. 343 B. καὶ τοῦ πάθους ὃ πέπονθε δι' αὐτοῦ ὁ Θεὸς τοῦ Θεοῦ, μέμνηται. p. 345 A. Θεὸς Θεοῦ υἱός. p. 357 D. οὐκ ἂν ἐξηρνεῖσθε αὐτὸν εἶναι Θεόν, τοῦ μόνου καὶ ἀγεννήτου καὶ ἀρρήτου Θεοῦ υἱόν. p. 355 D. ἀλλ' ἐκεῖνον τὸν κατὰ βουλὴν τὴν ἐκείνου καὶ Θεὸν ὄντα. p. 357 B

[2] τὸν γὰρ ἀπὸ ἀγεννήτου καὶ ἀρρήτου Θεοῦ λόγον μετὰ τὸν Θεὸν προσκυνοῦμεν καὶ ἀγαπῶμεν. Apol. II. p. 51 C. ὅτι γοῦν καὶ προσκυνητός ἐστι καὶ Θεὸς καὶ Χριστὸς ὑπὸ τοῦ ταῦτα ποιήσαντος μαρτυρούμενος. Dial. p. 287 B. See also p. 294 C. 302 B.

[3] καὶ Ἰησοῦς Χριστὸς μόνος ἰδίως υἱὸς τῷ Θεῷ γεγέννηται, Λόγος αὐτοῦ ὑπάρχων, καὶ πρωτότοκος, καὶ δύναμις. Apol. I. p. 68 C. υἱὸν αὐτοῦ (f. αὐτὸν) τοῦ ὄντως Θεοῦ μαθόντες. p. 60 D. Apol. II. p. 44 D. quoted in Note 1. p. 58. μονογενὴς γὰρ ὅτι ἦν τῷ πατρὶ τῶν ὅλων οὗτος, ἰδίως ἐξ αὐτοῦ Λόγος καὶ δύναμις γεγενημένος κ. τ ἑ. Dial. p. 332 C.

his ¹ Reason or Word, his ² First-Born or Begotten, his ³ Power, ⁴ his Thought or Intelligence, if the

---

[1] According to the passage quoted from the first Apology, Note 7. p. 62. Christ was the Λόγος before he was the Son and Messenger of God. ταῦτα ὁ Λόγος, Θεῖος (f. Θεὸς) ὢν, εἰργάσατο. Apol. I. p. 58 D. ὁ δὲ Λόγος τοῦ Θεοῦ ἐστιν ὁ υἱὸς αὐτοῦ. p. 95 D.

[2] γνόντες αὐτὸν πρωτότοκον μὲν τοῦ Θεοῦ, καὶ πρὸ πάντων τῶν κτισμάτων καὶ τῶν πατριαρχῶν, υἱόν. Dial. p. 326 E. See p. 310 B. 311 B. 367 D. 344 C. τῷ δὲ καὶ τὸν Λόγον, ὅ ἐστι πρῶτον γέννημα τοῦ Θεοῦ. Apol. I p. 66 E. νοεῖτε, ὦ ἀκροαταὶ, εἴ γε καὶ τὸν νοῦν προσέχετε, καὶ ὅτι γεγεννῆσθαι ὑπὸ τοῦ πατρὸς τοῦτο τὸ γέννημα πρὸ πάντων ἀπλῶς τῶν κτισμάτων ὁ Λόγος ἐδήλου· καὶ τὸ γεννώμενον τοῦ γεννῶντος ἀριθμῷ ἕτερόν ἐστιν, πᾶς ὁστισοῦν ὁμολογήσειε. Dial. p. 359 B. Justin uses the word generation in speaking of Christ both as begotten before all created things, and as born from the Virgin. See the passages quoted in Note 1. p. 58. as instances of the former use of this word, and the following examples of the latter : εἰ δὲ καὶ ἰδίως παρὰ τὴν κοινὴν γένεσιν γεγενῆσθαι αὐτὸν ἐκ Θεοῦ λέγομεν λόγον Θεοῦ κ. τ. ἑ. Apol. I. p. 67 E. εἰ δὲ διὰ παρθένου γεγεννῆσθαι φέρομεν. p. 68 B. δι' ἣν δ' αἰτίαν διὰ δυνάμεως τοῦ λόγου κατὰ τὴν τοῦ πατρὸς πάντων καὶ δεσπότου Θεοῦ βουλὴν, διὰ παρθένου ἄνθρωπος ἀπεκυήθη κ. τ. ἑ. p. 83 D. διὰ γὰρ παρθένου τῆς ἀπὸ τοῦ σπέρματος Ἰακὼβ, τοῦ γενομένου πατρὸς Ἰούδα, τοῦ δεδηλωμένου Ἰουδαίων πατρὸς, διὰ δυνάμεως Θεοῦ ἀπεκυήθη. p. 74 D. where διὰ δυνάμεως Θεοῦ is equivalent to διὰ δυνάμεως τοῦ λόγου in the passage before cited. See also Apol. II. p. 45 A. Dial. p 241 B. In p. 316 E. the word γένεσις is used with reference to the time when the Holy Spirit descended upon Christ at his baptism, and the voice from heaven declared him to be the Son of God, τότε γένεσιν αὐτοῦ λέγων γίγνεσθαι τοῖς ἀνθρώποις, ἐξότου ἡ γνῶσις αὐτοῦ ἔμελλε γίγνεσθαι, υἱός μου εἶ σὺ, ἐγὼ σήμερον γεγέννηκά σε.

[3] οὐ γὰρ σοφιστὴς ὑπῆρχεν, ἀλλὰ δύναμις Θεοῦ ὁ Λόγος αὐτοῦ ἦν. Apol. I. p. 61 D. ἡ δὲ πρώτη δύναμις μετὰ τὸν πατέρα πάντων καὶ δεσπότην Θεὸν, καὶ υἱὸς, ὁ Λόγος ἐστὶν, ὃς τίνα τρόπον σαρκοποιηθεὶς ἄνθρωπος γέγονεν, ἐν τοῖς ἑξῆς ἐροῦμεν. p. 74 B.

received reading is correct, his [1] Christ or Anointed, [2] his Glory, his Wisdom.

With reference to the part borne by him in conducting the Gospel Œconomy, he is styled, as we have already seen, the [3] Minister, and the [4] Angel or Messenger of God.

We have stated that Justin supposed the generation of the Son to have taken place without any abscission or division of the Essence or substance of the Father; and that he illustrated his notion by referring to a fire, which suffers no diminution though another fire is lighted from it. This comparison implies that the Father and Son are distinct, though of one substance. There were, how-

καὶ ὁ ἄγγελος τοῦ Θεοῦ, τουτέστιν ἡ δύναμις τοῦ Θεοῦ ἡ πεμφθεῖσα ἡμῖν διὰ Ἰησοῦ Χριστοῦ. Dial. p. 344 A.

[4] καὶ τοῦτο αὐτὸ, ὦ φίλοι, εἶπε καὶ διὰ Μωσέως ὁ τοῦ Θεοῦ Λόγος, μηνύων ἡμῖν, ὃν ἐδήλωσε, τὸν Θεὸν λέγειν τούτῳ αὐτῷ τῷ νοήματι ἐπὶ τῆς ποιήσεως τοῦ ἀνθρώπου. κ τ. ἑ. Dial p. 285 A. But Thirlby suggests that we should read γεννήματι.

[1] κατὰ τοῦ Χριστοῦ τοῦ Θεοῦ. Dial. p. 322 C. τὸν ἑαυτοῦ Χριστόν. D.

[2] ἥτις καὶ δόξα Κυρίου ὑπὸ τοῦ πνεύματος τοῦ ἁγίου καλεῖται, ποτὲ δὲ υἱὸς, ποτὲ δὲ σοφία, κ. τ. ἑ. Dial. p. 284 A. C δόξα τοῦ γεννήσαντος. D.

[3] See note 2. p. 60.

[4] καὶ ἄγγελος καλεῖται καὶ ἀπόστολος· αὐτὸς γὰρ ἀπαγγέλλει ὅσα δεῖ γνωσθῆναι, καὶ ἀποστέλλεται μηνύσων ὅσα ἀγγέλλεται. Apol. I. p. 95 D. See p. 60 A. Dial. p. 275 C. 276 D. 283 C. D. μεγάλης βουλῆς ἄγγελον. p. 301 C. 321 A 355 B. 356 C. In p. 251 B we find an enumeration of the names given to Christ in Scripture, βασιλεὺς, ἱερεὺς, Θεὸς, κύριος, ἄγγελος, ἄνθρωπος,

ever, in his day ¹those who contended that the power sent forth from the Father was inseparable from Him, as the light of the sun on the earth is inseparable from the sun in the heavens; so that when the sun sets, the light is withdrawn. In like manner the Father, when he wills, causes a power to proceed from himself, which he also recals at pleasure. Such was the power which appeared to Moses, Abraham, and Jacob, and was called a messenger or angel when it bore the commands of God to man; the glory of God, when it was seen ²under an incomprehensible appearance; a man, when it assumed the human form; and the Λόγος, when it repeated the words of the Father to man. The angels also were emanations from the Father of the same kind. In opposition to this opinion, Justin maintains that the angels have a distinct, and positive, and permanent existence, and are not resolved into the substance from which they issued; and that the power to which the word of prophecy gives the titles of God and Angel, is not merely the Father under a different name, but ³is numerically distinct from him.

ἀρχιστράτηγος, λίθος, παιδίον. See also 313 C. 327 C. 355 B.
αἰώνιος ἡμῖν νόμος καὶ τελευταῖος ὁ Χριστὸς ἐδόθη. p. 228 B.
242 A. 261 C 271 C 346 C.
¹ Dial. p. 358 A.
² ἐν ἀχωρήτῳ ποτὲ φαντασίᾳ.
³ οὐχ, ὡς τὸ τοῦ ἡλίου φῶς, ὀνόματι μόνον ἀριθμεῖται, ἀλλὰ καὶ ἀριθμῷ ἕτερόν τι ἐστίν, p. 358 C. Compare p. 276 E. ὅτι οὗτος ὅ τε τῷ Ἀβραὰμ καὶ τῷ Ἰακὼβ καὶ τῷ Μωσεῖ ὦφθαι λεγόμενος, καὶ γεγραμμένος Θεὸς, ἕτερός ἐστι τοῦ τα πάντα ποιήσαντος

With respect to the human nature of Christ, Justin uniformly speaks of him as [1] perfect man, but [2] without sin. He seems, however, to have thought that the divine nature in Christ was so blended with the human, as to be in a certain sense communicated to it. For, speaking of the moral precepts of Christ, he says that the cause of their perfection is to be sought in the nature of *him* by whom they were delivered. [3] μεγαλειότερα μὲν οὖν πάσης ἀνθρωπείου διδασκαλίας φαίνεται τὰ ἡμέτερα διὰ τοῦτο, λογικὸν τὸ ὅλον τὸν φανέντα (Thirlby would read διὰ τὸ λογικὸν ὅλον τὸν φανέντα, Pearson διὰ τοῦ

Θεοῦ, ἀριθμῷ λέγω, ἀλλ' οὐ γνώμῃ· οὐδὲν γάρ φημι αὐτὸν πεπραχέναι ποτὲ ἢ ἅπερ αὐτὸς ὁ τὸν κόσμον ποιήσας, ὑπὲρ ὃν ἄλλος οὐκ ἔστι Θεός, βεβούληται καὶ πρᾶξαι καὶ ὁμιλῆσαι. p. 285 D. πρός τινα καὶ ἀριθμῷ ὄντα ἕτερον, λογικὸν ὑπάρχοντα, and p. 359 B. quoted in Note 2, p. 64.

[1] καὶ ἀποδεικνύων ὅτι ἀληθῶς γέγονεν ἄνθρωπος ἀντιληπτικῶς παθών. (f ἀντιληπτικὸς παθῶν.) Dial. p 325 A καὶ δι' ἑαυτοῦ ὁμοιοπαθοῦς γενομένου καὶ διδάξαντος ταῦτα. Apol. II. p 49 A. καὶ γὰρ γεννηθεὶς δύναμιν τὴν αὐτοῦ ἔσχε, καὶ αὐξάνων κατὰ τὸ κοινὸν τῶν ἄλλων ἀπάντων ἀνθρώπων, χρώμενος τοῖς ἁρμόζουσιν, ἑκάστῃ αὐξήσει τὸ οἰκεῖον ἀπένειμε, τρεφόμενος τὰς πάσας τροφὰς, κ.τ.ἑ. p. 315 C. 328 E. 332 D. Justin founds a singular argument in proof of the supernatural birth of Christ on the words of Dan. vii. 13, 14. ὅταν γὰρ ὡς υἱὸν ἀνθρώπου λέγῃ Δανιὴλ τὸν παραλαμβάνοντα τὴν αἰώνιον βασιλείαν, οὐκ αὐτὸ τοῦτο αἰνίσσεται; τὸ γὰρ ὡς υἱὸν ἀνθρώπου εἰπεῖν, φαινόμενον μὲν καὶ γενόμενον ἄνθρωπον μηνύει, οὐκ ἐξ ἀνθρωπίνου δὲ σπέρματος ὑπάρχοντα δηλοῖ. p. 301 A. See p. 34. Note 1. See also p. 331 E. where there appears to be an allusion to the Docetæ. In p. 327 A. Justin assigns reasons why Christ called himself the Son of Man.
[2] ἀλλὰ πρὸς τὸ ἀναμάρτητος εἶναι. Dial. p. 330 A. D. See also p. 337 E. 234 D. 235 B. 241 B. 254 B.
[3] Apol. II. p. 48 B.

τὸ) δι' ἡμᾶς Χριστὸν γεγονέναι καὶ σῶμα καὶ λόγον καὶ ψυχήν. Where, whether we interpret καὶ λόγον of the Divine Nature, or suppose it equivalent to νοῦν as distinguished from ψυχὴν, Justin must be understood to say that Christ was λογικὸς as to the whole of his human nature. It should, however, be observed that, according to Justin, the whole human race participated of the Λόγος. In [1] the first Apology he supposes an objection of this nature to be made—that they who lived, before Christ entered upon his ministry and taught mankind how to believe and act, could not be held accountable for their actions; to which he answers—that Christ, the first-born of God, was the reason (Λόγος) of which the whole human race participated; so that all who lived according to reason (μετὰ λόγου) were Christians, even though they were reputed to be Atheists; for instance, Socrates, Heraclitus, and others, amongst the Greeks; Abraham, Ananias, Azarias, Misael, Elias, [2] amongst the barbarians. While on

[1] p. 83 B. Compare Apol. II p. 41 E. μετὰ λόγου ὀρθοῦ βιοῦσιν. Christ was in part known to Socrates, Apol. II. p. 48 E.

[2] ἐν βαρβάροις. As Justin here calls Abraham, &c. barbarians, in compliance with the prejudices of the heathens whom he is addressing, may not what he says respecting the seed of the Word, implanted in the breasts of all men, be said in accommodation to the same prejudices, with the view of procuring a more favourable reception for the doctrine of the Λόγος? Le Nourry and the Benedictine Editors have taken some pains to rescue Justin from the suspicion, founded on this passage, that he believed that the Gentiles could, by the mere light of reason,

the contrary, they who lived contrary to reason (ἄνευ λόγου) were bad men, and enemies of Christ; and, as Justin means his reader to infer, equally accountable with those who lived wickedly after Christ's coming. [1] Whatever right opinions the Gentile Philosophers entertained respecting the nature of the Deity, the relation in which man stands to him, and the duties arising out of that relation, were to be ascribed to this seed of the word implanted in their bosoms. But [2] to them

attain to eternal salvation. See Casaubon. Exercit. ad Baronii Annales I. 1. In Apol. I. p. 96 E. Justin says that Abraham, Isaac, &c. were the first who applied themselves to the study of divine things.

[1] οὐ γὰρ μόνον "Ελλησι διὰ Σωκράτους ὑπὸ λόγου ἠλέγχθη ταῦτα (the absurdities of the Gentile polytheism) ἀλλὰ καὶ ἐν βαρβάροις ὑπ' αὐτοῦ τοῦ λόγου μορφωθέντος, καὶ ἀνθρώπου γενομένου, καὶ Ἰησοῦ Χριστοῦ κληθέντος, Apol. I. p. 56 A. Here an opposition seems to be intended between Λόγος and ὁ Λόγος ; but it is not observed in other passages. διὰ τὸ ἔμφυτον παντὶ γένει ἀνθρώπων σπέρμα τοῦ λόγου. Apol. II. p. 46 C. οἱ γὰρ συγγραφεῖς πάντες διὰ τῆς ἐνούσης ἐμφύτου τοῦ λόγου σπορᾶς ἀμυδρῶς ἐδύναντο ὁρᾷν τὰ ὄντα. ἕτερον γάρ ἐστι σπέρμα τινὸς καὶ μίμημα κατὰ δύναμιν δοθέν· καὶ ἕτερον αὐτὸ οὗ, κατὰ χάριν τὴν ἀπ' ἐκείνου, ἡ μετουσία καὶ μίμησις γίγνεται. p. 51 D. ἀπὸ μέρους τοῦ σπερματικοῦ θείου λόγον. p. 51 C. ὅθεν παρὰ πᾶσι σπέρματα ἀληθείας δοκεῖ εἶναι. Apol. I. p. 82 A. As the word Λόγος in Justin's writings is used in three different senses, for the reason or word of God—the second Person in the Trinity ; for reason generally ; and for Speech or the Word spoken ; we may expect to find occasional difficulty in determining the precise sense in which it is used. See Casaubon ubi supra.

[2] τοὺς (μὴ) κατὰ σπερματικοῦ λόγου μέρος, ἀλλὰ κατὰ τὴν τοῦ παντὸς λόγον, ὅ ἐστι Χριστοῦ (l. Χριστὸς,) γνῶσιν καὶ θεωρίαν· Apol. II. p. 46 C. ὅσα γὰρ καλῶς ἀεὶ ἐφθέγξαντο καὶ εὗρον οἱ

was given only a small portion: the true believer in Christ alone possesses its fulness.

As it was the Λόγος who suggested to the Gentile Philosophers and Lawgivers whatever right notions they possessed, so was it also the Λόγος who inspired the ancient prophets. We [1] have already cited one passage to this effect; but the same statement occurs repeatedly in Justin's writings.

With respect to the third Person in the Trinity, we have seen that Justin represents the Holy Ghost, in conjunction with the Father and the Son, as an object of worship. The distinct personality of the Holy Spirit is also [2] incidentally asserted. It is,

φιλοσοφήσαντες ἢ νομοθετήσαντες, κατὰ λόγου μέρος εὑρέσεως καὶ θεωρίας ἐστὶ πονηθέντα αὐτοῖς. ἐπειδὴ δὲ οὐ πάντα τὰ τοῦ λόγου ἐγνώρισαν, ὅς ἐστι Χριστός, καὶ ἐναντία ἑαυτοῖς πολλάκις εἶπον. p. 48 C. οἱ πιστεύοντες αὐτῷ εἰσὶν ἄνθρωποι, ἐν οἷς οἰκεῖ τὸ παρὰ τοῦ Θεοῦ σπέρμα, ὁ Λόγος. Apol. I p. 74 B. ἐν οἷς ἀεὶ δυνάμει μὲν πάρεστι, καὶ ἐναργῶς δὲ παρέσται ἐν τῇ δευτέρᾳ αὐτοῦ παρουσίᾳ (ὁ Χριστός). Dial p 273 E.

[1] Apol. II. p. 49 A. quoted in Note 6. p. 62. See also Apol. I. p. 75 C. ὅτι δὲ οὐδενὶ ἄλλῳ θεοφοροῦνται οἱ προφητεύοντες, εἰ μὴ λόγῳ θείῳ, καὶ ὑμεῖς, ὡς ὑπολαμβάνω, φήσετε. p. 76 D. μὴ ἀπ' αὐτῶν τῶν ἐμπεπνευσμένων λέγεσθαι νομίσητε, ἀλλ' ἀπὸ τοῦ κινοῦντος αὐτοὺς θείου λόγου.

[2] καὶ ἀποκρίνεται αὐτοῖς τὸ πνεῦμα τὸ ἅγιον, ἢ ἀπὸ προσώπου τοῦ πατρὸς, ἢ ἀπὸ τοῦ ἰδίου κ. τ. ἑ. Dial. p. 255 C ἔσθ' ὅτε γὰρ τὸ ἅγιον πνεῦμα καὶ ἐναργῶς πράττεσθαί τι, ὁ τύπος τοῦ μέλλοντος γίγνεσθαι ἦν, ἐποίει· ἔσθ' ὅτε δὲ καὶ λόγους ἐφθέγξατο περὶ τῶν ἀποβαίνειν μελλόντων, φθεγγόμενος αὐτοὺς ὡς τότε γιγνο-

however, not unworthy of observation, that the passages most explicitly declaring the doctrine of the Trinity are found in the first Apology, not in the Dialogue with Trypho; in which Justin's principal object was to establish the pre-existence and divinity of Christ. When, therefore, he [1] alleges the passage in Genesis i. 26. " Let us make man in our image after our likeness," the only inference which he draws is, that the Almighty then addressed himself to some distinct rational being. In like manner, in alleging Genesis iii. 22. " Lo, Adam is become as one of us to know good and evil," he [2] proceeds no further than to conclude from the words " as one of us," that there were two persons *at least* in conference with each other; and he afterwards applies them solely to the Son. When the Holy Spirit is mentioned in the Dialogue, it is chiefly with reference to the inspiration of the Prophets, or to his operation on the hearts of men.

But though, in the passages above quoted, a distinct personality is ascribed to the Holy Ghost, we find others in which the Spirit and the Λόγος seem to be confounded. Thus, in allusion to Luke i. 35.

μένων ἢ καὶ γεγενημένων. p. 341 C. καὶ τὸ εἰπεῖν αὐτὸν τρίτον, ἐπειδὴ, ὡς προείπομεν, ἐπάνω τῶν ὑδάτων ἀνέγνω ὑπὸ Μωσεως εἰρημένον ἐπιφέρεσθαι τὸ τοῦ Θεοῦ πνεῦμα. Apol. I. p. 93 B.

[1] Dial. p. 285 D. quoted in Note 3. p. 66.

[2] οὐκοῦν εἰπὼν, ὡς εἷς ἐξ ἡμῶν, καὶ ἀριθμὸν τῶν ἀλλήλοις συνόντων, καὶ τὸ ἐλάχιστον δύο, μεμήνυκεν. Dial. p. 285 D.

"The Holy Ghost shall come upon thee, and the power of the Highest shall overshadow thee," Justin says, "It [1] is not allowed us to conceive that the Spirit and the power from God is any other than the Word, the first-begotten of God." Grotius, in his Note on Mark ii. 8. says, that the early Fathers frequently used the word πνεῦμα to signify the Divine Nature in Christ, and quotes this very passage from Justin in proof of the statement; and doubtless the word may without any over-refinement be there so understood. Perhaps, however, the idea present to their minds was, that as, in the mystery of the Incarnation, the Holy Ghost came upon the Virgin, and the power of the Highest overshadowed her, and the Λόγος thereby became flesh, the Holy Spirit, the power of the Highest, and the Λόγος were the same. But Justin attributes the inspiration of the ancient Prophets sometimes [2] to the Λόγος, sometimes to the Holy Spirit.

[1] τὸ πνεῦμα οὖν καὶ τὴν δύναμιν τὴν παρὰ τοῦ Θεοῦ οὐδὲν ἄλλο νοῆσαι θέμις, ἢ τὸν λόγον, ὃς καὶ πρωτότοκος τῷ Θεῷ ἐστι. Apol. I. p. 75 B. Compare this passage with Dial. p. 327 C. The ancients were very fond of contrasting Eve with the Virgin Mary. As, through Eve, a virgin, sin was brought into the world, so, through Mary, a virgin, has its power been destroyed. ἵνα καὶ δι' ἧς ὁδοῦ ἡ ἀπὸ τοῦ ὄφεως παρακοὴ τὴν ἀρχὴν ἔλαβε, διὰ ταύτης τῆς ὁδοῦ καὶ κατάλυσιν λάβῃ, παρθένος γὰρ οὖσα Εὔα καὶ ἄφθορος τὸν λόγον τὸν ἀπὸ τοῦ ὄφεως συλλαβοῦσα, παρακοὴν καὶ θάνατον ἔτεκε, κ. τ. ἑ. Eve conceived the word from the serpent, Mary the word from God.

[2] See Note 6, p. 62. and Note 1, p.70. καὶ πάλιν ὁ αὐτὸς προφήτης 'Ησαΐας, θεοφορούμενος τῷ πνεύματι τῷ προφητικῷ, ἔφη p. 76 A.

Here it is difficult to interpret the latter of the Divine Nature in Christ; and yet the two appear to be identified. I know no other mode of explaining this fact than by supposing that, as the Λόγος was the conductor of the whole Gospel œconomy, Justin deemed it a matter of indifference whether he said that the Prophets were inspired by the Λόγος, or by the Holy Spirit who was the immediate agent. The Holy Spirit is called in [1] Scripture the Spirit of Christ.

Had the work which Justin composed in confutation of the heretics of his day (Apol. I. p. 70 C.) come down to our hands, we should probably have obtained a clearer insight into his notions on these abstruse subjects. As it is, we cannot doubt that he maintained a real Trinity: whether he would have explained it precisely according to the Athanasian scheme, is not equally clear; but I have observed

For the Λόγος, see Dial. p. 268 B. C. 314 B. C. 370 C. For the Holy or Prophetic Spirit, Dial. p 242 C. 249 E. 271 D. 274 B. 275 C 277 B. D. 284 A. Apol I. p. 72 B. 94 E. In p. 243 C. we find λέγει γὰρ ὁ Θεὸς διὰ 'Ησαίου. The same Spirit who inspired the Prophets also anointed the Jewish Kings. Dial. p. 272 B. 313 C.

[1] Rom. viii. 9. Gal. iv. 6. Philip. i. 19. 1 Pet. i. 11. In the last passage the immediate reference is to the Inspiration of the Prophets In the following passage Justin says that the Prophets saw visions ἐν ἐκστάσει. τοῦτον δὲ αὐτὸν οὐκ ἐν τῇ ἀποκαλύψει αὐτοῦ ἑωράκει ὁ προφήτης, ὥσπερ οὐδὲ τὸν διάβολον καὶ τὸν τοῦ Κυρίου ἄγγελον οὐκ αὐτοψίᾳ ἐν καταστάσει ὧν ἑωράκει, ἀλλ' ἐν ἐκστάσει ἀποκαλύψεως αὐτῷ γεγενημένης. Dial. p. 343 A.

nothing in the Apologies or in the Dialogue with Trypho which appears to me to justify a positive assertion to the contrary. Those passages, which seem to imply an inferiority in Christ to the Father, may without any forced construction be understood of the part borne by Christ in conducting the Œconomy.

In [1] the first Chapter we mentioned that Justin accused the Jews of having erased from the prophecy of Jeremiah a passage which is not found in any copy, either Greek or Hebrew. The purport of the passage is, that the Lord God remembered the dead among the Israelites who were his, and descended to preach his salvation to them. Here we have an approach to the doctrine of Christ's descent into hell.

[1] p. 44. Note 2. observe the expression ἐν ᾅδου μένειν. p. 326 C.

CHAPTER III.

JUSTIN'S OPINIONS RESPECTING ORIGINAL SIN, THE FREEDOM OF THE WILL, GRACE, JUSTIFICATION, PREDESTINATION.

MAN, [1] according to Justin, was created an intelligent and rational being, capable of choosing the truth, and securing his own happiness, and consequently capable of transgression: for this [2] is the property of every thing created, that it is capable of virtue and vice; and on [3] this capacity of choosing

[1] καὶ τὴν ἀρχὴν νοερὸν καὶ δυνάμενον αἱρεῖσθαι τἀληθῆ, καὶ εὖ πράττειν, τὸ γένος τὸ ἀνθρώπινον πεποίηκεν, ὥστ' ἀναπολόγητον εἶναι τοῖς πᾶσιν ἀνθρώποις παρὰ τῷ Θεῷ· λογικοὶ γὰρ καὶ θεωρητικοὶ γεγένηνται. Apol. I. p. 71 B. In Dial. p. 259 A. the body of Adam is said to have been made the habitation of the Inspiration from God, τοῦ ἐμφυσήματος τοῦ παρὰ τοῦ Θεοῦ. See also p. 316 A. ἀλλ' ὡς ἐγίγνωσκε καλὸν εἶναι γενέσθαι, ἐποίησεν αὐτεξουσίους πρὸς δικαιοπραξίαν καὶ ἀγγέλους καὶ ἀνθρώπους, καὶ χρόνους ὥρισε μέχρις οὗ ἐγίγνωσκε καλὸν εἶναι τὸ αὐτεξούσιων ἔχειν αὐτούς· καὶ ὅτι (f. ὅτε) καλὸν εἶναι ὁμοίως ἐγνώριζε, καὶ καθολικὰς καὶ μερικὰς κρίσεις ἐποίει, πεφυλαγμένου μέντοι τοῦ αὐτεξουσίου. p. 329 A.

[2] γεννητοῦ δὲ παντὸς ἥδε ἡ φύσις, κακίας καὶ ἀρετῆς δεκτικὸν εἶναι κ. τ. ἑ. Apol. II. p. 45 E.

[3] τὸ δ' ἐξακολουθῆσαι οἷς φίλον αὐτῷ, αἱρουμένους δι' ὧν αὐτὸς ἐδωρήσατο λογικῶν δυνάμεων, πείθει τε καὶ εἰς πίστιν ἄγει ἡμᾶς. Apol. I. p. 58 C. Here we have something like preventing

good and evil, Justin rests the accountableness of men and angels. What were Justin's opinions respecting the change made by the fall in man's condition, with reference to this capacity of choosing good and evil, does not clearly appear. He [1] speaks of a concupiscence existing in every man, evil in all its tendencies, and various in its nature: and on one [2] occasion seems to distinguish between original and actual sin. He says [3] also that man, being born the child of necessity and ignorance, becomes by baptism the child of choice and knowledge; but the necessity and ignorance, in which man is said to be born, are not referred to the transgression of Adam.

grace καὶ δι' ἑαυτοὺς ἡμεῖς οἱ ἄνθρωποι, καὶ οἱ ἄγγελοι, ἐλεγχθησόμεθα πονηρευσάμενοι, ἐὰν μὴ φθάσαντες μεταθώμεθα. Dial. p. 370 C.

[1] σύμμαχον λαβόντες τὴν ἐν ἑκάστῳ κακὴν πρὸς πάντα καὶ ποικίλην φύσει ἐπιθυμίαν. Apol. I. p. 58 E.

[2] ἀλλ' ὑπὲρ τοῦ γένους τοῦ τῶν ἀνθρώπων, ὃ ἀπὸ τοῦ Ἀδὰμ ὑπὸ θάνατον καὶ πλάνην τὴν τοῦ ὄφεως ἐπεπτώκει, παρὰ τὴν ἰδίαν αἰτίαν ἑκάστου αὐτῶν πονηρευσαμένου. Dial. p. 316 A.

[3] ἐπειδὴ τὴν πρώτην γένεσιν ἡμῶν ἀγνοοῦντες κατ' ἀνάγκην γεγεννήμεθα ἐξ ὑγρᾶς σπορᾶς κατὰ μίξιν τὴν τῶν γονέων πρὸς ἀλλήλους, καὶ ἐν ἔθεσι φαύλοις καὶ πονηραῖς ἀνατροφαῖς γεγόναμεν, ὅπως μὴ ἀνάγκης τέκνα μηδὲ ἀγνοίας μένωμεν, ἀλλὰ προαιρέσεως καὶ ἐπιστήμης κ. τ. ἑ. Apol. I. p. 94 C. The opposition between the first and second birth in this passage implies that the baptised person is an adult. In Dial. p. 353 E. Justin says, that Adam, by his transgression, brought death upon himself; but Christians, if they keep God's commandments, can attain to a state of exemption from suffering, and of immortality, and are thought worthy to be called the Sons of God.

From the indistinctness of Justin's language respecting the effects of the Fall on the posterity of Adam, we may expect to find an equal indistinctness on the subject of grace. He insists, however, [1] repeatedly that man stands in need of illumination from above, in order to be enabled rightly to understand the Sacred Scriptures; and we find something resembling converting grace in Dial. p. 344 A.

On the subject of Justification, Justin is sufficiently clear and explicit. He uniformly assigns the merits or death of Christ as the cause, and faith as the medium by which we are justified. By Christ's [2] stripes we are healed; by [3] his stripes all are healed who approach the Father through him; by [4] his blood all who believe on him are

[1] Dial. p. 247 A. 250 C. οὐδὲ γὰρ δύναμις ἐμοὶ τοιαύτη τις ἐστὶν, ἀλλὰ χάρις παρὰ Θεοῦ μόνη εἰς τὸ συνιέναι τὰς γραφὰς αὐτοῦ ἐδόθη μοι· ἧς χάριτος καὶ πάντας κοινωνοὺς ἀμισθωτὶ καὶ ἀφθόνως παρακαλῶ γίγνεσθαι. p. 280 B. 305 A. εἰ οὖν τις μὴ μετὰ μεγαλῆς χάριτος τῆς παρὰ Θεοῦ λάβοι νοῆσαι τὰ εἰρημένα καὶ γεγενημένα ὑπὸ τῶν προφητῶν, οὐδὲν αὐτὸν ὀνήσει τὸ τὰς ῥήσεις δοκεῖν λέγειν. p. 319 B. 326 E 346 E. The inability of the Jews to understand the Scriptures was the effect of a judicial blindness inflicted on them by God, p. 274 E. Compare 287 E.

[2] μηδὲ χλευάζητε αὐτοῦ τοὺς μώλωπας, οἷς ἰαθῆναι πᾶσι δυνατὸν, ὡς καὶ ἡμεῖς ἰάθημεν. Dial. p. 366 D. See also p. 323 B.

[3] δι' οὗ τῶν μωλώπων ἴασις γίγνεται τοῖς δι' αὐτοῦ ἐπὶ τὸν πατέρα προσχωροῦσιν. Dial. p 234 E.

[4] προαγγελτικὸν ἦν τοῦ πάθους οὗ πάσχειν ἔμελλε, δι' αἵματος

purified; the [1] Father willed that he should bear for the whole human race the curses due to all; he [2] endured the servitude even of the cross in behalf of the various races of men, having purchased them by his blood and the mystery of the cross. The [3] names of Helper and Redeemer are applied to Christ; though with an immediate reference to the power of casting out dæmons in his name. With respect to the medium of justification, it is asserted that [4] men are purified by faith through the blood and death of Christ; and that [5] Abraham was not justified by circumcision, but by faith. In

καθαίρων τοὺς πιστεύοντας αὐτῷ. Apol. I. p. 74 A. Dial. p. 259 A. 273 E 338 D. δι' αὐτῶν παθόντα λόγον. 336 A.

[1] εἰ οὖν καὶ τὸν ἑαυτοῦ χριστὸν ὑπὲρ τῶν ἐκ παντὸς γένους ἀνθρώπων ὁ πατὴρ τῶν ὅλων τὰς πάντων κατάρας ἀναδέξασθαι ἐβουλήθη. Dial. p. 322 E. Observe the whole passage.

[2] ἐδούλευσε καὶ τὴν μέχρι σταυροῦ δουλείαν ὁ Χριστὸς ὑπὲρ τῶν ἐκ παντὸς γένους ποικίλων καὶ πολυειδῶν ἀνθρώπων, δι' αἵματος καὶ μυστηρίου τοῦ σταυροῦ κτησάμενος αὐτούς. Dial. p. 364 D.

[3] βοηθὸν γὰρ ἐκεῖνον καὶ λυτρωτὴν καλοῦμεν, οὗ καὶ τὴν τοῦ ὀνόματος ἰσχὺν καὶ τὰ δαιμόνια τρέμει κ. τ. ἑ. Dial. p. 247 C.

[4] καὶ μηκέτι αἵμασι τράγων καὶ προβάτων, ἢ σποδῷ δαμάλεως, ἢ σεμιδάλεως προσφοραῖς καθαριζομένους, ἀλλὰ πίστει διὰ τοῦ αἵματος τοῦ Χριστοῦ καὶ τοῦ θανάτου αὐτοῦ, ὃς διὰ τοῦτο ἀπέθανεν. Dial. p. 229 E. αἵματι σωτηρίῳ πεπιστεύκαμεν. p. 241 E 259 A. 273 E. 338 D.

[5] καὶ γὰρ αὐτὸς ὁ Ἀβραάμ, ἐν ἀκροβυστίᾳ ὢν, διὰ τὴν πίστιν ἣν ἐπίστευσε τῷ Θεῷ ἐδικαιώθη. Dial. p. 241 C. 319 E. Apol. I. p. 60 D. In p. 327 E. Justin says that the Fathers who hoped in God confessed Christ, δηλωτικά ἐστι τοῦ καὶ πατέρας αὐτὸν ὁμολογεῖν τοὺς ἐλπίσαντας ἐπὶ τὸν Θεόν.

[1] order, however, to secure the benefits arising from Christ's death, repentance and a renunciation of our past evil habits are necessary. [2] It has been already observed that Justin, in interpreting Genesis xlix. 10, says that the Holy Spirit calls those who have received remission of sins through Christ, his garments. We may not find in Justin those nice and subtle distinctions which controversy subsequently introduced into the question of justification; but the substance of the true doctrine is there—that man is justified on account of the merits of Christ through faith, of which faith a holy life is the fruit.

We have seen that Justin maintained such a degree of freedom in men as rendered them accountable for their actions. When, however, he is urging the argument from prophecy in [3] the first Apology, an objection of this kind seems to have occurred

---

[1] ἀπαλλαγὴν δὲ τοῦ θανάτου τοῖς μεταγιγνώσκουσιν ἀπὸ τῶν φαύλων καὶ πιστεύουσιν εἰς αὐτὸν ἐργάζεται. Dial. p. 327 E τοῦτο δέ ἐστιν ὡς, μετανοήσας ἐπὶ τοῖς ἁμαρτήμασι, τῶν ἁμαρτημάτων παρὰ τοῦ Θεοῦ λάβῃ ἄφεσιν· ἀλλ' οὐχ ὡς ὑμεῖς ἀπατᾶτε ἑαυτοὺς, καὶ ἄλλοι τινὲς ὑμῖν ὅμοιοι κατὰ τοῦτο, οἳ λέγουσιν ὅτι κἂν ἁμαρτωλοὶ ὦσι, Θεὸν δὲ γιγνώσκωσιν, οὐ μὴ λογίσηται αὐτοῖς Κύριος ἁμαρτίαν. p. 370 D. See also 267 A. and 259 D. where Christ is said to have been an offering for all sinners who would repent and live righteously.

[2] Dial. p. 273 E. quoted in p. 34. Note 1. A nearly similar thought occurs in p. 344 B.

[3] p. 80 D. Compare Tucker, Light of Nature, Vol. IV. p. 282.

to him—that events, in order to be predicted, must be fore-known—that what is fore-known must be irreversibly fixed—and consequently, that whatever happens, happens by a fatal necessity; men have nothing in their own power, and are not accountable for their conduct. In reply to this objection, and in order to show that men act well and ill by their own free choice, Justin argues thus:—" We see that the conduct of the same man is various at different times; is sometimes good, sometimes bad; but this could not be the case, if his character was fixed by a fatal necessity—if it was fated that he should be either good or bad. Nor would some men be good, and some bad: since in that case we should represent fate as at variance with itself; or place no distinction between virtue and vice, making them dependent only on opinion. This only is irreversibly fated—that they who choose what is good shall be rewarded; they who choose what is evil, punished. For man cannot be a fit object either of reward or punishment, if he is virtuous or wicked, not by choice, but by birth." In [1] another place he says, that events are foretold, not because they happen from a fatal necessity, but because God fore-knows what man will do. He [2] brings forward a cavil of the Jews, either real or supposed, to this effect—that if it was foretold

---

[1] p. 82 A. See Dial. p. 234 B.
[2] Dial. p. 370 A.

that Christ should die on the cross, and that they who caused his death should be Jews, the event could not fall out otherwise. To this he replies, that God is not the cause that men, of whom it is predicted that they shall be wicked, prove wicked: but they are themselves the cause; and if the Scripture foretels the punishment of certain angels and men, it is because God foreknows that they will be unchangeably wicked, not because he has made them so. He [1] illustrates his meaning by a reference to the prediction, that the Messiah should enter Jerusalem seated on an ass. That prediction, he says, did not cause him to be the Messiah, but pointed out to mankind a mark by which they might know that he was the Messiah. In all these passages there is no [2] mention of predestination: God foreknows events, but does not pre-ordain them. He acts, however, or rather forbears to act, in consequence of this fore-knowledge; for instance, he [3] defers the punishment of the devil and his

---

[1] Dial. p. 316 A.

[2] On one occasion Justin says, that through Christ we are called to a salvation prepared beforehand by the Father, δι' οὗ ἐκλήθημεν εἰς σωτηρίαν τὴν προητοιμασμένην παρὰ τοῦ πατρὸς ἡμῶν. Dial. p. 360 D.

[3] Apol. I. p. 71 B. καὶ γὰρ ἡ ἐπιμονὴ τοῦ μηδέπω τοῦτο πρᾶξαι τὸν Θεὸν διὰ τὸ ἀνθρώπινον γένος γεγένηται. προγιγνώσκει γάρ τινας ἐκ μετανοίας σωθήσεσθαι μέλλοντας, καί τινας μηδέπω ἴσως γεννηθέντας. See also p. 82 D. καὶ συντελεσθῇ ὁ ἀριθμὸς τῶν προεγνωσμένων αὐτῷ ἀγαθῶν γιγνομένων καὶ ἐναρέτων, δι' οὓς καὶ μηδέπω τὴν ἐπικύρωσιν πεποίηται. See also

angels, out of consideration to the human race; because he foreknows that many, now living or yet unborn, will repent and be saved; and he will not, therefore, bring on the consummation of all things until the number of those, foreknown to be good and virtuous, shall be accomplished. It should be observed that these remarks are for the most part introduced incidentally, and ought not, therefore, to be construed too strictly. [1] If Justin held the doctrine of predestination at all, it must have been in the Arminian sense—ex prævisis meritis.

On the subject of the Divine Providence, Justin held that it was not merely general, but extended to particular men and events. For, speaking of the philosophers, he says that the greater part of them never bestowed a thought on the inquiry, whether there was one God or many; and whether the Divine Providence extended to each individual

---

Apol II. p. 45 B. Dial. p. 258 A. In p. 261 B. and 297 A. Justin speaks of those who are foreknown to believe in Christ, and to exercise themselves in the fear of the Lord; and in p. 346 C. he says that the wonderful Providence of God was the cause that the Christians were found wiser and more pious than the Jews, through the calling of the new and eternal covenant. See also p. 364 C. κατὰ δὲ τὴν τάξιν καὶ κατὰ τὴν πρόγνωσιν, ὁποῖος ἕκαστος ἔσται, προλέλεκται, where the allusion is to Jacob's prediction respecting the character and fortune of his sons and their posterity.

[1] See Dial. p. 319 E. 370 C. 234 B.

or not, conceiving that such knowledge [1] contributed nothing towards happiness. Nay, he adds, *they endeavour to persuade us that God watches over the universe, and genera and species, but not over me and you and each individual; since, if he did, we should not pray to him day and night.* Justin's view of the subject is agreeable to the language of Scripture and to the dictates of common sense; for a Providence, like that above-described, is evidently no Providence at all; or at least can furnish no ground of love towards God—no motive to devotion. I do not think that this account of Justin's opinion is at variance with the fact that in another passage, to which I shall hereafter have occasion to refer, he says that God entrusted the care of the world to the angels.

[1] p. 217 E. The concluding words of this sentence are perhaps corrupt, certainly obscure,—ἐπεὶ οὐδ' ἂν ηὐχόμεϑα αὐτῷ δι' ὅλης νυκτὸς καὶ ἡμέρας. I follow the translation in Thirlby's edition; the Benedictines translate, neque fore ut eum tota nocte ac die precaremur, which is ambiguous. Justin uses the expression διοίκησιν τοῦ κόσμου with reference to the Divine Governance, p 246 E. In 91 D. ἐν τῇδε τῇ διοικήσει seems to be equivalent to *in this world.*

CHAPTER IV.

JUSTIN'S OPINIONS RESPECTING BAPTISM AND THE EUCHARIST, WITH A PARTICULAR REFERENCE TO A PASSAGE IN THE FIRST APOLOGY.

In the first Apology, p. 93 E. Justin tells the Emperors that he will detail to them the mode in which the Christian converts, being renewed through Christ, dedicate themselves to God. "As many," he says, "as are persuaded, and believe that what we teach is true, and undertake to conform their lives to our doctrine, are instructed to fast and pray, and entreat from God the remission of their past sins, we fasting and praying together with them. They are then conducted by us to a place where there is water, and are regenerated in the same manner in which we were ourselves regenerated. For they are then washed in the name of God the Father and Lord of the universe, and of our Saviour Jesus Christ, and of the Holy Spirit." Justin then alleges in proof of the necessity of this regeneration, John iii. 3. [1] Isai. i. 16. which he supposes to have

---

[1] This passage is again referred to in p. 81 D. and Dial. p. 229 E. where, in the words ἀλλὰ, ὡς εἰκὸς, πάλαι τοῦτο ἐκεῖνο τὸ σωτήριον λουτρὸν ἦν, ὃ εἵπετο τοῖς μεταγιγνώσκουσι, there appears to be an allusion to 1 Cor. x. 4. The Benedictine

been prophetic of Christian baptism; and states that the Apostles had transmitted both the mode of performing the rite and the reason on which the necessity for its observance rested. [1] "Since," he says, "at our first birth we were born without our knowledge or consent—in order that we may not remain the children of necessity and ignorance, but may become the children of choice and knowledge, and may obtain in the water remission of the sins which we have committed, the name of God the Father and Lord of the universe is pronounced over him who wishes to be regenerated, and has repented of his sins," &c. [2] Justin then runs off, as is his custom, into a long digression respecting the washings and other ceremonies introduced at the suggestion of the dæmons, into the religious worship of the Gentiles; in imitation either of what was actually enjoined in the Mosaic Law, or was foretold by the Prophets as afterwards to take place under the Christian dispensation. He proceeds to animadvert on the blindness of the Jews, who maintained that it was the Father, not the Son, who conversed with Moses and the Patriarchs; thereby

Editors, for εἴπετο, read εἶπε, τό. Compare p. 235 E. 342 B. 369 C. See also p. 263 C. 231 C.

[1] The passage is quoted in p. 76. Note 2.

[2] Justin observes that the name φωτισμὸς was given to baptism: καλεῖται δὲ τοῦτο τὸ λουτρὸν φωτισμὸς, ὡς φωτιζομένων τὴν διάνοιαν τῶν ταῦτα μανθανόντων. p. 94 D. φωτιζόμενοι διὰ τοῦ ὀνόματος τοῦ Χριστοῦ τούτου. Dial. p. 258 A. 351 A.

showing that they knew neither the Father nor the Son. Returning at length to the mode of initiating the new convert, he says, [1] "After we have thus washed *him* who has expressed his conviction, and assented to our doctrines, we take him to the place where those who are called brethren are assembled, in order that we may offer up earnest prayers in common for ourselves and for the baptized person, and for all others in every place, that, having learned the truth, we may be deemed worthy to be found walking in good works, and keeping the commandments, so that we may attain to eternal salvation. Having ended our prayers, we salute each other with a kiss. Bread is then brought to that brother who presides, and a cup of wine mixed with water; and he taking them, gives praise and glory to the Father of the universe, through the name of the Son and of the Holy Spirit; and employs some time in offering up thanks to him for having deemed us worthy of these gifts. The prayers and thanksgivings being ended, [2] all the people present express their assent by saying, Amen; which, in the Hebrew tongue, answers to γένοιτο in the Greek. The president having given thanks, and the people having expressed their assent, they who are called among us Deacons give to each of those present a portion of the bread and of the

---

[1] p. 97 B.   [2] πᾶς ὁ παρὼν λαός.

wine mixed with water, over which the thanksgiving was pronounced, and carry away a portion to those who are absent. And this food is called among us εὐχαριστία: of which no one is allowed to partake who does not believe that what we teach is true, and has not been washed with the laver (of baptism) for the remission of sins and unto regeneration, and does not live as Christ has enjoined. For we do not receive it as common bread and common drink; [1] but in the same manner as Jesus Christ our

[1] It is not easy to ascertain precisely what Justin meant in this passage, which runs thus in the original: ἀλλ' ὃν τρόπον διὰ λόγου Θεοῦ σαρκοποιηθεὶς Ἰησοῦς Χριστὸς ὁ σωτὴρ ἡμῶν καὶ σάρκα καὶ αἷμα ὑπὲρ σωτηρίας ἡμῶν ἔσχεν, οὕτως καὶ τὴν δι' εὐχῆς λόγου τοῦ παρ' αὐτοῦ εὐχαριστηθεῖσαν τροφὴν, ἐξ ἧς αἷμα καὶ σάρκες κατὰ μεταβολὴν τρέφονται ἡμῶν, ἐκείνου τοῦ σαρκοποιηθέντος Ἰησοῦ καὶ σάρκα καὶ αἷμα ἐδιδάχθημεν εἶναι. p. 98 A. The Commentators in general understand the words διὰ λόγου Θεοῦ of the Λόγος, or Word of God, and δι' εὐχῆς λόγου τοῦ παρ' αὐτοῦ of the prayer or blessing pronounced by Christ at the time of instituting the Eucharist. (We find λόγῳ εὐχῆς καὶ εὐχαριστίας, p. 60 C. In p. 88 C. τὸν παρὰ τοῦ Θεοῦ λόγον and in Dial. p. 328 E. τὸν παρ' αὐτοῦ λόγον means the word which the Prophets and Christ were commissioned to deliver from God.) Yet the expression, "Jesus Christ made flesh through the Word of God," has a strange sound. We should rather expect to find it said that Jesus Christ was the Word made flesh, ὁ Λόγος σαρκοποιηθεὶς, as in p. 74 B. See Dial. p. 264 A. 310 B. 326 E. In p. 83 D. however, it is said that Christ was born of the Virgin διὰ δυνάμεως τοῦ λόγου (διὰ δυνάμεως Θεοῦ, p. 74 D. See p. 64. Note 2. Compare p. 61 D. δύναμις Θεοῦ ὁ Λόγος αὐτοῦ ἦν, p. 75 B. τὸ πνεῦμα οὖν καὶ τὴν δύναμιν τὴν παρὰ τοῦ Θεοῦ οὐδὲν ἄλλο νοῆσαι θέμις, ἢ τὸν λόγον): Justin may, therefore, in like manner, have said that Christ was made flesh through the Word of God. As it appears to me,

Saviour, being made flesh through the word of God, had both flesh and blood for our salvation; so we are also taught that the food over which thanksgiving has been pronounced by the prayer of the word which came from him, by which food, undergoing the necessary change, our flesh and blood are nourished, we are taught, I say, that this food is the flesh and blood of the Incarnate Jesus. For the Apostles, in the memoirs composed by them, which are called Gospels, have declared that Jesus gave them this injunction—that having taken bread and given thanks, he said, *Do this in remembrance of me, this is my body;* and that, in like manner, having taken the cup and given thanks, he said, *This is my blood;* and that he distributed the bread and wine to them alone." Justin adds, that through the suggestion of wicked dæmons, bread and wine were placed before the persons to be initiated into the mysteries of Mithras, in imitation of the Eucharist.

He then proceeds to give an account of the meetings of the Christians on the Lord's day.

<small>Justin in this passage does not intend to compare the manner in which Jesus Christ, being made flesh by the Word of God, had flesh and blood for our sake, with that in which the bread and wine, over which the thanksgiving appointed by Christ has been pronounced, become the flesh and blood of Christ; but only to say that, as Christians were taught that Christ had flesh and blood, so were they also taught that the bread and wine in the Eucharist are the body and blood of Christ; ὃν τρόπον is merely equivalent to *as*.</small>

"Afterwards," he says, "we remind each other of these things, and they who are wealthy assist those who are in need, and we are always together; and over all our offerings we bless the Creator of all things, through his Son Jesus Christ, and through the Holy Spirit. And on the day called Sunday, there is an assembling together of all who dwell in the cities or country; and the Memoirs of the Apostles or the writings of the Prophets are read as long as circumstances permit. Then, when the reader has ceased, the president delivers a discourse, in which he admonishes and exhorts (all present) to the imitation of these good things. Then we all rise together and pray; and, as we before said, prayer being ended, bread and wine and water are brought, and the president offers prayers in like manner, and thanksgivings, [1] with his utmost power; and the people express their assent by saying, Amen: and the distribution of that over which the thanksgiving has been pronounced takes place to each, and each partakes, and a portion is sent to the absent by the Deacons. And they who are wealthy, and choose, give as much as they respectively deem fit; and whatever is collected is deposited with the president, who succours the orphans and widows, and those who through sickness or

---

[1] ὅση δύναμις αὐτῷ ἀναπέμπει. So ὅση δύναμις αἰνοῦντες. p. 60 C. The word ἀναπέμπει seems to imply that these prayers and thanksgivings were offered in a loud tone of voice.

any other cause are in want, and those who are in bonds, and the strangers sojourning among us, and, in a word, takes care of all who are in need. But we meet together on Sunday, because it is the first day, in which God, having wrought the necessary change in darkness and matter, made the world; and on this day Jesus Christ our Saviour rose from the dead. For he was crucified on the day before that of Saturn; and on the day after that of Saturn, which is the day of the Sun, having appeared to the Apostles and Disciples, he taught them the things which we now submit to your consideration."

To take the particulars stated in this passage in their order. We find [1] regeneration connected with the rite of baptism. In [2] the Dialogue, baptism is called the laver of repentance and of the knowledge of God, which was appointed for the sin of the people of God. It [3] is also opposed to the washings

[1] So in Dial. p. 367 D. ὁ γὰρ Χριστὸς, πρωτότοκος πάσης κτίσεως ὤν, καὶ ἀρχὴ πάλιν ἄλλου γένους γέγονεν, τοῦ ἀναγεννηθέντος ὑπ' αὐτοῦ δι' ὕδατος, καὶ πίστεως, καὶ ξύλου τοῦ τὸ μυστήριον τοῦ σταυροῦ ἔχοντος. In p. 312 C. τὸ μυστήριον πάλιν τῆς (τῆς πάλιν) γενέσεως ἡμῶν refers to the final restoration of the Jews. The following passage has been urged as affording presumptive proof that Infant Baptism was practised in Justin's time, καὶ πολλοί τινες καὶ πολλαὶ, ἑξηκοντοῦται καὶ ἑβδομηκοντοῦται, οἳ ἐκ παίδων ἐμαθητεύθησαν τῷ Χριστῷ, ἄφθοροι διαμένουσι. Apol. I. p. 62 A.

[2] p. 231 C. δι' ὕδατος ἀγνίσαι. p. 314 A.

[3] p. 229 D. 231 C. 235 E. 236 B. 263 C. 369 C. τίς ἐκείνου τοῦ βαπτίσματος χρεία ἁγίῳ πνεύματι βεβαπτισμένῳ: p 246 C.

of the Mosaic ritual, and to [1] circumcision. Conformably to the injunction of our blessed Lord, it was performed in the name of the Father, Son, and Holy Spirit; and the candidate was fitted for receiving it by prayer and fasting. After baptism, he was received into the congregation, and joined in prayer [2], and was admitted to a participation in the Eucharist, all present having first saluted each other with the kiss of peace.

With respect to the Eucharist, we find that in Justin's time [3] water was mixed with the wine; that the president, having taken the bread and the wine mixed with water into his hands, offered up praises and thanksgivings to God; that the Deacons then delivered the bread and wine to all present, and carried away a portion to those who were absent.

When we compare this account with the notices on the subject of the Eucharist in the Acts of the Apostles and the Epistles, we find that considerable alterations had taken place in the mode of celebration; occasioned probably by the necessity of

[1] p. 261 D.
[2] From a passage in the Dialogue, p. 318 A. it appears that, in Justin's opinion, prayer was most acceptable to God, when offered by the supplicant in a kneeling posture, and with his face bowed forwards to the earth.
[3] So Irenæus, L. iv. c. 57. temperamentum calicis.

correcting abuses and obviating inconveniences The first converts [1] appear daily, after their principal meal, to have taken bread and drunk wine in commemoration of the death of their Saviour; and it is probable that tables were prepared in the houses of the rich, at which the poorer brethren were received, and partook of the Eucharist. At a later period, the practice at [2] Corinth was that the brethren assembled together in some one appointed place, for the purpose of eating the Lord's Supper, still connecting it with their meal. Probably the abuses which prevailed there, and were condemned by St. Paul, or others of a similar nature, rendered it eventually expedient to make the celebration of the Eucharist entirely distinct from the meal; which appears, from the passage just cited, to have been the case in Justin's time.

As in those days nothing but unavoidable necessity could have prevented a Christian from attending the stated meetings, the custom of sending a portion of the consecrated elements to the absent probably originated in the charitable desire to testify to them that, though absent, they were present to the thoughts and affections of their brethren;

---

[1] Acts ii. 46. κλῶντές τε κατ' οἶκον ἄρτον, where κατ' οἶκον is evidently opposed to ἐν τῷ ἱερῷ.
[2] 1 Cor. xi. 20.

and to prevent them from losing their share in the benefits arising from the commemoration of the death of Christ. One inference we may draw from the custom—that the thanksgiving pronounced by the president was deemed necessary to give the bread and wine, so to speak, their sacramental character—to make them, as Justin expresses himself, no longer *common* bread and wine. [1] In Justin's description we find the Deacons employed, as from the account of the institution of the office in Acts vi. we might expect them to be employed, in distributing the bread and wine to the communicants.

On the ground that the bread and wine in the Eucharist are not common bread and wine, Justin says that none were allowed to receive them but baptized believers, who lived conformably to the precepts of Christ. His reason for saying that they are not common bread and wine is assigned in the passage quoted in p. 87. Note 1; from which

---

[1] In the Dialogue, p. 259 E. Justin says that the offering of fine flour made for those who were cleansed from the leprosy (Lev. xiv. 10.) was the type of the bread in the Eucharist, which Jesus Christ our Lord ordered to be offered in remembrance of the suffering which he underwent for those who are cleansed as to their souls from all wickedness; in order that we may give thanks to God for having created the world and all things in it for the sake of man, and for having delivered us from the wickedness in which we lived, and for having finally dissolved powers and principalities through Christ, who suffered according to his will.

[1] Le Nourry infers that Justin maintained the doctrine of Transubstantiation. It might, in my opinion, be more plausibly urged in favour of Consubstantiation: since Justin calls the consecrated elements bread and wine, though not common bread and wine. But in the [2] Dialogue with Trypho we find Justin stating that the bread in the Eucharist was commemorative of the body and the cup of the blood of Christ; and in [3] a subsequent passage he applies to them the expression dry and liquid food. We may, therefore, conclude that, when he calls them the body and blood of Christ, he speaks figuratively. He applies the word [4] θυσία

[1] Apparatus ad Bibliothecam maximam Veterum Patrum, p. 408.

[2] ὅτι μὲν οὖν καὶ ἐν ταύτῃ τῇ προφητείᾳ (Isaiah xxxiii. 13. et seq.) περὶ τοῦ ἄρτου ὃν παρέδωκεν ἡμῖν ὁ ἡμέτερος Χριστὸς ποιεῖν εἰς ἀνάμνησιν τοῦ τε σωματοποιήσασθαι (f. σεσωματοποιῆσθαι) αὐτὸν διὰ τοὺς πιστεύοντας εἰς αὐτόν, δι' οὓς καὶ παθητὸς γέγονε, καὶ περὶ τοῦ ποτηρίου ὃ εἰς ἀνάμνησιν τοῦ αἵματος αὐτοῦ παρέδωκεν εὐχαριστοῦντας ποιεῖν, φαίνεται. p. 296 E. See also p. 260 A. Justinus in Dialogo cum Tryphone dixit ἄρτον ποιεῖν, *panem facere vel conficere*, hoc est, Christi exemplo εὐλογεῖν καὶ εὐχαριστεῖν, benedictione et gratiarum actione consecrare in Sacramentum Corporis Christi. Alludit Justinus voce ποιεῖν ad vocem Christi apud Paulum, 1 Cor. xi. 24. τοῦτο ποιεῖτε εἰς τὴν ἐμὴν ἀνάμνησιν. Casaubon ad Baronii Annales, xvi. 33.

[3] ταῦτα γὰρ μόνα καὶ Χριστιανοὶ παρέλαβον ποιεῖν, καὶ ἐπ' ἀναμνήσει δὲ τῆς τροφῆς αὐτῶν ξηρᾶς τε καὶ ὑγρᾶς, ἐν ᾗ καὶ τοῦ πάθους ὃ πέπονθε δι' αὐτοῦ ὁ Θεὸς τοῦ Θεοῦ μέμνηται. p. 345 A. The passage is evidently corrupt. Thirlby proposes to read, ὃ πέπονθε δι' αὐτοὺς ὁ υἱὸς τοῦ Θεοῦ μέμνηνται. The language, however, is such as would scarcely have been used by a believer in the corporal presence.

[4] p. 260 C. Compare p. 344 D. πάντας οὖν οἳ (πάσας οὖν, Jebb.) διὰ τοῦ ὀνόματος τούτου θυσίας ἃς παρέδωκεν Ἰησοῦς ὁ

to the Eucharist, or rather to the thanksgivings and prayers which were offered up during the celebration of the rite; for he allows of none but spiritual sacrifices under the Christian dispensation. The account given by Justin of the intimate union which subsisted among the brethren, and of the readiness with which the rich contributed to the relief of the wants of the poor, proves that the spirit of love which distinguished the first converts still animated the members of the Christian community. They still distinguished each other by the endearing appellation of *brother*.

We learn, moreover, from the passage above-cited, that on the first day of the week, or, as Justin styles it, the [1] day of the sun, the brethren met

Χριστὸς γίγνεσθαι, τουτέστιν ἐπὶ τῇ εὐχαριστίᾳ τοῦ ἄρτου καὶ τοῦ ποτηρίου, τὰς ἐν παντὶ τόπῳ τῆς γῆς γιγνομένας ὑπὸ τῶν Χριστιανῶν προλαβὼν ὁ Θεὸς μαρτυρεῖ εὐαρέστους ὑπάρχειν αὐτῷ with p. 345 A. ὅτι μὲν οὖν καὶ εὐχαὶ καὶ εὐχαριστίαι, ὑπὸ τῶν ἀξίων γιγνόμεναι, τέλειαι μόναι καὶ εὐάρεστοί εἰσι τῷ Θεῷ θυσίαι, καὶ αὐτός φημι. See also p. 346 B. and Apol. I. p. 58 A. 60 C.

[1] The reader will observe that Justin calls the first day of the week ἡ τοῦ ἡλίου ἡμέρα, and the last ἡ κρονική. Dion Cassius in Pompeio, c. 6. says that the Romans derived the practice of assigning the names of the planets to different days from the Egyptians, and that it had become in a certain degree national among them, καὶ ἤδη καὶ τοῦτο σφίσι πάτριον τρόπον τινά ἐστιν. Whether the Egyptians, having received the computation of time by weeks from the Jews, applied the names of the seven heavenly bodies, then known to be immediately connected with our system, to the days of the week; or whether their observation of the heavenly bodies first led them to compute time by periods

together for the purposes of religious worship; and he assigns as the reason for the selection of that particular day, that on it God began the work of creation, and Christ rose from the dead. So long as the converts to the Gospel were principally of Jewish origin, it is reasonable to suppose that, as they attended the service of the temple, and frequented the Jewish synagogues, so they kept the Jewish sabbath; holding, however, meetings for religious worship on the first day of the week, in commemoration of Christ's resurrection from the dead. The admission of the Gentiles into the Church was quickly followed by the controversy respecting the necessity of observing the Mosaic ritual—a controversy carried on, as we collect from the writings of the New Testament, with great bitterness; one consequence of which was, that the

of seven days, may be doubtful: but it appears certain that the computation was made subservient to the purposes of astrology. Dion has recorded two explanations of the manner in which the names of the heavenly bodies came to be assigned to the different days. The early Christians, if of Jewish extraction, retained, if of Gentile, adopted the Scriptural computation by weeks; and finding the astronomical or astrological names of the days of the week generally received throughout the Roman Empire, in their Apologies addressed to the heathen, naturally used those names. Selden, in the 13th and following Chapters of the third Book of his work, De Jure naturali, &c. which we recommend to the careful perusal of those who, whatever be the side they espouse, shall hereafter engage in the controversy respecting the institution of the Sabbath, has collected all that can be found on this not uninteresting subject.

converts, whether Jew or Gentile, who believed that the injunctions of the Ceremonial Law were no longer obligatory, soon ceased to observe the Sabbath; some even went the length, as Justin [1] informs us, of attaching criminality to the observance, as bespeaking a species of return from Christianity to Judaism. Bearing, however, in mind that one reason assigned by Moses for the sanctification of the Sabbath was, that on the seventh day God rested from the work of creation, they added to the original reason for observing the [2] first day of the week—the commemoration of Christ's resurrection—another, that on that day God commenced the work of creation. Thus far, and thus far only, can it in my opinion be truly said, that the Lord's Day was substituted in the place of the Jewish Sabbath: at first it was observed in conjunction with the Sabbath, and with a reference only to the resurrection.

[1] The word $\sigma\alpha\beta\beta\alpha\tau\iota\zeta\epsilon\iota\nu$ is always used by Justin with a particular reference to the Jewish Law. p. 229 C. 236 E. 237 A. 238 A.

[2] In the Dialogue, p. 241 E. Justin says that a greater mystery was annexed by God to the eighth day than to the seventh. This mystery he afterwards states to be the command to circumcise on the eighth day, which was a type of the true circumcision from error and wickedness, received by Christians through Jesus Christ, who rose from the dead on the first day of the week, which, when the weekly circle is complete, corresponds to the eighth day, p. 260 C. The number of persons saved in the ark was also a symbol of the day on which Christ arose from the dead, being the eighth in number, but the first in power, p. 367 D.

H

In Justin's account of the Christian assemblies, we find mention of a President, Deacons, and a Reader. That the Deacons were regarded as fulfilling the same duties, as the ministers whose appointment is recorded in Acts vi. cannot, I think, be doubted. But should any person infer that, because Bishops and Presbyters are not expressly named by Justin, no minister with those titles then existed in the Church, his inference would not be warranted by the premises. Justin, it should be remembered, was addressing heathens, who could not be supposed to take any interest in the titles borne by the ministers of the new religion: nor did it form any part of Justin's plan to enter into minute details respecting the government or discipline of the Church. Tertullian, who in his other works frequently mentions Bishops, Priests, and Deacons, in his Apology, addressed to the governors of Proconsular Africa, uses language even more general than that of Justin. In one respect the President appears to have been regarded as occupying the place of an Apostle: for as the [1] early converts, who sold their lands and possessions, laid the price at the feet of the Apostles; so, according to Justin, whatever was collected for the use of the poor, at the meetings on the Lord's Day, was deposited in the hands of the President.

[1] Acts iv. 35.

CHAPTER V.

THE IMMORTALITY OF THE SOUL—THE RESURRECTION OF THE BODY—THE MILLENNIUM—FUTURE JUDGEMENT—ANGELS—DÆMONS.

IN the Introduction [1] to the Dialogue with Trypho, the old man, by whose discourse Justin was converted to Christianity, enters into a discussion respecting the soul. Having stated that the heathen Philosophers could not tell what the soul is, he proceeds to affirm that the soul is not immortal; "for if immortal, it must also be necessarily-existent, as some of the followers of Plato asserted, and as others erroneously asserted the world to be. Yet though not immortal, all souls do not die; for that would be a benefit to the bad; but the souls of the good exist in a happier, and those of the bad in a worse state, awaiting the day of judgement; when those which appear worthy of God will be exempt from death, and the rest be punished so long as God wills them to exist and to be punished. God

[1] p. 222 E.

alone is necessarily-existent and incorruptible, and on that very account is God; all other things, including the soul, are created and corruptible." He [1] afterwards arrives at the same conclusion by a different train of reasoning. "The soul," he says, "is either life, or has life. If it is life, it must cause something else, not itself, to live; as motion moves something else, not itself. No one can deny that the soul lives. If, then, it lives, it lives not as being life, but as partaking of life; and that which partakes is different from that of which it partakes. The soul partakes of life because God wills it to live; and in like manner it will cease to partake of life, when God wills it not to live. For its existence does not flow from itself, as the existence of God from himself. As man does not always exist, nor is the body always united to the soul, but, when this union is to be dissolved, the soul quits the body, and the man no longer exists; so when the soul is no longer to exist, the vital spirit departs from it, and it exists no longer, but returns thither whence it was taken."

Whether Justin wished to be considered as implicitly adopting these opinions of his Instructor, [2] appears to me doubtful; but, even if he did, it is

---

[1] p. 224 B.
[2] In the Dialogue, p 241 B. he refers to an argument which

evident that he meant not to deny the immortality of the soul, but only to say that it was not immortal in its own nature—that its immortality was the gift of God. In [1] a subsequent part of the Dialogue he quotes the fact—that the Witch of Endor called up Samuel's soul—to prove the existence of the soul after its separation from the body. In the [2] first Apology he says, that the souls of the wicked are in a state of sensation after death; and imitating Christ's example, [3] refers to the passages in which God calls himself the God of Abraham, Isaac, and Jacob, to prove that those Patriarchs, though dead, were still in being. His [4] notion seems to have been, that God conferred upon our first

he had received from his Instructor, ὃν παρ' ἐκείνου ἤκουσα τοῦ ἀνδρὸς, against the perpetual obligation of the Ceremonial Law. See p. 5. Note 1.

[1] p. 333 A.
[2] p. 66 D. τῷ δὲ κολάζεσθαι, ἐν αἰσθήσει καὶ μετὰ θάνατον οὔσας, τὰς τῶν ἀδίκων ψυχάς. See also p. 65 A. ὅτι καὶ μετα θάνατον ἐν αἰσθήσει εἰσὶν αἱ ψυχαί.
[3] p. 96 E. Compare Matthew xxii. 32.
[4] ἀλλὰ πρὸς τὸ ἀποδεῖξαι ὑμῖν ὅτι τὸ πνεῦμα τὸ ἅγιον ὀνειδίζει τοὺς ἀνθρώπους, τοὺς καὶ Θεῷ ὁμοίως ἀπαθεῖς καὶ ἀθανάτους, ἐὰν φυλάξωσι τὰ προστάγματα αὐτοῦ, γεγενημένους καὶ κατηξιωμένους ὑπ' αὐτοῦ υἱοὺς αὐτοῦ καλεῖσθαι, καὶ οὗτοι ὁμοίως τῷ Ἀδὰμ καὶ τῇ Εὔᾳ ἐξομοιούμενοι θάνατον ἑαυτοῖς ἐργάζονται. Dial. p. 353 E. referred to in p. 76. Note 3. See 265 D. οἳ ἐὰν ἀξίους τῷ ἐκείνου βουλεύματι ἑαυτοὺς δι' ἔργων δείξωσι, τῆς μετ' αὐτοῦ ἀναστροφῆς καταξιωθῆναι προσειλήφαμεν συμβασιλεύοντας, ἀφθάρτους καὶ ἀπαθεῖς γενομένους. Apol. I. p. 58 B. καὶ τοῦ πάλιν ἐν ἀφθαρσίᾳ γενέσθαι διὰ πίστιν τὴν ἐν αὐτῷ αἰτήσεις πέμποντες, p. 60 D.

parents the gifts of incorruptibility and immortality, which they lost by their transgression; but which may now be regained by us if we believe, and lead virtuous and holy lives.

We have seen that Justin's venerable Instructor speaks of the punishment of the wicked as enduring so long as God wills. Justin [1] always speaks of it as eternal. There is no absolute contradiction between the two statements; which may be reconciled by saying, that God wills the punishment to be eternal. But the former mode of expression implies the possibility, that the torments of the wicked may have an end, which the positive language of Justin seems to exclude. Previously to the final judgment, the [2] soul will be reunited to

[1] αἰωνίαν κόλασιν κολασθησομένων, ἀλλ' οὐχὶ χιλιονταετῆ περίοδον. Apol. I. p. 57 B. See also p. 59 B. 65 A 67 D. 83 B. Apol. II. p. 41 C. E. 45 E. 46 D. 47 D. Dial. 345 B. So also αἰώνιον κατάσχεσιν. 340 D. 349 B ἀπαύστως κολάζεσθαι. 264 B.

[2] Apol. I. p. 57 B. The passage is corrupt, but the meaning clear. p. 65 C. τὴν δὲ δευτέραν (παρουσίαν) ὅταν μετὰ δόξης ἐξ οὐρανῶν μετὰ τῆς ἀγγελικῆς αὐτοῦ στρατιᾶς παραγενήσεσθαι κεκήρυκται, ὅτε καὶ τὰ σώματα ἀνεγερεῖ πάντων τῶν γενομένων ἀνθρώπων, καὶ τῶν μὲν ἀξίων ἐνδύσει ἀφθαρσίαν, τῶν δ' ἀδίκων ἐν αἰσθήσει αἰωνίᾳ μετὰ τῶν φαύλων δαιμόνων εἰς τὸ αἰώνιον πῦρ πέμψει, p. 87 B. ὅτι κἄν τις ἐν λώβῃ τινὶ σώματος ὑπάρχων φύλαξ τῶν παραδεδομένων ὑπ' αὐτοῦ διδαγμάτων ὑπάρξῃ, ὁλόκληρον αὐτὸν ἐν τῇ δευτέρᾳ αὐτοῦ παρουσίᾳ, μετὰ τοῦ καὶ ἀθάνατον καὶ ἄφθαρτον καὶ ἀλύπητον ποιῆσαι, ἀναστήσει. Dial. p. 296 A. 359 D.

the body, which, in the case of the good, will not only be rendered immortal and incapable of suffering ; but even if, during this life, it laboured under any deformity or defect, it will then be raised in a state of complete integrity. The bodies of the bad will also be rendered immortal, in order to endure the eternity of suffering to which they are destined. The place of future punishment he calls by the name of [1] Gehenna.

In the [2] Dialogue with Trypho, Justin speaks of the appearance of *the man of sin* as immediately connected with the second coming of Christ in glory. His appearance was to be the prelude to severe persecutions against the Christians. Bishop [3] Pearson supposes Justin to have believed that

---

[1] ἡ δὲ γέεννά ἐστι τόπος ἔνθα κολάζεσθαι μέλλουσιν οἱ ἀδίκως βιώσαντες. Apol. I. p. 66 B.

[2] ἡ δὲ δευτέρα (παρουσία) ἐν ᾗ μετὰ δόξης ἀπὸ τῶν οὐρανῶν παρέσται, ὅταν καὶ ὁ τῆς ἀποστασίας ἄνθρωπος, ὁ καὶ εἰς τὸν ὕψιστον ἔξαλλα λαλῶν, ἐπὶ τῆς γῆς ἄνομα τολμήσῃ εἰς ἡμᾶς τοὺς Χριστιανούς, p. 336 E.

[3] The passage to which Pearson refers is as follows : ὅπερ γίγνεται ἐξότου εἰς τὸν οὐρανὸν ἀνελήφθη μετὰ τὸ ἐκ νεκρῶν ἀναστῆναι ὁ ἡμέτερος Κύριος Ἰησοῦς Χριστός, τῶν χρόνων συμπληρουμένων καὶ τοῦ βλάσφημα καὶ τολμηρὰ εἰς τὸν ὕψιστον μέλλοντος λαλεῖν ἤδη ἐπὶ θύραις ὄντος, (ὃν) καιρὸν καὶ καιροὺς καὶ ἥμισυ καιροῦ διακαθέξειν Δανιὴλ μηνύει. καὶ ὑμεῖς ἀγνοοῦντες πόσον χρόνον διακατέχειν μέλλει, ἄλλο ἡγεῖσθε· τὸν γὰρ καιρὸν ἑκατὸν ἔτη ἐξηγεῖσθε λέγεσθαι, εἰ δὲ τοῦτό ἐστιν, εἰς τὸ ἐλάχιστον τὸν τῆς ἀνομίας ἄνθρωπον τριακόσια πεντήκοντα ἔτη

this event was near at hand: this, however, does not strike me as a necessary conclusion from the words.

We have seen that, among other questions put by Trypho to Justin, [1] he asks whether the Christians really believed that Jerusalem would be rebuilt, and that they, as well as the Patriarchs, Prophets, and Jews, and Proselytes who lived before the coming of Christ, would be collected there. Justin replies that, although many pure (in doctrine) and pious Christians were of a different opinion, yet he himself, and as many Christians as were in every respect orthodox, ὀρθογνώμονες κατὰ πάντα, were assured [2] that they who believe in

βασιλεῦσαι δεῖ, ἵνα τὸ εἰρημένον ὑπὸ τοῦ ἁγίου Δανιὴλ, καὶ καιρῶν, (f. καὶ καιρούς) δύο μόνους καιροὺς λεγεσθαι ἀριθμήσωμεν, p. 250 A. Here we have a plain allusion to Daniel vii. 25. (xi. 36, &c.) 2 Thess. ii. 4, et seq. The last passage seems to have suggested the word διακατέχειν to Justin; but he employs it as relating to the time during which the man of sin was to have dominion; not to that during which he was to be restrained from appearing. See the use of the word κατέχειν. Apol. I. 82 D.

[1] c. 1. p. 38. Dial. p. 306 B. et seq. Compare p. 368 A. 369 A.

[2] To this resurrection Justin applies the words παλιγγενεσία, ἐν οἷς καὶ τὸ μυστήριον πάλιν τῆς γενέσεως (τῆς πάλιν γενέσεως) ἡμῶν, καὶ ἁπλῶς πάντων τῶν τὸν Χριστὸν ἐν Ἱερουσαλὴμ φανήσεσθαι προσδοκώντων, p. 312 C. Middleton has most unfairly charged Justin with maintaining that the Saints will pass the Millennium in the enjoyment of sensual pleasures.

Christ should rise in the flesh, 'and for the space of a thousand years inhabit Jerusalem, rebuilt and beautified, and enlarged. In confirmation of this opinion, he quotes Isaiah lxv. 17. and the book of Revelation, which he expressly ascribes to the Apostle St. John. At [1] the expiration of the period of one thousand years, the general resurrection was to take place; and [2] after the general resurrection and judgment, this whole frame of things was to be consumed by fire.

I will take the present opportunity of laying before the reader the different notices scattered over Justin's works respecting Angels and Dæmons. In [3] opposition to those who thought that Angels

---

Nothing of this kind is to be found in Justin's description: and in p. 346 B. he cautions Trypho against supposing that the Mosaic sacrifices will then be revived, or any but spiritual sacrifices offered; οὗ (τοῦ Χριστοῦ) ἐν τῇ πάλιν παρουσίᾳ μὴ δόξητε λέγειν Ἡσαίαν ἢ τοὺς ἄλλους προφήτας θυσίας ἀφ' αἱμάτων ἢ σπονδῶν ἐπὶ τὸ θυσιαστήριον ἀναφέρεσθαι, ἀλλὰ ἀληθινοὺς καὶ πνευματικοὺς αἴνους καὶ εὐχαριστίας. It has been observed, c. 1. p. 33. that Elias is to appear before Christ's second Advent.

[1] p. 308 B.

[2] Apol. I. p. 66 B. where Justin appeals to the authority of the Sibyl and Hystaspes, Apol. II. p. 45 C.

[3] Dial. p. 358 C. Compare p. 311 D. and 312 B. where Justin proves from Psalm cxlviii. 1, 2. that Angels are heavenly powers. They required food, but not such food as men require. Their food was manna, according to Psalm lxxviii. 24. Dial. p 279 D.

were only emanations, sent forth for a particular purpose, and then resolved again into that from which they issued, Justin ascribes to them a positive and permanent existence. To [1] certain of them God committed the charge of watching over men and over this nether world; but, [2] as they possessed freedom of will, and were capable of evil as well as good, they allowed themselves to be seduced into transgression by the beauty of women, from their intercourse with whom sprang Dæmons. These Apostate Angels [3] enslaved the human race by magical arts, by terrifying or by injuring them, by instructing them in sacrificial rites, and inducing them to offer incense and libations, which [4] became necessary to themselves after

---

[1] Apol. II. p. 44 A. referred to in c. I. p. 7. Note 12. Trypho appears to have been scandalized at the notion that an Angel could fall. Dial. p. 305 C. 306 A.

[2] Dial. p. 316 A. 370 A. In the former passage he seems to limit the freedom of men and Angels by saying that they were free to do that which God had empowered each to do, πράττειν ὅσα ἕκαστον ἐνεδυνάμωσε δύνασθαι ποιεῖν.

[3] See Apol. I. p. 61 A.

[4] οἳ καὶ παρὰ τῶν ἀλόγως βιούντων αἰτοῦσι θύματα καὶ θεραπείας. Apol. I. p. 59 D.

It should be observed that Justin makes a clear distinction between the worship of idols and that of the heavenly bodies. We have seen his notions respecting the origin of the former; (c. I. p. 7.) but he believed, and according to him Trypho also believed, that God actually permitted the heathen to worship the Sun and Moon as God. This notion was founded on a misinterpretation of the Septuagint Version of Deut. iv. 19. Dial. p. 274 B. 349 E

they were subjected to passions and lusts. Having enslaved mankind, they sowed among them murders, wars, adulteries, wantonness, and all kinds of wickedness. The Poets and Mythologists, ignorant that these evils were the work of the Angels and of the Dæmons, their offspring, ascribed them to the deities, whose names the Angels [1] appropriated to themselves at pleasure. In [2] order more securely to establish their dominion, the Dæmons employed every art to seduce men from the worship of the true God, adapting their temptations to the character of the individual: if he was of a low and grovelling temper, addressing themselves to his senses, and, as it were, nailing him to idols and earthly objects; if he was of a more contemplative cast, perplexing him with subtle inquiries, and urging him into impiety. With this view, also, after [4] Christ's ascent into heaven, they instigated different men, among them Simon the

---

[1] In the first Apology, p. 55 E. Justin gives a similar account, and says that men, being ignorant of the existence of wicked Dæmons, called them Gods, assigning to each the name which he had appropriated to himself. Compare p. 57 D, where he says that the images, the objects of worship in the heathen temples, bare the names and the forms of wicked dæmons. See also p. 67 D. In proof of this opinion he frequently appeals to Psalm xcvi. 5. οἱ θεοὶ τῶν ἐθνῶν δαιμόνια εἰσιν, as in Dial. p. 306 B.

[2] Apol. I. p. 92 B. The Devil enabled Pharaoh's magicians to work wonders. Dial. p. 294 E. 306 B. He also inspired the false Prophets. 325 A.

[3] Apol. I. p. 69 C.

Samaritan, to give themselves out for gods; as
[1] previously to Christ's appearance on earth, they
had suggested various fables to the Poets, founded
on what the holy Prophets had foretold respecting
the coming of Christ and the future punishment
of the wicked, to the end that men, having their
minds pre-occupied with those fables, might regard
the narrative of Christ's life and actions with less
reverence. In like manner, they caused various
rites to be introduced into the heathen mysteries,
bearing a resemblance to those which were to be
instituted under the Christian dispensation. Thus
from [2] Isaiah i. 16. which Justin refers to Baptism,
the worshippers in the heathen temples were instructed to sprinkle themselves before they made
their offerings; and [3] from what the dæmons had
learned respecting the future institution of the
Eucharist, bread and a cup of water were placed
before the candidates for initiation into the mys-

[1] Apol. I. p. 89 A. where Justin alleges several instances
of imitation, some of them sufficiently extravagant. Compare
p. 68 C. 90 A. 97 A. Dial. p. 297 B. 295 A. 294 E. The
Dæmons did not know that the Messiah was to be crucified, and
did not in consequence invent any fables with reference to the
crucifixion, p. 90 B.

[2] Apol. I. p. 94 E.

[3] Apol. I. p. 98 C. referred to in c. IV. p. 88. In the Dialogue, p. 304 B. Justin says that the practice of initiating the
votaries of Mithras in a place called a cave was derived from
Isaiah xxxiii. 16. οὗτος οἰκήσει ἐν ὑψηλῷ σπηλαίῳ πέτρας ἰσχυρᾶς.
from which passage he infers that Jesus was born in a cave near
Bethlehem. See Casaubon Exercit. ad Baronii Annales ii. 1.
See also p. 296 B.

teries of Mithras, as a part of the ceremony. [1] This imitation of the prophetic writings extended even to the precepts of righteousness inculcated in the Sacred Volume.

Actuated by a spirit of unremitting hostility against God and against goodness, the dæmons [2] instigated all the persecutions to which not only the Christians, but the virtuous among the heathen were exposed. [3] They also excited the Jews to put Christ to death. They [4] were the authors of the calumnious accusations brought against the Christians. To their suggestions were to be traced the [5] different heresies which had arisen in the Church; the [6] unjust and wicked laws which had been enacted in different states; in short, they were the authors of all evil existing in the world. Among [7] these evil Angels the serpent who de-

[1] οὗ καὶ τοὺς λόγους πάντας μιμήσασθαι ἐπεχείρησαν· δικαιοπραξίας γὰρ λόγους καὶ παρ' ἐκείνοις λέγεσθαι ἐτεχνάσαντο, p. 296 C.
[2] This opinion is repeatedly stated by Justin. See Apol. I. p. 55 D. 59 D. 82 B. Apol. II. p. 41 D. 45 D. 46 C. 50 B. Dial. 258 D. where it is said that the persecutions of the Christians will continue till Christ's second coming, 360 D.
[3] Apol. I. p. 96 A.
[4] Apol. I. p. 58 D. 68 D. Apol. II. p. 51 B.
[5] Apol. I. p 69 D. 91 A. 92 A.
[6] Apol. II. p. 48 A.
[7] παρ' ἡμῖν μὲν γὰρ ὁ ἀρχηγέτης τῶν κακῶν δαιμόνων ὄφις καλεῖται, καὶ σατανᾶς, καὶ διάβολος. Apol. I. p. 71 A. Compare Dial. p. 264 A. 304 D. 327 D. 331 B. 353 E. 354 E.

ceived Eve, called also in Scripture Satan, and the devil, was pre-eminent; [1] who, together with the other apostate Angels, and with wicked men, will be consigned to eternal flames at the consummation of all things.

With respect to dæmoniacal possessions, Justin says, that [2] the Christians, by adjuring Dæmons in the name of Christ, were enabled to work cures which the Jewish and heathen exorcists had in vain attempted. He here speaks as if the suffering party was really possessed by a Dæmon; but [3] on another occasion he classes possessed and insane persons together, and says that the souls of dead men had entered into them. There, however, is

---

[1] Apol. I. p. 71 B. 82 D. 87 B. Apol. II. p. 46 D. Dial. 361 C. This notion of Justin, that the punishment of the apostate Angels will not take place until the end of the world, has by some been stigmatized as heretical. See Le Nourry, p. 416. Perhaps Justin meant that all their power of doing mischief, and consequently their only source of gratification, would then be taken away, and they would exist for ever in a state of unmitigated misery.

[2] Apol. II. p. 45 A. 46 D. Dial. p. 247 C. 302 A. 311 B. In the last passage, Justin says that a dæmon would possibly obey, if adjured by a Jew in the name of the God of Abraham, of Isaac, and of Jacob. He speaks of the Dæmons as trembling at the name of Christ. ὃν καὶ τὰ δαιμόνια φρίσσει. p. 269 D. 350 B. 361 C.

[3] καὶ οἱ ψυχαῖς ἀποθανόντων λαμβανόμενοι καὶ ῥιπτούμενοι ἄνθρωποι, οὓς δαιμονιολήπτους καὶ μαινομένους καλοῦσι πάντες. Apol. I. p. 65 A.

no real contradiction; for he [1] supposed that wicked Angels hovered about the beds of dying men, on the watch to seize the parting soul; which being now brought within their power, was compelled to obey their bidding. The souls of the Prophets and holy men of old had thus fallen under the dominion of Dæmons; as was evident from the power, exerted by the Witch of Endor, of calling up the soul of Samuel; and the Dæmons could, by a similar exercise of power, cause them to possess the bodies of men.

[1] Dial. p. 332 E. Justin speaks as if a petition to be delivered in the hour of death from the power of evil spirits formed a special topic in the prayers of Christians.

CHAPTER VI.

THE CONDITION OF THE CHRISTIANS IN THE TIME OF JUSTIN, AND THE CAUSES OF THE RAPID DIFFUSION OF CHRISTIANITY.

IN the [1] Dialogue with Trypho we find Justin using the following language: "There is no race of men, whether of barbarians, or of Greeks, or bearing any other name, either because they live in wagons without fixed habitations, or in tents, leading a pastoral life, among whom prayers and thanksgivings are not offered to the Father and Maker of the universe through the name of the crucified Jesus." As Justin is then endeavouring to shew that the prediction of [2] Malachi, which speaks of the universal diffusion of true religion among the Gentiles in the days of the Messiah, was fulfilled in the actual state of Christianity, we must make allowance for some exaggeration in the description. We may interpret his language more strictly, when he says that new converts were continually added to the Church through the admiration excited by the

---

[1] p. 345 C. [2] i 11.

virtuous practice and enduring constancy of the Christians. He [1] states, with regard to himself, that in embracing Christianity, he was in no small degree influenced by observing, that the Christians, against whom so many calumnies were propagated, encountered death, and whatever else is deemed most dreadful, without fear. Such persons, he reasoned with himself, could not be leading wicked and dissipated lives. " For what lover of pleasure," he asks, " or intemperate man, or delighting to feed on human flesh, would embrace death, thereby to lose all that he deemed desirable? and would not rather strive, by every means, to evade the pursuit of the governors, in order that he might live for ever in this world? Much less would such a man denounce himself to the magistrate." On [2] another occasion he says, "It is evident that no one can terrify or enslave those who have believed in Jesus. For when condemned to be beheaded, to be crucified, to be cast to wild beasts, into chains, or into the flames, or to be otherwise tortured, they never swerve from the profession of their faith. Nay, the more frequently such punishments are inflicted, the greater the addition to the faithful and pious believers in the name of Jesus; as when you cut off the fruit-bearing parts of the vine, it puts forth other flourishing and fruitful branches."

[1] Apol. II. p. 50 A. Compare Apol I. p. 63 C.
[2] Dial. p. 337 B. 350 A. 360 D.

As the main object of the first Apology is to remove the unfavourable impression which had been made on the minds of the Emperors by the calumnious accusations circulated against the Christians, Justin naturally appeals to the moral precepts delivered by Christ, and to the fact that the Christians lived in conformity to them. [1] "We," he says, "follow the one unbegotten God, through the Son—we who formerly delighted in vicious excesses, but now are temperate and chaste—we who formerly had recourse to magical arts, but have now dedicated ourselves to the good and unbegotten God—we who formerly placed our greatest pleasure in acquiring wealth and possessions, but now bring all that we have into a common stock, and impart to every one in need—we who hated and destroyed each other, and, on account of the difference of manners, refused to live with men of a different tribe, now, since the appearance of Christ, live on terms of familiar intercourse with them, and pray for our enemies, and endeavour to persuade those who hate us without a cause to live conformably to the perfect precepts of Christ, to the end that they may become partakers with us of the same joyful hope of a reward from God the Ruler over all."

[1] Apol. I. p. 61 B. In the Dial. p. 309 A. Justin challenges his opponents to prove that the Christians were actuated by the love of gain, or glory, or pleasure.

But though many might [1] become favourably disposed to Christianity by contemplating the pure and blameless lives of its professors, and thus be induced at length to imitate the virtues which they admired, yet to the majority the Christians were the objects at once of hatred and contempt. They were regarded as the vilest [2] of men, and [3] treated with the greatest contumely and injustice. The most unnatural and revolting crimes were laid to their charge; they [4] were accused of feeding on human flesh, and, after their horrible repast, of extinguishing the lights, and indulging in a promiscuous intercourse. They were also [5] charged with atheism and impiety, because, as [6] Justin states, they would not worship the Gods of the Gentiles, or offer libations and sacrifices to dead men. No measure, which promised to accomplish their destruction, was rejected on account of its iniquity or atrocity; their [7] domestics were solicited to inform and to give evidence against them; and Justin in one place [8] states that murders were purposely

---

[1] Apol. I. p. 63 C.
[2] ἀνθρώποις οὐδενὸς ἀξίοις is Trypho's expression, p. 225 E. In p 347 B. Justin repels the charge, οὐκοῦν οὐκ εὐκαταφρόνητος δῆμος ἐσμὲν, οὐδὲ βάρβαρον φῦλον, οὐδὲ ὁποῖα Καρῶν ἢ Φρυγῶν ἔθνη.
[3] ἀδίκως μισουμένων καὶ ἐπηρεαζομένων. Apol. I. p. 53 B.
[4] Dial. p. 227 B.   [5] Apol. II. p. 47 A.
[6] Apol. I. p. 68 E.
[7] Dial. p. 254 A. Justin here alludes to Matt. x. 36.
[8] Apol. II. p. 50 B.

committed by others, in order that the Christians might be charged with the guilt; and that their servants, their children, or their wives were then put to the torture, in the hope that some expression might drop in the moment of agony, which might furnish matter of accusation against them. So strong was the current of public feeling against them, that Justin [1] ventures to ask of the Emperors no more than this—that when the Christians were brought before the tribunals, they should not be condemned merely because they were Christians; but should be dismissed, unless they were convicted of some crime. "I do not," he adds, "go the length of calling upon you to punish our accusers."

In [2] one of the passages above cited, allusion is made to Christians who denounced themselves to the magistrates. As Justin expresses no disapprobation of the practice, [3] M. Barbeyrac has inferred that he approved this extravagant display of zeal. M. Barbeyrac confirms his inference by appealing to [4] another passage in the same Apology, in which Justin supposes an objector to say, "If you (Chris-

---

[1] Apol. I. p. 56 E. Yet, in the Epistle of Adrian subjoined to the Apology, that Emperor directs that they who accused the Christians falsely shall be punished.
[2] Page 113.
[3] Traité de la Morale des Pères, c. 2. sect. 8.
[4] Apol. II. p. 43 C.

tians) are so eager to go to God, why do you not kill yourselves, and give us no further trouble?" Justin answers, "The reason why we do not destroy ourselves, and yet, when we are questioned, boldly confess that we are Christians, is this: We are taught that God did not make the world without an object, but for the sake of the human race; and that he delights in them who imitate his attributes, and is displeased with them who embrace what is evil either in word or deed. If, therefore, we all should destroy ourselves, we should, as far as depends on us, be the cause that no one would be born or instructed in the Divine doctrine, or even the cause that the whole human race would fail; and thus we should act in opposition to the will of God. But when we are questioned, we do not deny that we are Christians, because we are not conscious to ourselves of any evil; and because we think it impious not to speak the truth under every circumstance." M. Barbeyrac infers from this passage, that Justin did not consider a Christian to be really the cause of his own death, when, through an ill-regulated desire of martyrdom, he denounced himself. But when we inquire into the circumstances which gave rise to Justin's remark, we shall find that they have no connection with the case supposed by M. Barbeyrac. A Christian, named Ptolemy, was brought before Urbicus, the Prefect of Rome, and asked whether he was a Christian? On his replying in the affirmative, Urbicus ordered him to be led away to execution. Another Christian, named Lucius, who witnessed the transaction, immediately exclaimed to Urbicus, "What is the reason that you have ordered a man to be punished, who has been convicted of no crime whatever, but has merely confessed that he is a Christian? The judgement which you have pronounced befits neither a pious Emperor, nor the son of a philosophic Cæsar, nor the sacred senate." Urbicus made no other reply to this address than by saying to Lucius, "You also seem to be a Christian." Lucius admitted that he was, and Urbicus ordered him also to be led away to execution. Justin adds, that he thanked the governor for the sentence, knowing that he should now be delivered from the tyranny of such wicked rulers, and should go to the Father and King of heaven. It is evident that, in coming forward as he did, Lucius was not actuated by any desire of martyrdom, but was impelled by a feeling of indignation at the gross injustice of the Prefect's conduct towards Ptolemy. It is true that, when condemned to death, he expressed his joy at the prospect of quitting this world, and being admitted to the presence of his heavenly Father; but the desire of encountering death was not the motive which influenced him in addressing Urbicus. The case of a Christian who denounced himself to the magistrate through the desire of martyrdom does not seem to have been in Justin's contemplation. He states the case of a voluntary suicide on the one hand; of a Christian who, when questioned, denied that he was so on the other; and he condemns both. He argues that Christians would be culpable if they destroyed themselves. Why? because they would act in opposition to the will of God, who did not create the world without an object. The fair inference, therefore, would seem to be, that Justin would have condemned a Christian who exposed himself to death without an object. The [1] youth, who made the extraordinary proposal to the governor of Alexandria on which M. Barbeyrac has remarked, had an object in view —that of convincing the governor that the Christians did not practise in their assemblies those gross immoralities which were attributed to them. I mean not, however, to say that Justin does not sometimes use language which implies, on the part of the early converts, an [2] eagerness to court martyrdom: I am far from defending such language; but, as I [3] have elsewhere stated, there were circumstances in the situation of the first Christians which ought to prevent us from being too severe in condemning it.

[1] Apol. I. p. 71 D.
[2] Apol. I. p. 57 A. σπεύδομεν ἐπὶ τὸ ὁμολογεῖν.
[3] In my account of Tertullian's writings, p. 154.

M. Barbeyrac also says, that Justin entertained very exaggerated notions of the merit of celibacy. On one [1] occasion Justin, in order to point out the superiority of the precepts of Christ to those of the heathen Moralists, says, that with respect to chastity, they forbade practices which human laws allowed (for instance, the practice of divorcing a wife, and contracting another marriage), and that they controlled the inward desire, as well as the outward act. He then adds, that many persons of both sexes, who had been instructed in Christianity from their infancy, and had, when he wrote, attained the age of sixty or seventy, had led an uniform life of continence. On [2] another occasion Justin says, that the Christians either abstained from marriage altogether, or married with the sole view of having children. These passages, however, are not mentioned by M. Barbeyrac, who refers to the third Chapter of the Fragment of the Tract on the Resurrection of the Flesh, in which the Author distinctly applies the epithet *unlawful* ἄνομον to marriage. Grabe endeavours to get over the difficulty by saying that the word ἄνομον should be translated *indifferent;* because, as we have seen, Justin allowed

---

[1] Apol. I. p. 62 A.
[2] Apol. I. p. 71 D. In the Dialogue, p. 337 B. Justin seems to urge, as a proof of the superiority of the Christian morals, the fact that each man contented himself with a single wife.

that marriage might be contracted for the purpose of having children. But few, I think, will be satisfied with this interpretation. If the Fragment was really the work of Justin, we must conclude that, like other disputants, in his eagerness to answer the objections immediately before him, he did not stay to examine very accurately the soundness of his answer.

It is unnecessary to notice what M. Barbeyrac has said respecting Justin's opinions on the lawfulness of an oath; since, according to his own admission, Justin [1] has merely recited our Saviour's words.

Living so nearly as Justin did to the Apostolic age, it will naturally be asked whether, among other causes of the diffusion of Christianity, he specifies the exercise of miraculous powers by the Christians. He says, in general terms, that such [2] powers subsisted in the Church—that Christians were endowed with [3] the gift of prophecy—and in an enumeration of spiritual gifts conferred on Christians, he mentions that of [4] healing. We have seen, also, in a

[1] Apol. I. p. 63 D.
[2] Dial. p. 254 B. διά τε τῶν ἔργων, καὶ τῶν ἀπὸ τοῦ ὀνόματος αὐτοῦ καὶ νῦν γιγνομένων δυνάμεων.
[3] παρὰ γὰρ ἡμῖν καὶ μέχρι νῦν προφητικὰ χαρίσματά ἐστιν. Dial. p. 308 B. See also p. 315 B.
[4] Dial. p. 258 A.

[1] former chapter, that he ascribes to Christians the power of exorcising Dæmons. But he produces no particular instance of an exercise of miraculous power, and therefore affords us no opportunity of applying those tests by which the credibility of miracles must be tried. Had it only been generally stated by the Evangelists that Christ performed miracles, and had no particular miracles been recorded, how much less satisfactory would the Gospel narratives have appeared! how greatly the evidence in support of our Saviour's divine mission been diminished!

I know not that I can take a better opportunity than the present, of offering a few remarks on the arguments urged by Justin in proving the truth of the Christian Revelation. I [2] have elsewhere observed, that nothing can be more unreasonable than to censure the Apologies of the early Fathers, because they do not contain—what they never were designed to contain—a regular exposition of the Evidences of Christianity. They were composed with the view of removing the prejudices of the opponents of the New Religion, and instructing mankind in its real character and design. Whatever mention occurs of the Evidences of Christianity is merely incidental. In his dispute with

---

[1] Chapter V   [2] In my Volume on Tertullian, p. 134.

Trypho, Justin was naturally led to insist rather on the argument from prophecy, than on that from miracles. [1] A large portion of the Dialogue is occupied in shewing that the prophecies relating to the Messiah in the Old Testament were accomplished in Jesus. [2] Another argument urged by Justin is derived from the fulfilment of the predictions delivered by Jesus himself; to foretel future events being, as he [3] observes, the work of God alone. But though he appeals more frequently to the fulfilment of prophecy, he [4] occasionally introduces the mention of Christ's miracles; yet [5] as it might be said that they were performed by magical arts, he seems to have thought that, without the argument from prophecy, they would not of themselves be sufficient to establish the Divine Mission of Jesus. They who express surprise that the miracles wrought by Jesus and his Disciples did not produce instant conviction in the minds of all who witnessed them, have not sufficiently attended to the state of opinion either among the Jews or Gentiles. The

---

[1] See also Apol. I. p. 88 A. 73 B. et seq.

[2] Dial. p. 253 B. 254 A. 271 A. 308 C.

[3] ἐπειδὴ ἔργῳ φαίνεται γιγνόμενα ὅσα φθάσας γενέσθαι προεῖπεν, ὅπερ Θεοῦ ἔργον ἐστί. Apol. I. p. 60 A.

[4] Dial. p 254 B. In the first Apology, p. 73 A. both miracles and the fulfilment of prophecy are mentioned; but the argument turns rather on the latter. It was foretold that Christ would work miracles, Jesus worked miracles he was, therefore, the Christ.

[5] Apol. I p. 72 A.

distinction between their incredulity and that of modern sceptics is this. They readily admitted the fact, that an event out of the ordinary course of nature had occurred, but denied that it afforded conclusive proof of the Divine Mission of Him, through whose agency it was brought to pass. The modern sceptic takes a different course: he stops us at the very threshold, by asserting that no testimony whatever can outweigh the antecedent incredibility of the event.

CHAPTER VII.

THE HERESIES MENTIONED BY JUSTIN—MISCELLANEOUS OBSERVATIONS.

JUSTIN [1] mentions Simon, and says that he was a native of Samaria—that through the assistance of the Dæmons he performed magical miracles at Rome in the reign of Claudius Cæsar, and was in consequence regarded as a God—that a statue was erected in his honour, having the following inscription in Latin, [2] *Simoni Deo Sancto*—that nearly all the Samaritans, and a few of other nations, adored him as the [3] supreme God, and called a female, by name Helena, who then travelled about with him,

---

[1] Apol. I. p. 69 C. See also p. 91 B. Apol II. p. 52 A.

[2] This story respecting the statue erected in honour of Simon Magus has been repeated by several of the Fathers, and was generally received as true, until, in 1574, a statue was digged up in the Island of the Tiber, having an inscription commencing thus: Semoni Sanco Deo Fidio Sacrum. The majority of learned men have since been of opinion that Justin, deceived by the similarity of names, mistook a statue in honour of a Sabine deity for one erected to Simon Magus. Thirlby *affects* to defend Justin. Dr. Burton, in the Notes to his Bampton Lectures, p. 374, decides in favour of Justin's accuracy.

[3] τὸν πρῶτον θεόν. In the Dialogue, p. 349 D. Θεὸν ὑπεράνω πάσης ἀρχῆς, καὶ ἐξουσίας, καὶ δυνάμεως.

but had before been a prostitute, his first intelligence, τὴν ὑπ' αὐτοῦ ἔννοιαν πρώτην γενομένην.

Justin mentions, also, [1] Menander, another Samaritan, who was set on by the Dæmons, and when he resided at Antioch, deceived many by magical arts. He persuaded his followers that they should never die: and some in Justin's time still maintained the same doctrine.

A third heretic, [2] mentioned by Justin as his contemporary, is Marcion of Pontus, who taught that there was a God superior to the Creator of the Universe, and another Christ besides the Christ announced by the Prophets. He had, according to Justin, numerous followers.

Justin [3] mentions cursorily that there were heretical sects under the names of Marciani, Valentiniani, Basilidiani, Saturniliani, so called from the individuals who first broached the different heresies. He [4] speaks, or rather assents to Trypho, who speaks

---

[1] Apol. I. p. 69 E. 91 A.   [2] Apol. I. p. 70 A. 92 A.

[3] Dial. p. 253 E. The Marciani were probably the same as the Marcosii, so called from Marcus.

[4] Dial. p. 253 A. These were probably some of the Gnostic Sects. Justin couples the eating of things offered to idols with idolatry itself; and says that a Christian would rather suffer death than be guilty of either offence.

of Christians who, without scruple, ate food offered to idols.

We [1] have seen his own inference from the words in Genesis i. 26. " Let us make man in our image after our likeness ;" and iii. 22. " Lo Adam is become as one of us." [2] Some heretics affirmed that the Almighty addressed these words to the Angels, by whom the human body was made.

Justin speaks of two descriptions of Christians, who denied that the Jews would finally be restored to the land of their ancestors, and that Jerusalem would be rebuilt : one class, as we have seen, consisted of Christians, who were in other respects orthodox ; the other, [3] of heretics, who denied the resurrection of the dead, and affirmed that the soul, immediately on its separation from the body, was received into heaven.

It [4] has been already observed that Justin alludes to heretics, who affirmed that the power who appeared to Moses, Abraham, and Jacob, was only an emanation from the Father, bearing different names, according to the functions assigned him;

---

[1] p. 71.
[2] Dial p. 285 E. It appears from Irenæus I. c. 22. and Tertullian de Res. Carnis, c. 5. that Menander, Marcus, and Saturnilus affirmed the human body to be the workmanship of angels.   [3] p. 104. Dial. p. 307 A   [4] Page 66.

being inseparable from the Father, as the light of the Sun on the earth cannot be separated from the Sun in the heaven.

[1] Justin applies the name of sophists to certain persons, who contended that, when God said, in Genesis iii. 22. " Lo Adam is become as one of us," the expression was to be understood figuratively; not as spoken of two or more persons numerically distinct from each other.

We know, from the [2] assertion of Justin himself, that he composed a work against all the heresies which had arisen in the Church; but it has not reached our time.

Allusion has been made to a [3] passage in the first Apology, in which Justin appears to insinuate that the horrible crimes which were falsely charged upon the Christians in general by their adversaries, might perhaps be committed in the assemblies of the heretics.

Justin [4] twice appeals to the Acts of Pilate, in

[1] Dial. p. 359 A.   [2] Apol. I. p. 70 C.
[3] p. 13. Note 1. p. 70 B.
[4] Apol. I. p. 76 C. 84 C. Thirlby suspects that Justin was deceived by the fraud of some Christian who had falsified the genuine Acts, or misrepresented their contents. Both the circumstances to which Justin alludes are found in the spurious

order to shew that the predictions of the Prophets concerning the Messiah were accomplished in Jesus; first, with respect to the circumstances which attended his crucifixion; and secondly, with respect to the wonderful cures which he performed. Justin [1] appeals also to the records of the census made by Cyrenius, the first Procurator of Judea; in proof of the birth of Christ at Bethlehem, and of the time when the event occurred. He says [2] that Christ was thirty years of age, more or less, before he was baptized by John; and that [3] he worked at his father's trade, in order to inculcate the duties of justice and industry.

It has been frequently observed that Justin is not very accurate in his chronology. He [4] supposes that Ptolemy, the King of Egypt who caused the Septuagint Version to be made, was contemporary with Herod King of Judea. He says also, [5] if the reading is correct, that Christ suffered under

---

Acts of Pilate now extant. Respecting the Acts of Pilate, see Lardner, Heathen Testimonies, c. 2 Casaubon ad Baronii Annales, xvi. 154.

[1] Apol. I. p. 75 E. 83 B. Dial. p. 303 E.
[2] Dial. p. 315 D. [3] Dial. p. 316 C. See Mark vi. 3.
[4] Apol. I. p. 72 C.
[5] Dial. p. 272 A. καὶ γὰρ 'Ηρώδην, ἀφ' οὗ ἔπαθεν, 'Ασκαλωνίτην γεγονέναι λέγοντες. Perhaps, instead of ἀφ' οὗ ἔπαθεν, we should read ἀφ' οὗ ἐπαύσατο. Both ἔπαθεν and ἐπαύσατο occur in the preceding sentence, ὅτι οὖν οὐδέποτε ἐν τῷ γένει ὑμῶν ἐπαύσατο οὔτε προφήτης οὔτε ἄρχων, ἐξότου ἀρχὴν ἔλαβε,

Herod the Ascalonite. I say, if the reading is correct; for [1] in a subsequent passage he distinguishes very accurately between Herod the Great and Herod to whom Christ was sent by Pilate.

We may state, as another instance of Justin's views of chronology, that he [2] supposed Deucalion to be the same as Noah.

In speaking of the prophecies by which the coming of Christ was announced, he [3] says, that some were uttered 5000, some 3000, some 2000, some 1000, some 800 years before the event; and he immediately adds, that Moses was the first Prophet, and quotes the prediction of the dying Jacob. Pearson's remark on this passage is, *Mira Chronologia*. But when Justin called Moses the first Prophet, he seems to have meant that Moses was the first who recorded the prophecies of former ages; not to have asserted, as Pearson infers, that Moses lived 5000 years before Christ. [4] On another occasion he says, that David lived 1500 years before Christ. According to the received chronology,

---

μέχρις οὗ οὗτος Ἰησοῦς Χριστὸς καὶ γέγονε καὶ ἔπαθεν. Casaubon, i. 2. would omit the words ἀφ' οὗ ἔπαθεν, or read ἐφ' οὗ ἐγεννήθη, too arbitrary a change.

[1] p. 330 D. See Apol. I. p. 78 E.   [2] Apol. II. p. 45 C.
[3] Apol. I. p. 73 B. See p. 92 C. Dial. p. 247 B.
[4] Apol. I. p 80 C

Malachi prophesied about 400 years before Christ, and David lived between 1000 and 1100 years before Christ. In both cases it differs about 400 years from Justin's chronology, who places the last prophet 800, David 1500 years before Christ. Grabe supposes Justin to have placed an interval of 5500 years between the creation and the birth of Christ, and to have alluded to Adam when he spoke of a prophecy delivered 5000 years before Christ.

Justin [1] quotes the Sibyl and Hystaspes as saying, that all corruptible things will finally be consumed by fire. On [2] another occasion he states that the perusal of their books, as well as of those of the Prophets, had been prohibited through the instigation of the wicked Dæmons, lest the readers should be led to the knowledge of the truth; but that, notwithstanding the prohibition, the Christians continued to read them.

[1] Apol. I. p. 66 C.
[2] Apol. I. p. 82 C.   See Casaubon's remarks on this statement of Justin, Exercit. ad Baronii Annales, i. 11.

CHAPTER VIII.

AN EXAMINATION OF THE QUESTION, WHETHER JUSTIN QUOTED THE GOSPELS WHICH WE NOW HAVE?

[1] LARDNER, in his account of Justin, conceives it to be plain, " that our Gospels are the books Justin made use of, as authentic histories of Jesus Christ." Since, however, the controversy respecting the origin of the first three Gospels was raised in Germany, the correctness of the inference, which seemed so plain to Lardner, has been questioned; and in our own country, a Prelate, who occupies a place in the foremost rank of Biblical Critics, has expressed a decided opinion, " that Justin did not quote our Gospels." If I venture to state the reasons which induce me to withhold my assent from the opinion so expressed, I trust that I shall be acquitted of the rashness and presumption of *unnecessarily* opposing myself to one, for whose learning and acuteness I cannot but entertain the greatest respect. But, professing as I do, to give

---

[1] Credibility of the Gospel History, c. x. §. 9.

an account of the writings and opinions of Justin Martyr, the reader will reasonably expect from me some notice of this important question. The principal value of the writings of the Fathers consists, perhaps, in the testimony, which they bear to the authenticity of the books of the New Testament.

It is certain that the only book of the New Testament expressly referred to by Justin, is the Revelation, which he ascribes to the Apostle St. John. Yet it is scarcely possible to conceive that he had not, in the course of his travels, and during his residence at Rome, met with most of the other books which now compose our Canon. On the supposition that he had met with the present Gospels, the same reasons would have induced him to make his quotations from them, which induced the Church to admit them into the Canon, in preference to all the other narratives of our Saviour's life and ministry. If he did not quote them, we must either suppose that he was unacquainted with them; or we must admit that a document then existed, which Justin deemed to be of greater authenticity than our present Gospels, but which has since been lost.

[1] Dodwell, in his Dissertations on Irenæus, has

[1] Diss. I. c. xl.

stated the following reasons for thinking that the books from which Justin made his quotations were our present Gospels. [1] He calls them Gospels—[2] the passages which he quotes are extant in our Gospels, with very little variation, and the insertions of passages from Apocryphal Books are very rare—[3] the account which he gives of the origin of what he terms ἀπομνημονεύματα τῶν Ἀποστόλων corresponds with the origin of our Gospels, viz. that two were written by Apostles, and two by companions of the Apostles. Moreover [4] Irenæus, who was nearly contemporary with Justin, speaks as if it was a fact universally acknowledged, that there were only four Gospels; and assigns reasons

---

[1] οἱ ἀπόστολοι ἐν τοῖς γενομένοις ὑπ' αὐτῶν ἀπομνημονεύμασιν, ἃ καλεῖται εὐαγγέλια. Apol. I. p. 98 B. Bishop Marsh supposes the words ἃ καλεῖται εὐαγγέλια to be an interpolation.

[2] Dodwell's words are, Tum et ex ipso Justino qui e nostris Evangeliis loca plurima adduxit, et quidem id castissime, raro admodum immistis Apocryphis.

[3] ἐν γὰρ τοῖς ἀπομνημονεύμασιν ἅ φημι ὑπὸ τῶν Ἀποστόλων αὐτοῦ καὶ τῶν ἐκείνοις παρακολουθησάντων συντετάχθαι. Dial. p. 331 D. Dodwell's remark is, S Lucæ verba ipsa respexisse videtur, ἔδοξε κἀμοὶ παρηκολουθηκότι.

[4] Tatian, Justin's scholar, composed a Diatessaron. Eusebius Hist. Eccl L. iv. c. 29. Theodoret Hæret Fab. L. i. c. 20. The assertion, therefore, of Victor Capuanus that Tatian's harmony was called διὰ πέντε is either erroneous; or, with Ittigius, we must read πάντων for πέντε. According to Epiphanius Hær. 26 or 46, some called Tatian's Diatessaron the Gospel according to the Hebrews.

why there could neither be more nor less than four.

The learned [1] Prelate, however, to whom I have alluded, thinks that the expression ἀπομνημονεύματα τῶν Ἀποστόλων is wholly inapplicable to our present Gospels. For,

I. " The term Ἀπομνημονεύματα denotes not several works, each written by a different person, but simply one work." The title Ξενοφῶντος ἀπομνημονεύματα is used to denote a *single* work composed by a single author; consequently, ἀπομνημονεύματα τῶν Ἀποστόλων must mean a *single* work composed by more than one author. But is this a necessary inference? The title Ξενοφῶντος ἀπομνημονεύματα means a collection of such sayings and acts of Socrates as were remembered by Xenophon; in like manner, ἀπομνημονεύματα τῶν Ἀποστόλων means a collection of such sayings or acts of Christ as were remembered by the Apostles. But the recollections of each Apostle might be recorded in a separate book. One book might be entitled ἀπομνημονεύματα Ματθαίου, another, ἀπομνημονεύματα Ἰωάννου, while the general title might be ἀπομνημονεύματα τῶν Ἀποστόλων.

[1] See Bishop Marsh's Illustration of his Hypothesis, Appendix, Sect. 3.

II. "If Justin had departed from the common use of this title, and had meant to describe four different Gospels, written by four different authors, two of whom were not Apostles, he would surely not have adopted the title τῶν Ἀποστόλων, as applicable to all four; he would not have used the title *Memoirs by the Apostles*, if only two out of the twelve were concerned in drawing them up." The material part of this objection had been anticipated by [1] Bishop Pearson, who, in speaking of the passage of Eusebius, in which the account given by Papias of the origin of St. Mark's Gospel is recorded, observes that the Gospels of St. Mark and St. Luke were understood by the ancients to be ἀπομνημονεύματα Πέτρου καὶ Παύλου. The term ἀπομνημονεύματα τῶν Ἀποστόλων, therefore, applies to *them* as well as to the other two Gospels. But the learned Prelate seems to lay great stress on the article τῶν, and to infer from it that *all* the Apostles must have been concerned in drawing up the work. Let us, however, suppose that Justin had our present Gospels before him; by what more appropriate title could he refer to them, when addressing a heathen Emperor or a Jew, than by that of ἀπομνημονεύματα τῶν Ἀποστό-

---

[1] Sic Marci Evangelium credebant Veteres nihil aliud fuisse quam Petri ἀπομνημονεύματα. Vindiciæ Ignatianæ, Pars I. c. 6. p. 297. The passage of Eusebius is in Hist. Eccl. L. iii. c. 39.

λων? The fallacy, if I may venture to use the term, lies in assuming that Justin refers to a work actually existing under the title of ἀπομνημονεύματα τῶν Ἀποστόλων, whereas the expression is Justin's own, intended to convey to a heathen or a Jew a correct idea of the nature of the works which he quotes. The works were known to Christians by the title [1] εὐαγγέλια, as is evident from the clause which the learned Prelate wishes to expunge as spurious; and had Justin been addressing Christians, he would have used that title. But it is further urged, that "Justin's constant practice is to name the author from whom he quotes; and if we consult his numerous quotations from the Old Testament, we shall find that he does not content himself merely with saying, as it is written by the Prophets or by the Prophet, but that he adds by what Prophet." If this statement were more *strictly* correct than it is, satisfactory reasons might be assigned why Justin, in disputing with a Jew, should specify the book of the Old Testament to which he appeals, and yet not mention the particular Gospel

[1] See the quotation in p. 134. note 1. There are two other passages in which the word εὐαγγέλιον is used to signify a written Gospel: one in p. 227 C. where Trypho says that he had read the precepts delivered ἐν τῷ λεγομένῳ εὐαγγελίῳ; the other in p. 326 D. where Justin says, καὶ ἐν τῷ εὐαγγελίῳ δὲ γέγραπται εἰπὼν, Πάντα μοι παραδέδοται ὑπὸ τοῦ πατρὸς, καὶ οὐδεὶς γιγνώσκει τὸν Πατέρα εἰ μὴ ὁ υἱὸς, οὐδὲ τὸν υἱὸν εἰ μὴ ὁ Πατὴρ, καὶ οἷς ἂν ὁ υἱὸς ἀποκαλύψῃ, an evident quotation by memory from Matthew xi. 27.

which he is about to quote. In quoting the former, the object of Justin would be to influence Trypho's judgment, by appealing to an authority which the Jews held in the highest veneration; and he would naturally be minute and precise in his reference. But in quoting the New Testament, the authority of which was denied by the Jews, his object would be not so much to convince Trypho, as [1] to state certain facts; the same exactness of citation would consequently be useless. [2] On one occasion he appears almost to apologise for quoting the Sacred Books of the Christians. Should it be said, that in his first Apology, addressed to an heathen Emperor, Justin is no less exact in specifying the Prophet, whose book he quotes, we reply, that the principal object for which Justin there refers to the Books of the Old Testament, is, to show that the Prophecies respecting the Messiah were fulfilled in Jesus. It was important, therefore, to quote the precise words of the Prophecy; and

[1] Thus, in the first Apology, where he says that the Christians gave to the Prince of Evil Dæmons the titles Serpent, Satan, and Devil, he adds ὡς καὶ ἐκ τῶν ἡμετέρων συγγραμμάτων ἐρευνήσαντες μαθεῖν δύνασθε. p. 71 A.

[2] ἐπειδὴ γὰρ ἀνέγνως, ὦ Τρύφων, ὡς αὐτὸς ὁμολογήσας ἔφης, τὰ ὑπ' ἐκείνου τοῦ σωτῆρος ἡμῶν διδαχθέντα, οὐκ ἄτοπον νομίζω πεποιηκέναι καὶ βραχέα τῶν ἐκείνου λόγια πρὸς τοῖς προφητικοῖς ἐπιμνησθείς. p. 235 D. If Trypho had not admitted that he had read the precepts delivered by Christ, Justin would have thought it unseasonable to quote them.

Justin, with the view of proving that he does quote accurately, introduces his quotations by a short history of the Septuagint Version; in order that the Emperor may, by referring to a work so generally known, satisfy himself of their correctness. The difference between the two cases is, that, in quoting the Old Testament, Justin appeals to an authority;—in quoting the New, he does not: and this difference sufficiently accounts for the different manner in which the quotations are made.

III. Another objection is, that Justin is very exact in his quotations from the Old Testament; from which circumstance it is inferred, that, if he had quoted our present Gospels, the same verbal coincidence would have been found in the quotations from them. But is Justin really so exact in his quotations from the Old Testament as this objection represents? In [1] Apol. I. he ascribes to Zephaniah a passage which is found in Zechariah ix. 9. and which he himself gives to Zechariah, in the [2] Dialogue with Trypho. In [3] another pas-

[1] p. 76 D. The latter part of the quotation agrees more nearly with the quotation of the same passage in Matt. xxi. 5. than with the Septuagint. There is not a verbal coincidence in the two quotations by Justin

[2] p. 273 A. In p. 268 B. he gives Malachi iv. 5 to Zechariah.

[3] p. 74 C. In p. 269 B. he mixes together Numbers xxvii. 18. 20. xi. 17. and Deut. xxxiv. 9.

sage he has mixed together Numbers xxiv. 17. Isaiah xi. 1. and li. 5. In ¹ another he appears to have mixed together Isaiah vii. 14. and Matthew i. 23. In ² another he professes to quote the Prophet Micah, v. 2., but gives the words precisely as they stand in Matthew ii. 6. In ³ another he has mixed together Isaiah lxv. 2. and lviii. 2. In ⁴ another he ascribes to Isaiah a passage, part of which is found in Jeremiah xxvii. 3. In ⁵ another he ascribes to Jeremiah a passage which is found in Daniel. These instances, to which many ⁶ others might be added, are surely sufficient to prove that

¹ p. 74 E.
² p. 75 D.
³ p. 76 A.
⁴ p. 84 B.   See also p. 89 A.
⁵ p. 86 E.
⁶ In p. 344 B. Justin states a circumstance respecting Jesus, the High Priest mentioned in Zechariah iii which is not found in Scripture. In p. 232 D. he assigns to Hosea a passage which, in other places, he rightly gives to Zechariah. In p. 367 C. we find ὅτι ἐν τῷ Ἡσαίᾳ λέλεκται ὑπὸ τοῦ Θεοῦ πρὸς τὴν Ἱερουσαλὴμ, ὅτι ἐπὶ τοῦ κατακλυσμοῦ τοῦ Νῶε ἔσωσά σε, which Thirlby, with reason, conjectures to be an erroneous quotation from memory of Isaiah liv. 8, 9. One of Middleton's charges against Justin is founded upon his negligent mode of quoting Scripture ; and it is remarkable, that all the instances are taken from the Old Testament. Enquiry, p. 161. In Apol. I. p. 95 A. Justin speaks of Moses as feeding his uncle's flock, τοῦ πρὸς μητρὸς θείου, in Arabia. See Thirlby's Note. He says also, that, as the bodies of the younger Israelites grew during their journey through the wilderness, their clothes grew also, ἀλλὰ καὶ τὰ τῶν νεωτέρων (ἐνδύματα) συνηύξανε, Dial. p. 361 D. See Deuteron. viii. 4.

Justin is not *uniformly* accurate in his quotations from the Old Testament. The strictest verbal coincidence is observable in the quotations from the Psalms; for which [1] Thirlby seems satisfactorily to account, by remarking that the Psalms always formed a considerable part of the service of the Church, and thus were impressed more accurately on the memories of Christians.

Let us now consider in detail the passages in which Justin expressly refers to the ἀπομνημονεύματα τῶν Ἀποστόλων. Apol. I. p. 75 A. καὶ ὁ ἀποσταλεὶς δὲ πρὸς αὐτὴν τὴν παρθένον κατ' ἐκεῖνο τοῦ καιροῦ εὐηγγελίσατο αὐτὴν εἰπὼν, Ἰδοὺ συλλήψει ἐν γαστρὶ ἐκ πνεύματος ἁγίου, καὶ τέξει υἱὸν, καὶ υἱὸς ὑψίστου κληθήσεται, καὶ καλέσεις τὸ ὄνομα αὐτοῦ Ἰησοῦν· αὐτὸς γὰρ σώσει τὸν λαὸν αὐτοῦ ἀπὸ τῶν ἁμαρτιῶν αὐτῶν, ὡς οἱ ἀπομνημονεύσαντες πάντα τὰ περὶ τοῦ σωτῆρος ἡμῶν Ἰησοῦ Χριστοῦ ἐδίδαξαν. The former part of this quotation is found, though the words are not precisely in the same order, in Luke i. 31, 32; the latter in Matthew i. 21. Justin joined the two quotations together, perhaps from error of memory, perhaps by design.

P. 98 B. οἱ γὰρ Ἀπόστολοι ἐν τοῖς γενομένοις ὑπ'

---

[1] p. 239 E.

αὐτῶν ἀπομνημονεύμασιν, ἃ καλεῖται εὐαγγέλια, οὕτως παρέδωκαν ἐντετάλθαι αὐτοῖς τὸν Ἰησοῦν λαβόντα ἄρτον, εὐχαριστήσαντα εἰπεῖν, τοῦτο ποιεῖτε εἰς τὴν ἀνάμνησίν μου· τοῦτ' ἐστι τὸ σῶμά μου. καὶ τὸ ποτήριον ὁμοίως λαβόντα καὶ εὐχαριστήσαντα εἰπεῖν, τοῦτό ἐστι τὸ αἷμά μου· καὶ μόνοις αὐτοῖς μεταδοῦναι. Here Justin evidently means to give the sense, not the exact words, of Scripture.

P. 98 D. In this place there is no quotation; but Justin states that the ἀπομνημονεύματα τῶν Ἀποστόλων, or the συγγράμματα τῶν Προφητῶν, were read in the assemblies of the Christians every Sunday. Unless, therefore, the ἀπομνημονεύματα here alluded to were our present Gospels, we must suppose that a work, esteemed to be of so high authority as to be publicly read in the Church, had wholly disappeared in the interval between Justin and Irenæus, who recognised only our present Gospels. Is this probable?

Dial. p. 328 B. οἱ γὰρ θεωροῦντες αὐτὸν ἐσταυρωμένον τὰς κεφαλὰς ἕκαστος ἐκίνουν, καὶ τὰ χείλη διέστρεφον, καὶ τοῖς μυξωτῆρσιν ἐν ἄλλοις (l. ἀλλήλοις) διερινοῦντες ἔλεγον εἰρωνευόμενοι ταῦτα, ἃ καὶ ἐν τοῖς ἀπομνημονεύμασι τῶν Ἀποστόλων αὐτοῦ γέγραπται, Υἱὸν Θεοῦ ἑαυτὸν ἔλεγε, καταβὰς περιπατείτω, σωσάτω αὐτὸν ὁ Θεός. Justin in this instance has evidently, in quoting from memory, mixed up with Matthew xxvii. 42. words from Psalm xxi. 7. to which he had just referred.

P. 329 C. σιγήσαντος αὐτοῦ καὶ μηκέτι ἐπὶ Πιλάτου ἀποκρίνασθαι μηδὲν μηδενὶ βουλομένου, ὡς ἐν τοῖς ἀπομνημονεύμασι τῶν Ἀποστόλων αὐτοῦ δεδήλωται. This is a reference, not a quotation.

P. 331 B. καὶ γὰρ οὗτος ὁ διάβολος ἅμα τῷ ἀναβῆναι αὐτὸν ἀπὸ τοῦ ποταμοῦ τοῦ Ἰορδάνου, τῆς φωνῆς αὐτῷ λεχθείσης, Υἱός μου εἶ σύ, ἐγὼ σήμερον γεγέννηκά σε, ἐν τοῖς ἀπομνημονεύμασι τῶν Ἀποστόλων γέγραπται προσελθὼν αὐτῷ καὶ πειράζων μεχρὶ τοῦ εἰπεῖν αὐτῷ, Προσκύνησόν μοι· καὶ ἀποκρίνασθαι αὐτῷ τὸν Χριστόν, Ὕπαγε ὀπίσω μου, Σατανᾶ, Κύριον τὸν Θεόν σου προσκυνήσεις καὶ αὐτῷ μόνῳ λατρεύσεις. In this passage Justin appears to have referred to Luke iii. 22. iv. 8. but, quoting from memory, to have cited the words of Psalm ii. 7. instead of Luke iii. 22. Is there not also reason for suspecting that Justin, in arguing with a Jew, might think that he added weight to his argument, by substituting for the actual words of the Gospel, words from the Old Testament, which the Jews themselves interpreted of the Messiah [1]? It ought, however, to be observed, that the Codex Bezæ in Luke iii. 22. gives the words

[1] Compare p. 316 D.

as Justin quotes them; and that [1] Clemens Alexandrinus, who certainly quoted our Gospels, gives them in the same manner. They appear also to have been extant in the Gospel used by the Ebionites [2].

P. 331 D. ἐν γὰρ τοῖς ἀπομνημονεύμασιν, ἅ φημι ὑπὸ τῶν Ἀποστόλων αὐτοῦ καὶ τῶν ἐκείνοις παρακολουθησάντων συντετάχθαι, ὅτι ἱδρὼς, ὡσεὶ θρόμβοι, κατεχεῖτο αὐτοῦ εὐχομένου καὶ λέγοντος, Παρελθέτω, εἰ δυνατὸν, τὸ ποτήριον τοῦτο. Here Justin evidently quotes Matthew xxvi. 39. though he adds from Luke xxii. 44. a circumstance which gives great weight to his argument; his purpose being then to show that the prediction in Psalm xxii. 14. was actually accomplished in Christ's sufferings.

P. 332 B. ὅπερ καὶ ἐν τοῖς ἀπομνημονεύμασι τῶν Ἀποστόλων αὐτοῦ γέγραπται γενόμενον. And shortly after, ὡς ἀπὸ τῶν ἀπομνημονευμάτων ἐμάθομεν. Here are only references.

[1] αὐτίκα γοῦν βαπτιζομένῳ τῷ Κυρίῳ ἀπ' οὐρανῶν ἐπήχησε φωνὴ μάρτυς ἠγαπημένου· Υἱός μου εἶ σὺ ἀγαπητὸς, ἐγὼ σήμερον γεγέννηκά σε. Pædag. L. ı. c. 6. p. 113. Ed. Pot.
[2] Epiphanius Hær. x. or xxi. §. 13. καὶ φωνὴ ἐγένετο ἐκ τοῦ οὐρανοῦ, λέγουσα, σύ μου εἶ υἱὸς ὁ ἀγαπητὸς, ἐν σοὶ ηὐδόκησα. καὶ πάλιν, ἐγὼ σήμερον γεγέννηκά σε. In §. 3. Epiphanius says, that the Ebionites used the Gospel of St. Matthew (but corrupted and mutilated, §. 13.), and called it the Gospel according to the Hebrews, affirming that Matthew alone wrote in Hebrew.

P. 333 B. καὶ γὰρ ἀποδιδοὺς τὸ πνεῦμα ἐπὶ τῷ σταυρῷ εἶπε, Πάτερ, εἰς χεῖράς σου παρατίθεμαι τὸ πνεῦμά μου, ὡς καὶ ἐκ τῶν ἀπομνημονευμάτων καὶ τοῦτο ἔμαθον. This quotation agrees with Luke xxiii. 46. In the received Text we find παραθήσομαι, instead of παρατίθεμαι ; but the latter is marked as a various reading. Again, ταῦτα εἰρηκέναι ἐν τοῖς ἀπομνημονεύμασι γέγραπται, ἐὰν μὴ περισσεύσῃ ὑμῶν ἡ δικαιοσύνη πλεῖον τῶν γραμματέων καὶ φαρισαίων, οὐ μὴ εἰσέλθητε εἰς τὴν βασιλείαν τῶν οὐρανῶν, which agrees with Matt. v. 20.

P. 333 D. ὡς καὶ ἐν τοῖς ἀπομνημονεύμασι τῶν Ἀποστόλων δηλοῦται γεγενημένον. Here is only a reference.

P. 333 E. καὶ τὸ εἰπεῖν μετωνομακέναι αὐτὸν Πέτρον ἕνα τῶν Ἀποστόλων, καὶ γεγράφθαι ἐν τοῖς ἀπομνημονεύμασιν αὐτοῦ γεγενημένον καὶ τοῦτο, μετὰ τοῦ καὶ ἄλλους δύο ἀδελφοὺς, υἱοὺς Ζεβεδαίου ὄντας, μετωνομακέναι ὀνόματι τοῦ Βοανεργὲς, ὅ ἐστιν, υἱοὶ βροντῆς, σημαντικὸν ἦν τοῦ αὐτὸν ἐκεῖνον εἶναι. Here, although there is no quotation, there is an evident allusion to Mark iii. 17.

P. 334 B. ἀνατείλαντος οὖν καὶ ἐν οὐρανῷ ἅμα τῷ γεννηθῆναι αὐτὸν ἀστέρος, ὡς γέγραπται ἐν τοῖς ἀπομνημονεύμασι τῶν Ἀποστόλων αὐτοῦ, οἱ ἀπὸ Ἀραβίας μάγοι, ἐκ τούτου ἐπιγνόντες, παρεγένοντο καὶ προσεκύνησαν αὐτῷ. καὶ ὅτι τῇ τρίτῃ ἡμέρᾳ ἔμελλεν ἀναστήσεσθαι μετὰ τὸ σταυρωθῆναι, γέγραπται ἐν τοῖς ἀπομνημονεύμασιν, ὅτι οἱ ἀπὸ τοῦ γένους ὑμῶν συζητοῦντες αὐτῷ ἔλεγον (ὅτι) Δεῖξον ἡμῖν σημεῖον, καὶ ἀπεκρίνατο αὐτοῖς, Γενεὰ πονηρὰ καὶ μοιχαλὶς σημεῖον ἐπιζητεῖ, καὶ σημεῖον οὐ δοθήσεται αὐτοῖς, εἰ μὴ τὸ σημεῖον Ἰωνᾶ.

In the former part of the passage, though there is no quotation, there is a manifest reference to the second chapter of St. Matthew: and in the latter part there is an almost exact verbal coincidence with Matthew xii. 39.

P. 327 B. καὶ υἱὸν Θεοῦ γεγραμμένον αὐτὸν ἐν τοῖς ἀπομνημονεύμασι τῶν Ἀποστόλων αὐτοῦ ἔχοντες. Here is no quotation.

The inference which I am disposed to draw from the consideration of the above passages, is, not that Justin quoted a Narrative of our Saviour's Life and Ministry, agreeing in substance with our present Gospels, though differing from them in expression; but that he quoted our present Gospels from memory. This inference is, as it appears to me, equally deducible from those passages which he quotes without any express reference to the ἀπομνημονεύματα τῶν Ἀποστόλων. It is, moreover, necessary always to bear in mind, as has been already observed, that Justin does not appeal to the New Testament, as an authority; he wishes merely to give a true representation of the doctrines and precepts of the Gospel; and for this purpose, it was sufficient to express the meaning without any scrupulous regard to verbal accuracy.

IV. It is objected that "Justin has quoted from his Memoirs by the Apostles, what does not exist, either in sense or substance, in any of our four Gospels." In p. 315 D. we read καὶ τότε ἐλθόντος τοῦ Ἰησοῦ ἐπὶ τὸν Ἰορδάνην ποταμὸν, ἔνθα ὁ Ἰωάννης ἐβάπτιζε, κατελθόντος τοῦ Ἰησοῦ ἐπὶ τὸ ὕδωρ, καὶ πῦρ ἀνήφθη ἐν τῷ Ἰορδάνῃ, καὶ ἀναδύντος αὐτοῦ ἀπὸ τοῦ ὕδατος, ὡς περιστερὰν τὸ ἅγιον πνεῦμα ἐπιπτῆναι ἐπ᾽ αὐτὸν ἔγραψαν οἱ ἀπόστολοι αὐτοῦ τούτου τοῦ Χριστοῦ ἡμῶν. The construction of this sentence is not very clear, and it has, in consequence, been conjectured that we ought, instead of ἀνήφθη, to read ἀνῆφθαι. Grabe,[1] who has discussed the passage at considerable length, retains the old reading, and wishes to restrict the words ἔγραψαν οἱ Ἀπόστολοι to the latter part of the sentence, so that the authority of the Apostles is appealed to *only* in confirmation of the descent of the Holy Spirit in the shape of a dove. This fact Grabe supposes Justin to have obtained from the present Gospels, and to have added the statement respecting the

[1] Spicil. T. I. p. 19.

fire from tradition. [1] Lardner appears disposed to acquiesce in this solution of the difficulty, which derives support from the fact, that, in quoting from the Old Testament, Justin sometimes mixes up statements not found in the Sacred Volume. I have [2] already referred to a statement respecting Joshua, the High-Priest, who, according to Justin, is said to have been clothed in filthy garments, because he had married a fornicatress; a statement of which there is no vestige in the Prophet Zechariah. I referred also to the following statement, in p. 361 D. respecting the children of Israel in their journey through the wilderness, ὧν καὶ οἱ ἱμάντες τῶν ὑποδημάτων οὐκ ἐρράγησαν, οὐδὲ αὐτὰ τὰ ὑποδήματα ἐπαλαιώθη, οὐδὲ τὰ ἐνδύματα κατετρίβη, ἀλλὰ καὶ τὰ τῶν νεωτέρων συνηύξανε, where manifestly referring to Deut. viii. 4. and xxix. 5. he has mixed up facts derived from some other source than Scripture. It is not, therefore, improbable that Justin obtained the statement respecting the fire from tradition, and added it to the Gospel narrative. The learned Prelate, however, whose opinions on this subject I am venturing to controvert, thinks

---

[1] Credibility, c. 10. §. 8.
[2] See p. 140. note 8 Thirlby supposes Justin either to have confounded Joshua with Hosea, who was commanded to take such a wife, c. i 2 or to have had in his mind Ezra, c. x. 18. where the sons of Jeshua, the son of Jozadak, are said to have had *strange* wives

that Justin quoted the Gospel according to the Hebrews, which was also called the Gospel according to the twelve. For, according to [1] Epiphanius, it was recorded in that Gospel, that after Christ had ascended out of the water, and the Holy Spirit had descended, and the voice had come from heaven, a great light shone around the place. It has been observed, that in Justin the fire is said to have been lighted when Jesus descended into the water; whereas, in the Gospel according to the Hebrews, the light shone after Jesus had come up out of the water; a difference, not merely of words, but of fact. The learned Prelate, however, considers this difference of no importance. To [2] Dodwell it appeared of so much weight, that he was induced to conclude from it, that Justin did not quote the Ebionite Gospel, but obtained the account from tradition. Lardner suggests that the words πῦρ ἀνήφθη may be nothing more than a particular explication of the words ἀνεῴχθησαν οἱ οὐρανοὶ in our present Gospels. Is

---

[1] Part of the passage is quoted in p. 144. note 1. καὶ ὡς ἀνῆλθεν ἀπὸ τοῦ ὕδατος, κ. τ. ἑ. ———— καὶ εὐθὺς περιέλαμψε τὸν τόπον φῶς μέγα. The author of the Tract De Baptismo Hæreticorum, printed with Cyprian's works, says that a similar account was given in an heretical forgery extant under the title, Prædicatio Petri. Item, quum baptizaretur, ignem super aquam visum. *Quod in Evangelio nullo est scriptum*, p. 30. Ed. Oxon.

[2] Diss. in Irenæum, II §. 9.

it not more likely, that they arose out of the declaration of the Baptist, that he who was to come after him would baptise with the Holy Ghost and *with fire?*

The learned Prelate urges another [1] passage, in which Justin quotes a saying of our Lord, not to be found in our present Gospels, διὸ καὶ ὁ ἡμέτερος Κύριος Ἰησοῦς Χριστὸς εἶπεν, Ἐν οἷς ἂν ὑμᾶς καταλάβω, ἐν τούτοις καὶ κρινῶ. This saying of our Lord is also quoted by [2] Clemens Alexandrinus; and, because Clemens has on another occasion expressly quoted the Gospel according to the Hebrews, the learned Prelate argues that both he and Justin obtained the saying from that Gospel. But this is surely to draw conclusions from very insufficient premises. We find in [3] the Acts of the Apostles a saying of our Lord, not recorded in the Gospels; why might not the saying in question have been handed down in the same manner by [4] tradition?

I will conclude my remarks on this interesting

---

[1] Dial. p. 267 A.
[2] Quis dives salvetur? §. 40. T. II p. 957. Ed. Pot. Clemens does not ascribe the saying expressly to Christ.
[3] c. 20 v 35
[4] See Jones on the Canon, T. I Appendix, Part 2 §. 12. Grabe, Spicil. T. I. p. 327.

question, with the words of an [1] able writer, who, at the same time that he protests against a gross misrepresentation which had been made of the learned Prelate's opinion, thus expresses his dissent from the opinion itself. " In fact, the modern German Divines appear to have been the first who thought the verbal diversity of Justin's quotations from the present Text of the Evangelists to be of any consequence. As a question of criticism, I own it is a difficult one; and, did I think that Justin had not quoted our present Books, I should not hesitate a moment to avow it. But when we reflect that there is no difference in the *facts* mentioned; that the verbal coincidence is sometimes exact, and sometimes so great as to appear exact in a translation; that Justin calls his books by the name of Gospels, and says that they were written by Apostles and Apostolick men, which precisely corresponds with ours, two of which are by Apostles, and two by Apostolick men; and that Irenæus makes no mention of any other Books so similar to ours, as Justin's were, if they be not the same: when we reflect on these things, we shall find it hard to believe that Justin quoted any other Gospels than ours. If, however, it be thought necessary, notwithstanding all this, to grant that he

---

[1] Everett, Defence of Christianity, &c. p. 474.

did not quote our Books, then it will be an inference scarcely less favourable to Christianity, that a set of Sacred Writings, different from ours, did yet testify to the truth of the same facts."

CHAPTER IX.

CONTAINING ILLUSTRATIONS OF THE PRECEDING CHAPTERS FROM THE WRITINGS OF TATIAN, ATHENAGORAS, AND THEOPHILUS, OF ANTIOCH, WITH ADDITIONAL REMARKS.

Page 10. note 1. TATIAN uses the words θεολογεῖν, θεοποιεῖν to signify what we express by the word *Deify*. p. 149 D. 157 B. Athenagoras uses θεολογεῖν in a sense approaching more nearly to that in which it is used in the Hortatory Address. Legatio, p. 18 D. 24 C. θεοποιεῖν means to Deify, in 24 B. D.

P. 12. [1] In the Dialogue with Trypho, Justin alludes to the charge which was brought against the Christians, of eating human flesh, and of indulging in the most horrible sensuality. [2] Tatian alludes to the same charge, and complains of the injustice of condemning the Christians merely because they were Christians. [3] Athenagoras com-

[1] p. 227 B. referred to in chapter VI note 4. p. 115.
[2] p. 149 B. 158 D. 162 D. 164 A
[3] Legatio, sub in, p 2 C. 3 A. 4 C. 7 D. 34 D. 38 B.

plains that the Christians were not allowed the liberty, which all other subjects of the Roman empire enjoyed, of worshipping the gods whom they preferred; and that they were persecuted only on account of their name: he affirms also, that no proof was ever brought forward that they were guilty of the crimes laid to their charge. The same calumnies are noticed by [1] Theophilus.

P. 12. note 2. [2] Theophilus also plays upon the words Χριστὸς and Χρηστός.

P. 13. In Apol. I. p. 64 D. Justin says, that the Christians prayed for the Emperors. So also Athenagoras, Leg. sub fin. Theophilus, L. i. p. 76 D.

P. 22. note 1. [3] Athenagoras speaks of the κοινὴ καὶ φυσικὴ ἔννοια. We find also τὰ αἰώνια δίκαια, Dial. p. 246 A.

P. 48. note 3. [4] Athenagoras quotes the same passage from the second Epistle of Plato, and thus argues upon it, ἆρ' οὖν ὁ τὸν ἀΐδιον νοῦν καὶ λόγῳ καταλαμβανόμενον περινοήσας Θεὸν, καὶ τὰ ἐπισυμ-

---
[1] L. iii p. 119 B. 126 D.
[2] ἐγὼ μὲν οὖν ὁμολογῶ εἶναι Χριστιανὸς, καὶ φορῶ τὸ Θεοφιλὲς ὄνομα τοῦτο, ἐλπίζων εὔχρηστος εἶναι τῷ Θεῷ. L. i. p. 69 B. Compare p. 77 B.
[3] De Mort. Res. p. 54 D.
[4] Legatio, p. 26 A

βεβηκότα αὐτῷ ἐξειπὼν, τὸ ὄντως ὂν, τὸ μονοφυὲς, τὸ ἀγαθὸν ἀπ' αὐτοῦ ἀποχεόμενον, ὅπερ ἐστὶν ἀλήθεια· καὶ περὶ πρώτης δυνάμεως· καὶ ὡς περὶ τὸν πάντων βασιλέα πάντα ἐστὶ, καὶ ἐκείνου ἕνεκεν πάντα, καὶ ἐκεῖνο αἴτιον πάντων· καὶ περὶ δύο καὶ τρία· δεύτερον δὲ περὶ, τὰ δεύτερα· καὶ τρίτον περὶ, τὰ τρίτα· περὶ τῶν ἐκ τῶν αἰσθητῶν γῆς τε καὶ οὐρανοῦ λεγομένων γεγονέναι μεῖζον ἢ καθ' ἑαυτὸν τἀληθὲς μαθεῖν ἐνόμισεν; ἢ οὐκ ἔστιν εἰπεῖν. He had just before said, Πλάτων δὲ τὰ ἄλλα ἐπέχων, καὶ αὐτὸς εἴς τε τὸν ἀγέννητον Θεὸν καὶ τοὺς ὑπὸ τοῦ ἀγεννήτου εἰς κόσμον τοῦ οὐρανοῦ γεγονότας, τούς τε πλανήτας καὶ τοὺς ἀπλανεῖς ἀστέρας, καὶ εἰς Δαίμονας τέμνει· περὶ ὧν Δαιμόνων αὐτὸς ἀπαξιῶν λέγειν τοῖς περὶ αὐτῶν εἰρηκόσιν προσέχειν ἀξιοῖ. Then follows a quotation from the [1] Timæus of Plato. If Athenagoras had supposed that the writings of the Greek Philosopher contained any intimations of the doctrine of the Trinity, here, surely, was a favourable opportunity for introducing the subject: but he is silent.

P. 53. [2] Athenagoras, in like manner, appeals to the belief of the Christians in the Doctrine of the Trinity, for the purpose of defending them against the charge of Atheism, τίς οὖν οὐκ ἂν ἀπορήσαι, λέγοντας Θεὸν πατέρα καὶ υἱὸν Θεὸν καὶ πνεῦμα ἅγιον, δεικνύντας αὐτῶν καὶ τὴν ἐν τῇ ἑνώσει δύναμιν,

[1] Tom. III. p. 40. Ed. Serr.
[2] Legatio, p. 11 A.

καὶ τὴν ἐν τῇ τάξει διαίρεσιν, ἀκούσας ἀθέους καλουμένους; he had before said, [1] οὐδὲ ἡμεῖς ἄθεοι, ὑφ' οὗ λόγῳ δεδημιούργηται καὶ τῷ παρ' αὐτοῦ πνεύματι συνέχεται τὰ πάντα, τοῦτον εἰδότες καὶ κρατοῦντες Θεόν. In [2] a subsequent passage we find ὑπὸ μόνου δὲ παραπεμπόμενοι τούτου, ὃν ἴσως (f. ἴσασι) Θεὸν, καὶ τὸν παρ' αὐτοῦ λόγον εἰδέναι, τίς ἡ τοῦ παιδὸς πρὸς τὸν πατέρα ἑνότης, τίς ἡ τοῦ πατρὸς πρὸς τὸν υἱὸν κοινωνία, τί τὸ πνεῦμα, τίς ἡ τῶν τοσούτων ἕνωσις καὶ διαίρεσις, ἑνουμένων τοῦ πνεύματος, τοῦ παιδὸς, τοῦ πατρός. And [3] again, ὡς γὰρ Θεὸν φαμὲν, καὶ υἱὸν τὸν λόγον αὐτοῦ, καὶ πνεῦμα ἅγιον, ἑνούμενα μὲν κατὰ δύναμιν, τὸν πατέρα, τὸν υἱὸν, τὸ πνεῦμα· ὅτι νοῦς, λόγος, σοφία υἱὸς τοῦ πατρός· καὶ ἀπόρροια, ὡς φῶς ἀπὸ πυρὸς, τὸ πνεῦμα. With respect to Theophilus, it is well known that he is the earliest Christian writer who has used the word τριάς. In his second book he is commenting on the work of Creation, as described in the first chapter of Genesis. Having assigned a reason why the Sun and Moon were not created till the fourth day, he goes on to say that the Sun is a type of God, the Moon, of man; and then adds, [4] ὡσαύτως καὶ αἱ τρεῖς ἡμέραι (f. ins. πρὸ) τῶν φωστήρων γεγονυῖαι τύποι εἰσὶ τῆς τριάδος, τοῦ Θεοῦ, καὶ τοῦ λόγου αὐτοῦ, καὶ τῆς σοφίας αὐτοῦ. τετάρτῳ δὲ τύπῳ (f. τόπῳ) ἐστὶν ἄνθρωπος ὁ προσδεὴς

---

[1] Legatio, p. 7 A.
[2] p. 12 C.
[3] p. 27 A.
[4] p. 94 D.

τοῦ φωτὸς, ἵνα ᾖ Θεὸς, λόγος, σοφία, ἄνθρωπος. It is not very easy to discover wherein the correspondence between the types and antitypes consists; one thing, however, is certain, that, according to the notions of Theophilus, God, his Word, and his Wisdom, constitute a Trinity, and, it should seem, a Trinity of Persons; for man, whom he afterwards adds, is a person. One remarkable circumstance is, that Theophilus assigns to the third Person the title [1] σοφία, which is usually assigned by the early Fathers to the [2] second; as in the passage just quoted from Athenagoras.

Page 54. note 1. Immediately after [3] one of the passages just quoted from Athenagoras, follow these words, καὶ οὐκ ἐπὶ τούτοις τὸ θεολογικὸν ἡμῶν ἵσταται μέρος, ἀλλὰ καὶ πλῆθος Ἀγγέλων καὶ λειτουργῶν φαμὲν, οὓς ὁ ποιητὴς καὶ δημιουργὸς κόσμου Θεὸς διὰ τοῦ παρ' αὑτοῦ λόγου διένειμε καὶ διέταξε περί τε τὰ

[1] Compare L. ι. p. 74 B. ὁ Θεὸς διὰ τοῦ λόγου αὐτοῦ καὶ τῆς σοφίας ἐποίησε τὰ πάντα. τῷ γὰρ λόγῳ αὐτοῦ ἐστερεώθησαν οἱ οὐρανοὶ, καὶ τῷ πνεύματι αὐτοῦ πᾶσα ἡ δύναμις αὐτῶν. I give the passage as it stands in the Benedictine Edition; the latter part is a quotation from Psalm xxxiii. Again, L. ii p. 96 D. ἔτι μὴν καὶ ὡς βοηθείας χρῄζων ὁ Θεὸς εὑρίσκεται λέγων, ποιήσωμεν ἄνθρωπον κατ' εἰκόνα καὶ καθ' ὁμοίωσιν· οὐκ ἄλλῳ δέ τινι εἴρηκε, ποιήσωμεν, ἀλλ' ἢ τῷ ἑαυτοῦ λόγῳ καὶ τῇ ἑαυτοῦ σοφίᾳ.

[2] Theophilus himself gives the title σοφία to the second person in L. ii. p. 88 C. 100 A. and to God *absolutely*, L. i. p. 71 B.

[3] Legatio, p 11 A

στοιχεῖα εἶναι καὶ τοὺς οὐρανοὺς, καὶ τὸν κόσμον καὶ τὰ ἐν αὐτῷ, καὶ τὴν τούτων εὐταξίαν. Here Athenagoras says nothing of any worship to be paid to angels, though his words seem to imply that, in order fully to state the notions of the Christians respecting the Deity, it was necessary to add that they believed in the existence of a multitude of Angels who were to have their attention continually directed to the elements, heavens, &c. We should bear in mind that Justin and Athenagoras were replying to a charge of Atheism; and they appear to have thought that they strengthened their case by saying, " We not only believe in God, but also that he has subject to him a multitude of ministering Angels." It is to be observed, that, according to the statement of Athenagoras, God distributed to those Angels their various offices through the instrumentality of the Λόγος; so that they were, in fact, the ministers of the Λόγος.

P. 56. note 1. Thus Tatian, [1] Θεὸς ὁ καθ' ἡμᾶς οὐκ ἔχει σύστασιν ἐν χρόνῳ, μόνος ἄναρχος ὤν, καὶ αὐτὸς ὑπάρχων τῶν ὅλων ἀρχή. Again, [2] τὸν ἀνωνόμαστον Θεόν. Again, [3] ὑπὸ τοῦ πάντων δημιουργοῦ. Again, [4] ὁ δὲ τῶν ὅλων δεσπότης. Unless, as was before remarked, it should be thought that some

[1] p. 144 C.
[2] p. 144 D.
[3] p. 145 D.
[4] p. 151 D.

of these passages are to be understood of God *absolutely*. In Athenagoras we find, [1] ἕνα Θεὸν—τὸν τοῦδε τοῦ παντὸς ποιητὴν, αὐτὸν μὲν οὐ γενόμενον (ὅτι τὸ ὂν οὐ γίγνεται, ἀλλὰ τὸ μὴ ὂν) πάντα δὲ διὰ τοῦ παρ' αὐτοῦ λόγου πεποιηκότα, &c. Again, [2] ἕνα τὸν δημιουργὸν τῶν ὅλων νοῶν ἀγέννητον Θεόν. Again, [3] ὁ τοῦδε τοῦ παντὸς δημιουργὸς καὶ πατήρ. Again, [4] ἀποπίπτουσι τῷ (l. τοῦ) λόγῳ θεωρητοῦ Θεοῦ. Theophilus, in like manner, uses the expressions [5] ὁ Θεὸς ἀγέννητος ὢν καὶ ἀναλλοίωτος—[6] τὸν ποιητὴν καὶ δημιουργὸν τῶν ὅλων—ὁ μέν τοί γε Θεὸς καὶ πατὴρ καὶ κτιστὴς τῶν ὅλων.

Page 56. note 3. Theophilus [7] supposes the following objection to be made: " You say that God cannot be limited to a place; yet you say that he walked in Paradise." Theophilus answers, " It is true that God cannot be limited to a place, or be found in a place; for he has no place of his rest (Isaiah lvi. 1). But his Word, by whom he made all things, being his Power and Wisdom, assuming the person of the Father and Lord of the universe,

[1] Legatio, p. 5 C.
[2] p. 7 A. See also p. 10 A.
[3] p. 13 B.
[4] p. 24 B. See p. 5 B. 26 A.
[5] p. 82 C. See 71 C.
[6] p. 110 B. See p 122 D 89 A.
[7] L. ii. p. 100 A. Theophilus calls God τόπος τῶν ὅλων, L. 2. p. 81 D. and ἑαυτοῦ τόπος, p. 88 B.

came into Paradise in the person of God, and conversed with Adam. For the Divine Scripture itself instructs us that Adam said that he heard a voice; but what is this voice else than the Word of God, who is his Son."

Page 57. Tatian [1] thus states his view of the

[1] Θεὸς ἦν ἐν ἀρχῇ· τὴν δὲ ἀρχὴν Λόγου δύναμιν παρειλήφαμεν· ὁ γὰρ δεσπότης τῶν ὅλων, αὐτὸς ὑπάρχων τοῦ παντὸς ἡ ὑπόστασις, κατὰ μὲν τὴν μηδέπω γεγενημένην ποίησιν μόνος ἦν· καθὸ δὲ πᾶσα δύναμις ὁρατῶν τε καὶ ἀοράτων αὐτὸς ὑπόστασις ἦν, σὺν αὐτῷ τὰ πάντα· σὺν αὐτῷ γὰρ διὰ λογικῆς δυνάμεως αὐτὸς καὶ ὁ λόγος, ὃς ἦν ἐν αὐτῷ, ὑπέστησε θελήματι δὲ τῆς ἁπλότητος αὐτοῦ προπηδᾷ λόγος· ὁ δὲ λόγος, οὐ κατὰ κενοῦ χωρήσας, ἔργον πρωτότοκον τοῦ πνεύματος (f. πατρὸς) γίγνεται· τοῦτον ἴσμεν τοῦ κόσμου τὴν ἀρχήν. γέγονε δὲ κατὰ μερισμὸν, οὐ κατὰ ἀποκοπήν. τὸ γὰρ ἀποτμηθὲν τοῦ πρώτου κεχώρισται· τὸ δὲ μερισθὲν οἰκονομίας τὴν αἵρεσιν προσλαβὸν οὐκ ἐνδεᾶ τὸν ὅθεν εἴληπται πεποίηκεν. ὥσπερ γὰρ ἀπὸ μιᾶς δᾳδὸς ἀνάπτεται μὲν πυρὰ πολλὰ, τῆς δὲ πρώτης δᾳδὸς διὰ τὴν ἔξαψιν τῶν πολλῶν δᾳδῶν οὐκ ἐλαττοῦται τὸ φῶς· οὕτω καὶ ὁ λόγος, προελθὼν ἐκ τῆς τοῦ πατρὸς δυνάμεως, οὐκ ἄλογον πεποίηκε τὸν γεγεννηκότα. καὶ γὰρ αὐτὸς ἐγὼ λαλῶ, καὶ ὑμεῖς ἀκούετε, καὶ οὐ δήπου διὰ τῆς μεταβάσεως τοῦ λόγου κενὸς ὁ προσομιλῶν λόγου γίγνομαι· προβαλλόμενος δὲ τὴν ἐμαυτοῦ φωνὴν, διακοσμεῖν τὴν ἐν ὑμῖν ἀκόσμητον ὕλην προῄρημαι. καὶ καθάπερ ὁ λόγος, ἐν ἀρχῇ γεννηθεὶς, ἀντεγέννησε τὴν καθ' ἡμᾶς ποίησιν, αὐτὸς ἑαυτῷ τὴν ὕλην δημιουργήσας· οὕτω κἀγὼ κατὰ τὴν τοῦ λόγου μίμησιν ἀναγεννηθεὶς, καὶ τὴν τοῦ ἀληθοῦς κατάληψιν πεποιημένος, μεταρρυθμίζω τῆς συγγενοῦς ὕλης τὴν σύγχυσιν, p. 145 A. This difficult passage has furnished ample room for discussion. Petavius, and the author of the Dissertation on Tatian, in the Oxford edition, thought that by λόγου δύναμιν, was meant the same as by λογικῆς δυνάμεως which follows, that is, the power of Reason by which God produces all things; in other words, that, before the emission of the Λόγος, he existed only in *posse*, not in *esse*. Bull, on the contrary, and Le Nourry

Christian doctrine respecting the second Person in the Trinity. "God was in the beginning; but we understand the beginning to be the power of the Word. For the Lord of all things,

contend, that by λόγου δύναμις we must understand the power of the Word, that is, the Word himself, referring in support of this interpretation, to ἡ δὲ τοῦ λόγου δύναμις in p. 146 D. The expression λογικῆς δυνάμεως occurs again in p. 146 B. Λόγος γὰρ ὁ ἐπουράνιως, πνεῦμα γεγονὼς ἀπὸ τοῦ πατρὸς, καὶ Λόγος ἐκ τῆς λογικῆς δυνάμεως, where the Oxford Editor translates ἐκ τῆς λογικῆς δυνάμεως, Ex potentiâ divinâ τοῦ λόγου productrice. Petavius also differs from Bull respecting the translation of the words διὰ λογικῆς δυνάμεως αὐτὸς καὶ ὁ Λόγος, ὃς ἦν ἐν αὐτῷ, ὑπέστησε, which the former renders *per rationalem vim Λόγος ipse, qui in eo erat, extitit* the latter *per rationalem potentiam tum ipse, tum Λόγος qui in ipso erat, substitit*. I have followed Petavius, thinking his translation more agreeable both to the construction of the sentence, and to the whole scope of the passage; being further confirmed in this opinion by a corresponding passage of Tertullian, quoted by the Oxford Editor, *Ante omnia Deus erat solus, quia nihil aliud extrinsecus præter illum. Cæterum ne tum quidem solus. habebat enim secum, quam habebat in semetipso, Rationem suam scilicet,* contra Praxeam, c. 5. The Oxford Editor suggests very plausibly that we should read αὐτοῦ instead of αὐτός. In p. 155 D. Tatian speaks of Dæmons who were smitten, λόγῳ Θεοῦ δυνάμεως. We find λόγου δυνάμει, p. 157 C. with reference to the healing of diseases. Bull translates the words θελήματι δὲ τῆς ἁπλότητος αὐτοῦ literally by the words *Voluntate autem simplicitatis suæ*, and Waterland is angry with Whitby for not allowing the words to appear as they lie in the author, without the mean artifice of giving them a false turn. *By the will of his simplicity the Word proceeded forth*, Tom. III. p. 271. I wish that Bull and Waterland had told us the exact meaning which ought to be attached to the words. *By the will of his simplicity* I conceive that Tatian meant to express the simplicity of the Divine Nature, and the consequent unity of the Divine Will.

being himself the substance of all things, with reference to the Creation which did not yet exist, was alone; but inasmuch as he comprehended all power, and all things, visible and invisible, subsisted in him, all things were with him. For with him also by a Rational Power subsisted the Word, who was in him. By the unity of his will the Word went forth; and the Word going forth not ineffectually (but so as to produce an effect, viz. the creation of the Universe,) became the first-born work of the Father. Him (the Word) we know to be the beginning of the Universe.

He was begotten by division, not by abscission. For that which is cut off is separated from the original; but that which is divided, voluntarily taking its part in the Œconomy, does not impoverish him from whom it is taken. As many fires are lighted from one torch, yet the light of the first torch is not diminished by the lighting of many from it; so the Word (or Reason) proceeding from the power of the Father, did not render him who begat destitute of Word (or Reason). For I speak, and you hear; yet I who converse am not, by the transfer of the words, rendered destitute of the word; but sending forth my voice, I design to reduce into order the confused matter in you. And as the Word, being begotten in the beginning, begat in turn the Creation in which we are, having formed matter for his own use; so I also, being begotten again after the imitation of the Word, and having arrived at the comprehension of the truth, reduce into order the confusion of kindred matter." In this passage we find the notion respecting the subsistence of the Λόγος from eternity in a state of most intimate union with the Father, which [1] I have stated to be common among the Ante-Nicene Fathers, but not to be clearly expressed by Justin. When, too, Tatian says that the Λόγος was not only *in*, but *with* the Father, he appears to intend to express a distinct personality. [2] Waterland has observed, that he speaks only of a *temporal* generation. In order to explain the mode of it, he uses the same illustration of a fire, which Justin had used; he distinguishes, however, between the words μερίζειν and ἀποτέμνειν, which Justin has used indifferently. The inference apparently intended to be drawn from the comparison with a fire is, that the substance of the Father was not divided in consequence of the generation of the Λόγος. The intent of the subsequent illustration, taken from the human voice, is less clear, and the illustration itself open, perhaps, to some objection. It [3] is also used by Justin.

It will be observed, that Tatian calls the Λόγος

---

[1] p. 58.   [2] Vol. III. p. 270.   [3] Dial. p. 284 B.

the beginning of the Universe, τοῦτον ἴσμεν τοῦ κόσμου τὴν ἀρχήν. This title I conceive to have been derived from Prov. viii. 22. Κύριος ἔκτισέ με ἀρχὴν ὁδῶν αὐτοῦ εἰς τὰ ἔργα αὐτοῦ, which is [1] twice quoted by Justin in proof of the generation of the Word to create the world; though he does not apply the title ἀρχὴ to the Λόγος. Bull supposes Tatian to have meant by the word ἀρχὴ the Idea and Exemplar of the Universe, which was always present to the Deity; and [2] thus in one sense it might be said that the Universe was present to the Deity before the creation; in its ἀρχὴ, or principle, or idea, that is, in the Λόγος. If this was Tatian's meaning, we must allow that he has expressed it very imperfectly; yet I seem to discover more traces of the influence of Gentile philosophy on his language and opinions, than on those of his master Justin.

Let us proceed to Athenagoras. Defending the Christians against the charge of Atheism, he [3] says,

[1] Dial. p. 284 D 359 A
[2] Sed et hoc voluit significare Tatianus, Deo ante conditum mundum etiam ipsum quodammodo mundum præsentem fuisse; quum ipsi revera præsens fuerit ὁ Λόγος mundi principium, qui et idea est et exemplar, sive ars divina, quâ Pater universa, quum voluit, molitus est Def. Fid. Nic Sect. III. c. 6.
[3] τὸ μὲν οὖν ἄθεοι μὴ εἶναι, ἕνα τὸν ἀγέννητον καὶ ἀίδιον καὶ ἀόρατον καὶ ἀπαθῆ καὶ ἀκατάληπτον καὶ ἀχώρητον, νῷ μόνῳ καὶ λόγῳ καταλαμβανόμενον, φωτὶ καὶ κάλλει καὶ πνεύματι καὶ δυνάμει ἀνεκδιηγήτῳ περιεχόμενον, ὑφ' οὗ γεγένηται τὸ πᾶν διὰ τοῦ αὐτοῦ λόγου καὶ διακεκόσμηται καὶ συγκρατεῖται, Θεὸν

" I have sufficiently shewn that we are not Atheists; we who hold one God, Unbegotten, Eternal, Invisible, not subject to suffering, incomprehensible, not circumscribed by place, conceived only by the mind and reason, surrounded by ineffable light and beauty, and Spirit and Power, by whom, through his Word, every thing was made and adorned, and is preserved. We acknowledge also a Son of God; and let no one think it ridiculous that there should be a Son of God. For we deem not of God and the Father, or of the Son, as the Poets fable, who represent the Gods as no better than men. The Word of the Father, is the Son of God, in idea and operation.

άγοντες, ικανώς μοι δέδεικται. νοούμεν γαρ και υιόν του Θεού· και μή μοι γελοϊόν τις νομίση το υιόν είναι τω Θεώ. ου γαρ, ως ποιηταί μυθοποιούσιν, ουδέν βελτίους των ανθρώπων δεικνύντες τους θεούς, ή περί του Θεού και πατρός, ή περί του υιού πεφρονήκαμεν· αλλ' έστιν ο υιός του Θεού Λόγος του πατρός, εν ιδέα και ενεργεία. προς αυτού γαρ και δι' αυτού πάντα εγένετο, ενός όντος του πατρός και του υιού· όντος δε του υιού εν πατρί, και πατρός εν υιώ, ενότητι και δυνάμει πνεύματος· νους και Λόγος του πατρός, ο υιός του Θεού. ει δε δι' υπερβολήν συνέσεως σκοπείν υμίν έπεισιν ο παις τί βούλεται, ερώ δια βραχέων· πρώτον γέννημα είναι τω πατρί, ουχ ως γενόμενον (εξ αρχής γαρ ο Θεός, νους αΐδιος ων, είχεν αυτός εν εαυτώ τον λόγον, αϊδίως λογικός ων) αλλ' ως των υλικών ξυμπάντων, άποιου φύσεως και γης (f. οποίας φύσεως και γένους) οχείας υποκειμένων δίκην, μεμιγμένων των παχυμεστέρων προς τα κουφότερα επ' αυτοίς, ιδέα και ενέργεια είναι προελθών. συνάδει δε τω λόγω και το προφητικόν πνεύμα. Κύριος γαρ, φησίν, έκτισέ με, αρχήν οδών αυτού εις έργα αυτού. καί τοι και αυτό το ενεργούν τοις εκφωνούσι προφητικώς άγιον πνεύμα, απόρροιαν είναι φαμέν του Θεού, απορρέον και επαναφερόμενον, ως ακτίνα ηλίου. Leg. p. 10 A.

For by him and through him were all things made, the Father and the Son being one: the Son being in the Father, and the Father in the Son, by the unity and power of the Spirit. The Mind and Word of God is the Son of God."

"But if you (O Emperors) through the excellence of your understanding, are desirous to enquire what the Son means, I will briefly explain myself. He is the first-begotten to the Father, not as if made; (for from the beginning, God, being the eternal Mind, had within himself the Word, or Reason, being from eternity rational,) but as if proceeding forth to be the idea and operating cause of all material things, of whatever nature and kind, which are subjected as a vehicle to him, the denser parts being mixed with the lighter. The prophetic Spirit agrees with what I say; *The Lord,* he says, *formed me the beginning of his ways to his works.* Though we also say that the Holy Spirit, who works in those who speak prophetically, is an emanation from the Deity, flowing forth and reflected, as a ray of the sun."

In [1] another passage, Athenagoras says to the

---

[1] ἔχοιτε ἀφ' ἑαυτῶν καὶ τὴν ἐπουράνιον βασιλείαν ἐξετάζειν, ὡς γὰρ ὑμῖν, πατρὶ καὶ υἱῷ, πάντα κεχείρωται, ἄνωθεν τὴν βασιλείαν εἰληφόσι (βασιλέως γὰρ ψυχὴ ἐν χειρὶ Θεοῦ, φησὶ τὸ προφητικὸν πνεῦμα) οὕτως ἑνὶ τῷ Θεῷ καὶ τῷ παρ' αὐτοῦ

emperors whom he is addressing, " You may estimate the heavenly empire by your own; for as all things are subject to you, father and son, who have received the empire from above (for the prophetic Spirit says, that the soul of the king is in the hand of God, Prov. xxi. 1.) so all things are subject to one God and to his Word, who is conceived to be the Son, inseparable from him."

In the former of these passages we find the subsistence of the Λόγος from eternity in a state of intimate union with the Father expressly declared; and though Athenagoras does not use the term, yet, as [1] Bull has observed, he evidently had in his mind the notion, which was afterwards conveyed by the term περιχώρησις or Circumincession; a word designed to express the mutual penetration, if I may so express myself, of the three Persons of the Trinity—the entireness of their union. We find also the notion that the Λόγος was the idea or exemplar of all created things; and that he was begotten in order to be the agent in the work of creation. Still we find mention only of a temporal generation. The illustration contained in the second passage has been noticed by [2] Gibbon: he calls it profane and.

λόγῳ, υἱῷ νοουμένῳ ἀμερίστῳ, πάντα ὑποτέτακται. Legatio, p. 17 D. We find in p. 15 C. πάντα γὰρ ὁ Θεός ἐστιν αὐτὸς αὑτῷ, φῶς ἀπρόσιτον, κόσμος τέλειος, πνεῦμα, δύναμις, λόγος.

[1] Def. Fid. Nic. Sect. iv. c. 4.
[2] Chapter xxi. note 50.

absurd, and says with a sneer, that it has been alleged without censure by Bull. But the object of Athenagoras in employing it was, not to explain the mode of subsistence of the Father and Son, but to shew that the monarchy, as it was termed—the unity of the Divine Government—was not infringed by the distinction of Persons in the Godhead. Bull produces the passage in order to clear Athenagoras from the charge of Sabellianism; and undoubtedly a Sabellian would not have used the illustration. Such, however, are the difficulties inherent in the very nature of the subject, that it is scarcely possible for a writer so to guard his expressions as not to be open to cavil. How apt soever an illustration may be in one point of view, it may be most inapplicable in another, and lead to most inconvenient consequences.

Let us now consider the language of Theophilus. [1] Speaking of the Prophets, he says, "First they

---

[1] καὶ πρῶτον μὲν συμφώνως ἐδίδαξαν ἡμᾶς, ὅτι ἐξ οὐκ ὄντων τὰ πάντα ἐποίησεν. οὐ γάρ τι τῷ Θεῷ συνήκμασεν· ἀλλ' αὐτὸς ἑαυτοῦ τόπος ὤν, καὶ ἀνενδεὴς ὤν, καὶ ὑπερέχων πρὸ τῶν αἰώνων, ἠθέλησεν ἄνθρωπον ποιῆσαι ᾧ γνωσθῇ. τούτῳ οὖν προητοίμασε τὸν κόσμον. ὁ γὰρ γενητὸς καὶ προσδεής ἐστιν ὁ δὲ ἀγενητὸς οὐδενὸς προσδεῖται. ἔχων οὖν ὁ Θεὸς τὸν ἑαυτοῦ λόγον ἐνδιάθετον ἐν τοῖς ἰδίοις σπλάγχνοις ἐγέννησεν αὐτὸν, μετὰ τῆς ἑαυτοῦ σοφίας ἐξερευξάμενος πρὸ τῶν ὅλων. τοῦτον τὸν λόγον ἔσχεν ὑπουργὸν τῶν ὑπ' αὐτοῦ γεγενημένων, καὶ δι' αὐτοῦ τὰ πάντα πεποίηκεν· οὗτος λέγεται ἀρχὴ, ὅτι ἄρχει καὶ κυριεύει πάντων τῶν δι' αὐτοῦ δεδημιουργημένων. οὗτος οὖν ὢν πνεῦμα

taught us with one consent that God made all things out of nothing. For nothing was contemporaneous with God. But he being his own place, and wanting nothing, and existing before the ages, willed to make man by whom he might be known. For him, therefore, he prepared the world. For he that is created, stands in need (of another); but he that is increate, wants nothing. God, therefore, having his own Word internal within his own bowels, begat him, emitting him in conjunction with his wisdom before all things. He had this Word as his minister in the work of creation, and by him he made all things. He is called the beginning, because he is the commencement and ruler over all things created by him. He, therefore, being the Spirit of God, and the beginning, and the wisdom, and the power of the Most High, descended into the Prophets, and through them spake of the creation of the world and of all other things. For the prophets were not when the world was made; but the wisdom of God who was in him, and his Holy Word who was always present with him."

Θεοῦ, καὶ ἀρχὴ, καὶ σοφία, καὶ δύναμις ὑψίστου κατήρχετο εἰς τοὺς προφήτας, καὶ δι' αὐτῶν ἐλάλει τὰ περὶ τῆς ποιήσεως τοῦ κόσμου καὶ τῶν λοιπῶν ἁπάντων. οὐ γὰρ ἦσαν οἱ προφῆται ὅτε ὁ κόσμος ἐγένετο, ἀλλὰ ἡ σοφία ἡ ἐν αὐτῷ οὖσα ἡ τοῦ Θεοῦ, καὶ ὁ Λόγος ὁ ἅγιος αὐτοῦ ὁ ἀεὶ συμπαρὼν αὐτῷ. L. ii. p. 88 B. In p. 92 D. we find ἡ διάταξις οὖν τοῦ Θεοῦ τοῦτό ἐστιν, ὁ λόγος αὐτοῦ φαίνων ὥσπερ λύχνος κ.τ.ἑ. See p. 93 B.

In [1] another passage he says, "For the Sacred Scripture represents to us Adam saying, that he heard the voice (of God): but what else is the voice, than the Word of God, who is his Son? Not as the poets and writers of fables talk of the sons of gods, born from intercourse with women; but as the truth represents the Word, always internal in the heart of God. For before any thing was created, God had him as his Counsellor, being his mind and intelligence; but when God willed to create what he had designed, he begat this Word to go forth, to be the first-born of all creation; not being himself emptied of the Word, but having begotten and always conversing with the Word."

Here again we find the notion of the subsistence of the Word from eternity in a state of most intimate union with God, and of his subsequent generation to create the world. We have observed that Theophilus is the earliest Christian author in whose

---

[1] καὶ γὰρ αὐτὴ ἡ θεία γραφὴ διδάσκει ἡμᾶς τὸν 'Αδὰμ λέγοντα τῆς φωνῆς ἀκηκοέναι· φωνὴ δὲ τί ἄλλο ἐστὶν ἀλλ' ἢ ὁ Λόγος ὁ τοῦ Θεοῦ, ὅς ἐστι καὶ υἱὸς αὐτοῦ. οὐχ ὡς οἱ ποιηταὶ καὶ μυθογράφοι λέγουσιν υἱοὺς θεῶν ἐκ συνουσίας γεννωμένους· ἀλλὰ ὡς ἀλήθεια διηγεῖται, τὸν λογον, τὸν ὄντα διαπαντὸς ἐνδιάθετον ἐν καρδίᾳ Θεοῦ. πρὸ γάρ τι γίγνεσθαι, τοῦτον εἶχε σύμβουλον, ἑαυτοῦ νοῦν καὶ φρόνησιν ὄντα ὁπότε δὲ ἠθέλησεν ὁ Θεὸς ποιῆσαι ὅσα ἐβουλεύσατο, τοῦτον τὸν λόγον ἐγέννησε προφορικὸν, πρωτότοκον πάσης κτίσεως, οὐ κενωθεὶς αὐτὸς τοῦ λόγου, ἀλλὰ λόγον γεννήσας, καὶ τῷ λόγῳ αὐτοῦ διαπαντὸς ὁμιλῶν. L. ii. p. 100 A.

writings the word τριὰς occurs; he is the first also who distinguishes expressly between the Λόγος ἐνδιάθετος and προφορικὸς, the internal and emitted Word. Theophilus also, like Tatian, applies the title ἀρχὴ to the Λόγος with a [1] particular reference to Proverbs viii. and Genesis i.

Page 61, note 1. I have observed in this note that, because Justin speaks of the world as created out of matter without form, we must not, therefore, suppose him to have maintained the eternity of matter. The Benedictine editors are extremely anxious to clear him from the suspicion of having entertained such an opinion, and with this view refer to passages in the Hortatory Address to the Gentiles. But having already declared my doubts of the genuineness of that tract, I cannot rely upon the passages quoted from it. As, however, [2] Justin's

---

[1] p. 88 D. So in p. 92 B. ἐν ἀρχῇ ἐποίησεν ὁ Θεὸς τὸν οὐρανὸν, τουτέστι, διὰ τῆς ἀρχῆς γεγενῆσθαι τὸν οὐρανὸν, καθὼς ἔφθημεν δεδηλωκέναι. In a description of the Deity, p. 71 A. we find the following remarkable passage: εἰ γὰρ φῶς αὐτὸν εἴπω, ποίημα αὐτοῦ λέγω· εἰ λόγον εἴπω, ἀρχὴν αὐτοῦ λέγω· νοῦν ἐὰν εἴπω, φρόνησιν αὐτοῦ λέγω· πνεῦμα ἐὰν εἴπω, ἀναπνοὴν αὐτοῦ λέγω· σοφίαν ἐὰν εἴπω, γέννημα αὐτοῦ λέγω· ἰσχὺν ἐὰν εἴπω, κράτος αὐτοῦ λέγω· δύναμιν ἐὰν εἴπω, ἐνέργειαν αὐτοῦ λέγω· πρόνοιαν ἐὰν εἴπω, ἀγαθοσύνην αὐτοῦ λέγω· βασιλείαν ἐὰν εἴπω, δόξαν αὐτοῦ λέγω· κύριον ἐὰν εἴπω, ἑαυτὸν λέγω· πατέρα ἐὰν εἴπω, τὰ πάντα αὐτοῦ λέγω· πῦρ ἐὰν εἴπω, τὴν ὀργὴν αὐτοῦ λέγω. See also p. 73 D. L. 3. p. 122 D.

[2] Dial. p. 223 A. See Beausobre, Histoire du Manichéisme, L. 5. cc. 2. 4, 5.

instructor applauds him for saying, in opposition to the Platonists, that the world was not eternal, we may reasonably infer that he did not maintain the eternity of matter.

If we turn to Tatian, we shall find him expressly affirming that matter had a beginning. [1] οὔτε γὰρ ἄναρχος ἡ ὕλη καθάπερ ὁ Θεὸς, οὐδὲ διὰ τὸ ἄναρχον καὶ αὐτὴ ἰσοδύναμος τῷ Θεῷ· γεννητὴ δὲ, καὶ οὐχ ὑπό του ἄλλου γεγονυῖα, μόνου δὲ ὑπὸ τοῦ πάντων δημιουργοῦ προβεβλημένη.

Athenagoras, in like manner distinguishing between the Divine Nature and Matter, says, that the former is increate and eternal, the latter created and corruptible, [2] τὸ μὲν γὰρ θεῖον ἀγένητον εἶναι καὶ ἀΐδιον, νῷ μόνῳ καὶ λόγῳ θεωρούμενον· τὴν δὲ ὕλην γενητὴν καὶ φθαρτήν. In [3] another place he says, that God

[1] p. 145 C. He had just before said of the Λόγος, αὐτὸς ἑαυτῷ τὴν ὕλην δημιουργήσας. In another place he says, that all matter was sent forth or emitted by God; some of it to be considered as being without form before a separation had taken place; some as being adorned and reduced to order after the separation, p. 151 A. See Beausobre, L. 5. c. 5.

[2] Legatio, p. 5 B. So p. 23 A. λήσομεν ἑαυτοὺς ἰσότιμον τὴν ὕλην τὴν φθαρτὴν καὶ ῥευστὴν καὶ μεταβλητὴν τῷ ἀγεννήτῳ, καὶ ἀϊδίῳ, καὶ διαπαντὸς συμφώνῳ ποιοῦντες Θεῷ.

[3] εἰ δὲ διεστᾶσιν (ὕλη καὶ Θεὸς) πάμπολυ ἀπ' ἀλλήλων, καὶ τοσοῦτον ὅσον τεχνίτης καὶ ἡ πρὸς τὴν τέχνην αὐτοῦ παρασκευή —καὶ ἡ πανδεχὴς ὕλη ἄνευ τοῦ Θεοῦ τοῦ δημιουργοῦ διάκρισιν καὶ σχῆμα καὶ κόσμον οὐκ ἐλάμβανεν, p. 14 D. Beausobre justly remarks that this passage is not irreconcileable to a belief in the eternity of matter. L. 5. c. 5.

and matter differ as widely from each other, as the artisan and the materials upon which he employs his art.

Theophilus says expressly, that God produced all things from a state of non-existence into a state of existence, [1] τὰ πάντα ὁ Θεὸς ἐποίησεν ἐξ οὐκ ὄντων εἰς τὸ εἶναι. In another place he asks, "[2] What mighty power do we ascribe to God, if we say that he made the world out of subject matter? An artisan, if materials are given him, makes what he chooses. But the power of God is displayed in this—that he makes what he chooses out of nothing." He [3] afterwards says, that, according to the scriptural representation, God made the world out of matter which had been produced by him.

Page 61, note 2. The word οἰκονομία is used by Tatian, but not with any reference to the Gospel Dispensation. In a passage quoted in note 2, p. 159, he says, that whatever is only divided takes its part in the Œconomy, οἰκονομίας τὴν αἵρεσιν προσλαβόν. In

---

[1] L. i. p. 72 A. Compare p. 75 A. L. ii. p. 88 B. 92 B.

[2] τί δὲ μέγα εἰ ὁ Θεὸς ἐξ ὑποκειμενης ὕλης ἐποίει τὸν κόσμον; καὶ γὰρ τεχνίτης ἄνθρωπος, ἐπὰν ὕλην λάβῃ ἀπό τινος, ἐξ αὐτῆς ὅσα βούλεται ποιεῖ. Θεοῦ δὲ ἡ δύναμις ἐν τούτῳ φανεροῦται, ἵνα ἐξ οὐκ ὄντων ποιῇ ὅσα βούλεται, L. ii. p. 82 C.

[3] ταῦτα ἐν πρώτοις διδάσκει ἡ θεία γραφὴ τρόπῳ τινὶ ὕλην γενητὴν ὑπὸ τοῦ Θεοῦ γεγονυῖαν, ἀφ' ἧς πεποίηκε καὶ δεδημιούργηκεν ὁ Θεὸς τὸν κόσμον, p. 89 A.

[1] another place he speaks of those who trust to the Œconomy of matter, ὕλης οἰκονομίᾳ, meaning those who ascribe the cure of diseases to combinations of matter; and when [2] he is ridiculing the astrologers, he calls the constellations the dispensers of fate, τῆς εἱμαρμένης οἰκονόμους.

Athenagoras uses the word in a sense which bears a nearer resemblance to that in which I have supposed Justin to use it. Speaking of the assumption of the human form by the heathen deities, he says, [3] κἂν σάρκα θεὸς κατὰ θείαν οἰκονομίαν λάβῃ, ἤδη δοῦλός ἐστιν ἐπιθυμίας.

Theophilus, speaking of earthly monarchs, [4] says, that "they are not made to be worshipped, but to receive appropriate honour; for they are not gods, but men appointed by God; not to be worshipped, but to give righteous judgments,—for they are in

[1] p. 157 B. In p. 151 B. Tatian speaks of the human body as being μιᾶς οἰκονομίας, and shortly after we find ἐντοσθίων οἰκονομία, and κατ' οἰκονομίαν συμφωνίας. Speaking of those writers who turned the heathen mythology and the Iliad into allegory, he says that they introduced the Greeks and Barbarians as contending χάριν οἰκονομίας, p. 160 B.
[2] p. 149 B. 150 A.
[3] Legatio, p. 21 D.
[4] ὅτι οὐκ εἰς τὸ προσκυνεῖσθαι γέγονεν, ἀλλὰ εἰς τὸ τιμᾶσθαι τῇ νομίμῳ τιμῇ. Θεὸς γὰρ οὐκ ἔστιν, ἀλλὰ ἄνθρωπος ὑπὸ Θεοῦ τεταγμένος, οὐκ εἰς τὸ προσκυνεῖσθαι, ἀλλὰ εἰς τὸ δικαίως κρίνειν· τρόπῳ γάρ τινι παρὰ Θεοῦ οἰκονομίαν πεπίστευται, L. i. p. 76 D.

a manner entrusted with an administration by God." He says, [1] on another occasion, that no person is able worthily to explain the whole œconomy of the six days of creation. He says [2] also, that the disposition of the stars in the work of creation contains the œconomy and order of just and pious men, who observe the commandments of God; and in alluding to the narrative in Scripture, respecting Cain and Abel, he talks of the œconomy of the narrative [3] τὴν οἰκονομίαν τῆς ἐξηγήσεως.

Page 63. Tatian gives the title of God to Christ, and calls him, [4] in one instance, the God who suffered; in [5] another, God who appeared in the form of man.

[6] Athenagoras also gives the title of God to the Son; and Theophilus, referring to John i. 1. [7] says expressly that the Word is God.

---

[1] L. ii. p. 91 B.   [2] p. 94 D.   [3] p 105 B.

[4] He is speaking of the Holy Spirit, whom he calls τὸν διάκονον τοῦ πεπονθότος Θεοῦ, p. 153 A.

[5] Θεὸν ἐν ἀνθρώπου μορφῇ γεγονέναι καταγγέλλοντες, p. 159 C. In another passage he calls upon the heathen to renounce the Dæmons, and to follow the only God, to whom he applies what St. John (i. 3) says of the Λόγος. All things were made by him, and without him was not any thing made, ἀλλὰ παραιτησάμενοι τοὺς δαίμονας Θεῷ τῷ μόνῳ κατακολουθήσατε· πάντα ὑπ' αὐτοῦ, καὶ χωρὶς αὐτοῦ γέγονεν οὐδὲ ἕν, p. 158 D.

[6] See the first passage quoted in page 155.

[7] Θεὸς οὖν ὢν ὁ Λόγος καὶ ἐκ Θεοῦ πεφυκώς, L. ii. p. 100 C.

Page 68. Bull, [1] speaking of the περιχώρησις, or Circumincession of the three Persons in the Trinity, says, " that some of the ancients also ascribe a περιχώρησις to the two natures in Christ; but that in so doing, they do not speak accurately. For since περιχώρησις, in its strict sense, is the union of things entering in all respects into each other (which is signified by the preposition περὶ), in order to justify the use of the term, no one of the things so united should be without or beyond the other; but wheresoever one of them is, there the other should also be. But in Christ, though the Divine Nature enters in every respect into the human, the human does not in turn enter into the Divine; for the human is finite and limited,—the Divine infinite and unlimited; so that the human cannot be wheresoever the Divine is." There is, in other words, a perfect περιχώρησις of persons in the Divine Nature, but not a perfect περιχώρησις of natures in the person of Christ. Still, according to Bull's view, Justin is correct in saying, that the Divine Nature pervaded, or perfectly entered into the human.

Justin puts into the mouth of the old man who converted him to Christianity, the following question: " What then is our relationship to God? Is

[1] Def. Fid. Nic. Sect. iv. c. 4.

the soul divine, and immortal, and a part of that Royal Intelligence? αὐτοῦ ἐκείνου τοῦ βασιλικοῦ νοῦ μέρος." Dial. p. 221 E. So Tatian, p. 146 C. says, that man obtains immortality by partaking of a portion of God. Θεοῦ μοίραν. See Beausobre, Lib. 6. c. 5.

That partial insight into the truth, which the Gentile Poets and Philosophers possessed, and which, according to Justin, they obtained through their participation in the Λόγος, is traced by Athenagoras to what he terms their " sympathy with the breath of God." ποιηταὶ μὲν γὰρ καὶ φιλόσοφοι, ὡς καὶ τοῖς ἄλλοις ἐπέβαλον στοχαστικῶς, κινηθέντες μὲν, κατὰ συμπάθειαν τῆς παρὰ τοῦ Θεοῦ πνοῆς, ὑπὸ τῆς (αὐτὸς) αὐτοῦ ψυχῆς ἕκαστος ζητῆσαι, εἰ δυνατὸς εὑρεῖν καὶ νοῆσαι τὴν ἀλήθειαν· τοσοῦτον δὲ δυνηθέντες ὅσον περινοῆσαι, οὐχ εὕρηνται ὂν (f. Θεὸν) οὐ παρὰ Θεοῦ ἀξιώσαντες μαθεῖν, ἀλλὰ παρ' αὐτοῦ ἕκαστος, Legatio, p. 7 D.

P. 69. We have [1] seen that Athenagoras calls the Holy Spirit an emanation from God, flowing forth and reflected like a ray of the sun. In [2] another place he says, that the Holy Spirit is an emanation, as light from a fire. [3] Justin, on

---

[1] Leg. p. 10 D. quoted in note 1, p. 164.
[2] καὶ ἀπόρροια, ὡς φῶς ἀπὸ πυρός, τὸ πνεῦμα, Leg. p. 27 A.
[3] See p. 66.

the contrary, in speaking of the generation of the Son, expressly censures those who compared it to the emission of a ray from the sun; and uses the illustration of a fire lighted from another fire. We have here another instance of the difficulty of bringing forward, on this mysterious subject, any illustration, to which an objection may not be made. Justin's illustration better conveys the notion of a distinction of persons; that of Athenagoras, the notion of an unity of substance. But they who are disposed to raise cavils will say, that the former tends to Tritheism; the latter to Sabellianism.

I [1] have observed that Theophilus speaks explicitly of a Trinity; and, as it should seem, of a real Trinity—a Trinity of Persons. Yet we [2] find him speaking of the Spirit of God, as surrounded or confined by the hand of God; and [3] saying, that the Spirit of God, which moved on the face

---

[1] See p. 157.

[2] οὕτως ἡ πᾶσα κτίσις περιέχεται ὑπὸ πνεύματος Θεοῦ, καὶ τὸ πνεῦμα τὸ περιέχον σὺν τῇ κτίσει περιέχεται ὑπὸ χειρὸς Θεοῦ. L. i. p. 72 C.

[3] πνεῦμα δὲ τὸ ἐπιφερόμενον ἐπάνω τοῦ ὕδατος, ὃ ἔδωκεν ὁ Θεὸς εἰς ζωογόνησιν τῇ κτίσει, καθάπερ ἀνθρώπῳ ψυχήν, L. ii. p. 92 C. Compare p. 74 A. ὁ θεμελιώσας τὴν γῆν ἐπὶ τῶν ὑδάτων, καὶ δοὺς πνεῦμα τὸ τρέφον αὐτήν· οὗ ἡ πνοὴ ζωογονεῖ τὸ πᾶν. In p. 110 B. Theophilus calls God τροφέα πάσης πνοῆς. πνεῦμα Θεοῦ in p. 78 D. corresponds to τὸ πνεῦμα τὸ ἅγιον in p. 106 C.

of the waters in the work of creation, was given by God in order to vivify it, as the soul is given to man. Justin, as [1] we have seen, supposed the Spirit of God, in the first chapter of Genesis, to be the Holy Spirit,—an application of the passage, to which Theophilus appears to have been a stranger.

Page 72. The opinion of Athenagoras respecting the inspiration of the Prophets, was, that [2] the Spirit from God moved their mouths, like instruments; or, [3] as he expresses himself in another

[1] See p. 55.

[2] ἔχομεν Προφήτας μάρτυρας, οἳ πνεύματι ἐνθέῳ ἐκπεφωνήκασι καὶ περὶ τοῦ Θεοῦ καὶ περὶ τῶν τοῦ Θεοῦ. εἴποιτε δ᾽ ἂν καὶ ὑμεῖς, συνέσει καὶ τῇ περὶ τὸ ὄντως θεῖον εὐσεβείᾳ τοὺς ἄλλους προὔχοντες, ὡς ἔστιν ἄλογον, παραλιπόντας πιστεύειν τῷ παρὰ τοῦ Θεοῦ πνεύματι, ὡς ὄργανα κεκινηκότι τὰ τῶν Προφητῶν στόματα, προσέχειν δόξαις ἀνθρωπίναις, Legatio, p. 8 A. Tatian's description of the prophetic writings, p. 165 B. deserves attention.

[3] καὶ τῶν λοιπῶν προφητῶν, οἳ κατ᾽ ἔκστασιν τῶν ἐν αὐτοῖς λογισμῶν, κινήσαντος αὐτοὺς τοῦ θείου πνεύματος, ἃ ἐνηργοῦντο ἐξεφώνησαν· συγχρησαμένου τοῦ πνεύματος, ὡσεὶ καὶ αὐλητὴς αὐλὸν, ἐμπνεῦσαι, p. 9 D. Here Athenagoras says, that the Prophets spoke κατ᾽ ἔκστασιν, in a state of rapture or ecstasy. On this point he agreed with Montanus, though I see no reason for suspecting, with Tillemont, that he ever attached himself to the Montanists. See the Preface of the Benedictine Editors, Part III. c. 14. Justin, speaking of the Prophet Zechariah, says, τοῦτον δὲ αὐτὸν οὐκ ἐν τῇ ἀποκαλύψει αὐτοῦ ἑωράκει ὁ προφήτης, ὥσπερ οὐδὲ τὸν διάβολον καὶ τὸν τοῦ Κυρίου ἄγγελον οὐκ αὐτοψίᾳ, ἐν καταστάσει ὢν, ἑωράκει, ἀλλ᾽ ἐν ἐκστάσει ἀποκαλύψεως αὐτῷ γεγενημένης, Dial. p. 343 A. quoted in p. 73, note 1. The difference between the two representations seems to be, that, ac-

place, that the Spirit made use of the Prophet, as a player on the pipe does of the pipe.

The language of Theophilus on this subject differs not widely from that of Athenagoras. He speaks of the Prophets as [1] inspired by the Holy Spirit, or by God himself; so [2] that, being holy and just, they were deemed worthy to be made the instruments of God, and to partake of his wisdom.

The account of the Prophets given by Justin, or, rather, by the Old Man who converted him to Christianity, is, that "[3] long before all those

cording to Justin, the Prophet was in a state of rapture when he saw the vision which he recorded: according to Athenagoras, when he delivered or wrote the prophecy.

[1] L. i. p. 78 D. L. ii. p. 106. C. 110 A. 111 C. 128 B. See also p. 88 C. quoted in p. 168, note 1, and 88 D. Μωσῆς δὲ—μᾶλλον δὲ ὁ λόγος ὁ τοῦ Θεοῦ, ὡς δι' ὀργάνου, δι' αὐτοῦ φησίν. In these passages the inspiration of the prophets is attributed to the λόγος πάντες οἱ πνευματοφόροι. p. 100 C L. iii. p. 125 A.

[2] οἱ δὲ τοῦ Θεοῦ ἄνθρωποι, πνευματοφόροι πνεύματος ἁγίου καὶ προφῆται γενόμενοι, ὑπ' αὐτοῦ τοῦ Θεοῦ ἐμπνευσθέντες καὶ σοφισθέντες, ἐγένοντο θεοδίδακτοι καὶ ὅσιοι καὶ δίκαιοι. διὸ καὶ κατηξιώθησαν τὴν ἀντιμισθίαν ταύτην λαβεῖν, ὄργανα Θεοῦ γενόμενοι, καὶ χωρήσαντες σοφίαν τὴν παρ' αὐτοῦ, δι' ἧς σοφίας εἶπον καὶ τὰ περὶ τῆς κτίσεως τοῦ κόσμου καὶ τῶν λοιπῶν ἁπάντων, L. ii. p. 87 D.

[3] ἐγένοντό τινες πρὸ πολλοῦ χρόνου πάντων τούτων τῶν νομιζομένων φιλοσόφων παλαιότεροι, μακάριοι, καὶ δίκαιοι, καὶ θεοφιλεῖς, θείῳ πνεύματι λαλήσαντες, καὶ τὰ μέλλοντα θεσπίσαντες, ἃ δὴ νῦν γίγνεται· προφήτας δὲ αὐτοὺς καλοῦσιν· οὗτοι μόνοι τὸ ἀληθὲς καὶ εἶδον καὶ ἐξεῖπον ἀνθρώποις, μήτ' εὐλαβηθέντες

who are deemed philosophers, lived blessed and just men, lovers of God, who spake by the Holy Spirit, and foretold future things, which are now happening. They are called Prophets. They alone saw the truth, and told it to men; neither respecting nor fearing any one, nor influenced by the love of glory; but speaking those things only which they heard and saw, being filled with the Holy Spirit."

The author of the Hortatory Address to the Greeks [1] says, that " it was only necessary for the Prophets to surrender themselves entirely to the operation of the Divine Spirit; that the Divine quill descending from heaven, and using the instrumentality of just men, as of a harp or lyre, should reveal to us the knowledge of Divine and Heavenly things."

Page 74. Tatian gives the following account of the Creation and fall of Angels and men. "The [2] heavenly Λόγος, being a Spirit from the Father,

μήτε δυσωπηθέντες τινά, μὴ ἡττημένοι δόξης, ἀλλὰ μόνα ταῦτα εἰπόντες ἃ ἤκουσαν καὶ ἃ εἶδον, ἁγίῳ πληρωθέντες πνεύματι. Dial. p. 224 D.

[1] ἀλλὰ καθαροὺς ἑαυτοὺς τῇ τοῦ θείου πνεύματος παρασχεῖν ἐνεργείᾳ, ἵν' αὐτὸ τὸ θεῖον ἐξ οὐρανοῦ κατιὸν πλῆκτρον, ὥσπερ ὀργάνῳ κιθάρας τινὸς ἢ λύρας, τοῖς δικαίοις ἀνδράσι χρώμενος, τὴν τῶν θείων ἡμῖν καὶ οὐρανίων ἀποκαλύψῃ γνῶσιν, p. 9 B.

[2] p 146 B.

and the Λόγος from the Rational Power, in imitation of the Father who begat him, made man the image of immortality; that, as incorruption is with God, so man, partaking of a portion of God, might also have immortality. The Λόγος, before the creation of man, was the Creator of Angels. Each species was created free, not being good in its own nature, which is the property of God alone; but capable, in the case of man, of perfection through freedom of choice,—so that the wicked might be justly punished, being wicked through their own fault; and the good might be justly praised on account of their good deeds,—not having, in the exercise of their freedom, transgressed the will of God. Such was the case with respect to Angels and men."

" But the power of the Word, possessing within himself a prescience of futurity, not by any fatal necessity, but by (foreseeing) the determination of those who were free to choose predicted future events; restraining men from wickedness by prohibitions, and praising those who persevered in goodness. And when men followed one, who, on account of the priority of his birth, was more subtle than the rest, and set him up as God, though he opposed himself to the law of God, the power of the Word excluded both the author of this madness, and all his followers, from intercourse with himself.

And he who was made in the image of God, the more powerful Spirit being withdrawn from him, became mortal; and the first-born Angel, through his transgression and ignorance, was manifested as a Dæmon; and they who imitated his phantasms, became a host of Dæmons, and through (the abuse of) their freedom were delivered over to their own folly." He then proceeds to say, that the Dæmons introduced the doctrine of fate, and connected it with astrology.

In order that we may understand what Tatian means by the withdrawing of the more powerful Spirit, we must turn to [1] another passage, in which he says, " We recognise two different Spirits: one, which is called the soul; the other, greater than the soul, the image and likeness of God. Both those Spirits were united in the first men ($ἀνθρώποις$ $τοῖς$ $πρώτοις$), so that in one respect they were material; in another, superior to matter." He then goes on to say, that the universe is material; and though its parts differ, according to their different

---

[1] p. 150 D. Tatian, on one occasion, says, that " God is a Spirit; not the Spirit pervading matter, but the preparer of the Spirits in matter and of its forms," p. 144 C.: in another, that " the Spirit pervading matter is inferior to the Diviner Spirit," p. 144 D. Compare what is said in my work on Clement of Alexandria, respecting the principal and subject Spirit, p. 235. To those who are devoid of the Spirit, Tatian gives the title of $ψυχικοί$, p 154 C. See p. 155 B.

degrees of beauty, yet the whole is pervaded by a material Spirit. [1] There is a Spirit in the stars, in Angels, in plants and water, in men, in animals, which, though one and the same, is thus variously modified. As, then, the soul partakes of this material Spirit, it is not immortal in its own nature, but mortal. It may, however, not die. It dies, and is dissolved with the body, when it knows not the truth—again, it does not die, although it is dissolved for a time, when it has acquired the knowledge of God. "The soul, therefore," Tatian [2] proceeds, " did

[1] p. 152 A. The soul is called πολυμερής, p. 153 B.
[2] p. 152 C. καθ' εαυτὴν γὰρ σκότος ἐστὶν (ἡ ψυχὴ) καὶ οὐδὲν ἐν αὐτῇ φωτεινόν. καὶ τοῦτό ἐστιν ἄρα τὸ εἰρημένον, ἡ σκοτία τὸ φῶς οὐ καταλαμβάνει. ψυχὴ γὰρ οὐκ αὐτὴ τὸ πνεῦμα ἔσωσεν, ἐσώθη δὲ ὑπ' αὐτοῦ, καὶ τὸ φῶς τὴν σκοτίαν κατέλαβεν. ὁ λόγος μέν ἐστι τὸ τοῦ Θεοῦ φῶς, σκότος δὲ ἡ ἀνεπιστήμων ψυχή. διὰ τοῦτο μόνη μὲν διαιτωμένη πρὸς τὴν ὕλην νεύει κάτω, συναποθνήσκουσα τῇ σαρκί. συζυγίαν δὲ κεκτημένη τὴν τοῦ θείου πνεύματος οὐκ ἔστιν ἀβοήθητος· ἀνέρχεται δὲ πρὸς ἅπερ αὐτὴν ὁδηγεῖ χωρία τὸ πνεῦμα. τοῦ μὲν γάρ ἐστιν ἄνω τὸ οἰκητήριον. τῆς δὲ κάτωθέν ἐστιν ἡ γένεσις· (See p. 151 A. ὡς εἶναι κοινὴν πάντων γένεσιν.) γέγονε μὲν οὖν συνδίαιτον ἀρχῆθεν τὸ πνεῦμα τῇ ψυχῇ· τὸ δὲ πνεῦμα ταύτην ἕπεσθαι μὴ βουλομένην αὐτῷ καταλέλοιπεν, ἡ δὲ ὥσπερ ἔναυσμα τῆς δυνάμεως αὐτοῦ κεκτημένη καὶ διὰ τὸν χωρισμὸν τὰ τέλεια καθορᾶν μὴ δυναμένη, ζητοῦσα τὸν Θεόν, κατὰ πλάνην πολλοὺς θεοὺς ἀνετύπωσε, τοῖς ἀντισοφιστεύουσι δαίμοσι κατακολουθήσασα. πνεῦμα δὲ τοῦ Θεοῦ παρὰ πᾶσιν μὲν οὐκ ἔστι· παρὰ δέ τισι τοῖς δικαίως πολιτευομένοις καταγόμενον, καὶ συμπλεκόμενον τῇ ψυχῇ, διὰ προαγορεύσεων ταῖς λοιπαῖς ψυχαῖς τὸ κεκρυμμένον ἀνήγγειλε. καὶ αἱ μὲν πειθόμεναι σοφίᾳ σφίσιν αὐταῖς ἐφείλκοντο πνεῦμα συγγενές. αἱ δὲ μὴ πειθόμεναι καὶ τὸν διάκονον τοῦ πεπονθότος Θεοῦ παραιτούμεναι θεόμαχοι μᾶλλον, ἤπερ θεοσεβεῖς, ἀνεφαίνοντο.

Beausobre has given the following translation of this passage,

not save the Spirit, but was saved by it; and the light comprehended the darkness. The Word is the light of God; and the ignorant soul, darkness. On which account, when it is alone, it bends downwards towards matter, dying together with the flesh. Histoire du Manichéisme, L. 4. c. 3. " L'ame de sa nature," dit Tatien, " n'est que tenèbres, et n'a rien de la lumière. De là ce mot de l'Ecriture, *Les tenèbres n'embrassent point la lumière*, car l'Esprit n'est pas sauvé par l'ame, mais c'est lui qui sauve l'ame, et c'est *la lumière qui embrasse les tenèbres*. La Raison est la lumière de Dieu : les tenèbres sont une ame qui est dans l'ignorance. C'est pourquoi quand elle est seule, elle s'abaisse aux choses matérielles, et meurt avec la chair. Mais quand elle est unie avec l'Esprit elle monte au lieu où elle est conduite par l'Esprit. En effet, le siège de l'Esprit est le Ciel, mais le siège de l'ame est la nature matérielle (in the original τῆς δὲ κάτωθέν ἐστιν ἡ γένεσις. Beausobre defends his translation by a reference to James iii 6. καὶ φλογίζουσα τὸν τρόχον τῆς γενέσεως. But γένεσις seems rather to mean in this place nature, as rendered in our Version. See Grotius in loco, and τὴν παλαιὰν γένεσιν, p. 150 D) Au commencement, l'Esprit étoit familièrement uni avec l'ame, et vivoit, pour ainsi dire, avec elle : mais n'ayant pas voulu suivre les lumières de l'Esprit, il la laissa. Cependant, elle conserva encore comme une étincelle de feu caché sous la cendre; mais à cause de la séparation de l'Esprit, elle n'a pas la force d'appercevoir les choses parfaites. En cherchant Dieu, elle s'est égarée, et en a imaginé plusieurs, séduite par la fraude des Démons." Beausobre's comment on the passage is, " L'ame est donc l'ouvrage du Créateur : l'Esprit est un don de Dieu Voilà les différens genres, ou les différentes natures de Basilide. Le Créateur ne connoissoit que la première, et ne commença à savoir, qu'il y en a une plus excellente et plus parfaite, que lorsque l'Esprit descendit sur Jésus." In my work on Clement of Alexandria, p. 272, note 1, I have said, with reference to this comment, that Beausobre appears to put interpretations on some of the expressions which the words will not bear. On further consideration, I do not change my opinion.

But having obtained an union with the Divine Spirit, it is no longer destitute of aid, but ascends to the places to which the Spirit conducts it. For the dwelling-place of the Spirit is above; the origin of the soul from below. In the beginning, then, the Spirit dwelt with the soul, but quitted it, because it refused to follow the Spirit. But the soul, retaining some spark as it were of the power of the Spirit, being unable, through its separation from the Spirit, to see that which is perfect, erring in its search after God, figured to itself many gods, following the fraudulent devices of the Dæmons. But the Spirit of God is not with all; sojourning only with some who lived righteous lives, and united with their souls, it declared, by means of predictions, secret things to other souls; some of them obeying wisdom, drew down to themselves a kindred Spirit[1]: while those which did not obey, but rejected the minister of God who suffered, proved rather adversaries, than worshippers, of God."

"It is, then," he [2] afterwards says, " our business to recover that which we have lost, and to unite the soul to the Holy Spirit, and earnestly to aim at an union with God." After some other further remarks

[1] As Tatian here speaks of a kindred spirit, so p. 145 D. he talks of a kindred matter.
[2] p. 153 D.

on the soul of man, Tatian proceeds: "[1] Man alone is the image and likeness of God; that man, I mean, who does not live like animals, but, raised far above humanity, draws near to God himself. The point to which I must now address myself is, to explain of what kind the image and likeness of God is. That which admits not of comparison is nothing but the Self-existent itself: that which is compared to the Self-existent is different from it, but like to it. The perfect God is without flesh, but man is flesh. The soul is the bond of the flesh, and the flesh holds together the soul. Such is the form of the constitution (of man) if God chooses to dwell in it by his [2] Ambassador, the Spiri , that it may be his temple. But if it is not so, man excels the beasts only in uttering articulate sounds: in all other respects he is of the same conversation as they; being no longer the likeness of God."

In [3] another place Tatian says, that "the perfect Spirit is, so to speak, the wings of the soul, which the soul casting off through sin, fluttered like a newly-fledged bird, and fell to the ground. Passing from its heavenly society, it longed for an intercourse with inferior things. The Dæmons quitted

---

[1] We have seen that in the passage quoted in page 183, Tatian calls the more powerful Spirit, the image and likeness of God.

[2] διὰ τοῦ πρεσβεύοντος πνεύματος, p. 154 B.

[3] p. 158 D.

their original abode : the first-created human beings were driven out. The former were expelled from heaven; the latter from earth, not this earth, but one better than this. It is our duty, then, henceforward to aspire to our ancient state, and to cast down every obstacle which impedes our progress." And [1] again : " We have learned that, of which we were ignorant, through the Prophets ; who, being persuaded that the Spirit together with the soul will receive immortality—the heavenly covering of mortality—foretold things which other souls knew not; and it is possible for every one that is naked to obtain this covering, and to return to his ancient kindred.

Tatian is particularly careful to guard against the notion that man fell by any fatal necessity. " We were not created," he [2] says, " to die ; but

---

[1] p. 159 B. The meaning of this passage is not very clear, οἵτινες ἅμα τῇ ψυχῇ πεπεισμένοι ὅτι πνεῦμα τὸ οὐράνιον ἐπένδυμα τῆς θνητότητος, τὴν ἀθανασίαν, κεκτήσεται. The Benedictine Editors wish to substitute σῶμα for πνεῦμα. Tatian says in another place, " Men, after the loss of immortality, have vanquished death by dying (to the world) through faith ; and a calling has been given to them through repentance, according to the words of Scripture, ' They were made a little lower than the angels,' (Psalm viii. 5.) It is possible for the vanquished to vanquish in turn, by renouncing the condition of death; and what that is, they who wish for immortality may easily see," p. 154 D. See also p. 155 C. θώρακι πνεύματος ἐπουρανίου καθωπλισμένος.

[2] p. 150 D.

we die through our own fault. Our freedom has destroyed us. When we were free, we became slaves: we were sold through sin. Nothing evil was made by God: we brought forth wickedness; and they who brought it forth are able in turn to renounce it." In [1] another passage he says, that "the sin of man was the cause of evil in the natural world."

The inference from these different passages seems to be that, according to Tatian, in man were originally united a spirit and a soul; the former of purely celestial origin, the latter material; or, to speak perhaps more accurately, a [2] portion of that inferior spirit which pervades matter. Man being, with reference to this material soul, peccable, abused the freedom with which he was endowed; and listening to the suggestions of wicked Dæmons, refused to follow the guidance of the heavenly Spirit, which in consequence quitted him. Thus deserted by the Divine Spirit, he became mortal: and by his sin all evil, moral and natural, was introduced into the world. As, however, he fell by the abuse of his freedom, so by the right use of it he may rise again, and reunite himself to the Heavenly

[1] p. 158 D.
[2] See the passage p. 144 D quoted in p. 183, note 1. Tatian speaks of the evaporation of this material Spirit, when the flesh is annihilated by fire, p. 146 A. κἂν πῦρ ἐξαφανίσῃ τὸ σάρκιον, ἐξατμισθεῖσαν τὴν ὕλην ὁ κόσμος κεχώρηκεν.

Spirit; and thus replace himself in his original state of innocence and happiness. It must be confessed that this account of the original state, and of the fall of man, savours more of the spirit of Gentile philosophy than of Scripture: yet in one respect it differs not greatly from that scheme, which assigns as the cause of the fall—that God withdrew the special influences of his presence from our first parents.

I find in Athenagoras little that has any direct bearing on these subjects. [1] On one occasion he is censuring those who thought that they sufficiently established the truth of a future resurrection, by saying, that it was necessary to the final judgement of mankind. "This argument," he says, "is clearly shewn to be inconclusive by the fact, that, although all rise again, all do not rise to judgement. For if to answer the ends of justice is the sole cause of the resurrection; then they, who have neither done good nor evil, that is, very young children, need not rise." Here the future condemnation of man is made to depend entirely on the commission of actual sin. In [2] another place he says, that "man, according to the design of his Maker, pursues a regular course with reference to his nature by

---

[1] De Mort. Res. p. 55 D. Athenagoras says that the soul is immortal, Leg. p. 30 D.
[2] Legatio, p. 29 A.

birth, which is common to all; and the disposition of his members, which does not transgress its peculiar law; and the end of life, which is the same to all; but, according to the determinations of his own reason, and the operation of the Ruler who has obtained dominion over him, and of the attendant Dæmons, he is carried in different directions; although the power of reasoning is common to all." The [1] Ruler to whom Athenagoras here alludes is a Power, or Spirit, who is conversant with and pervades matter; and being opposed to God, induced man to abuse the freedom with which he was endowed, and led him into transgression. On the subject of the Divine Providence, Athenagoras says, [2] that " they who admit God to be the Creator of the Universe must, if they mean to abide by their own principles, refer the custody and Providence over all things to his wisdom and justice. Under this persuasion they must think that every

---

[1] p. 27 A. D Athenagoras speaks of a material Spirit, Legatio, p. 30 C. 27 B

[2] ὅτι δεῖ τοὺς ποιητὴν τὸν θεὸν τοῦδε τοῦ παντὸς παραδεξαμένους τῇ τούτου σοφίᾳ καὶ δικαιοσύνῃ τὴν τῶν γενομένων ἁπάντων ἀνατιθέναι φυλακήν τε καὶ πρόνοιαν, εἴγε ταῖς ἰδίαις ἀρχαῖς παραμένειν ἐθέλοιεν· ταῦτα δὲ περὶ τούτων φρονοῦντας μηδὲν ἡγεῖσθαι μήτε τῶν κατὰ γῆν μήτε τῶν κατ' οὐρανὸν ἀνεπιτρόπευτον μηδ' ἀπρονόητον, ἀλλ' ἐπὶ πᾶν ἀφανὲς ὁμοίως καὶ φαινόμενον, μικρόν τε καὶ μεῖζον, διήκουσαν γιγνώσκειν τὴν παρὰ τοῦ ποιήσαντος ἐπιμέλειαν. δεῖται γὰρ πάντα τὰ γενόμενα τῆς παρὰ τοῦ ποιήσαντος ἐπιμελείας· ἰδίως δὲ ἕκαστον καθ' ὃ πέφυκε καὶ πρὸς ὃ πέφυκεν. De Mort. Res. p. 60 B.

thing, both in earth and heaven, is directed and governed by Providence; and that the care of the Creator extends to all things alike, whether unseen or seen, whether small or great. For all created things *in general* stand in need of the care of the Creator: and each *in particular* according to its nature and the end for which it was created." He asserts the same doctrine in [1] another place; although, like Justin, he ascribes to God a general superintendance over the Universe; and says, that the Angels were appointed to watch over the different parts.

Theophilus, [2] speaking of wild beasts and noxious animals, affirms that "nothing evil proceeded from God: all things were originally good, very good. But man by his transgression affected other living things with evil; for when he transgressed, they transgressed with him.—When, however, man shall return to his original state, and cease to do evil, they also shall return to their original gentleness." A considerable portion of the second book consists of a comment on the account of the Creation, given in the book of Genesis. [3] Speaking of the creation of man, Theophilus alleges, as a proof of his superior dignity, that, whereas God created all

[1] Legatio, p. 29 A. 27 C.
[2] Lib. ii. p. 96 B.
[3] p. 96 C. There is a description of Paradise, p 97 D. See also p. 101 B.

other things by a word, he considered the creation of man a work worthy of his own hands; and as if he even stood in need of assistance, said to his Word and Wisdom, " Let *us* make man," &c. [1] Man after his creation was placed in Paradise, the means of improvement being afforded him, so that he might go on to perfection; and being at length [2] declared a god, might ascend into heaven. For he was created in a sort of intermediate state; neither wholly mortal, nor wholly immortal, but capable of both conditions. [3] Adam was forbidden to eat of the fruit of the tree of knowledge, because, being yet in a state of infancy, he could not worthily receive knowledge. Some appear to have thought that the fruit of the tree of knowledge

[1] p. 101 D. Theophilus says that Adam was not forbidden to eat of the fruit of the tree of life. He repeats his notion respecting this intermediate state of man in p. 103 C. "If God had created man immortal, he would have made him a god, if mortal, God would have appeared to be the author of his death. Man was, therefore, made capable of both conditions: that, keeping the commandment of God, he might receive immortality as a reward, and become a god; or, disobeying God, might be the author to himself of death." Theophilus says that the majority deemed the soul immortal, because God breathed the breath of life into Adam's nostrils, p. 97 C.

[2] ἔτι δὲ καὶ θεὸς ἀναδειχθείς. Justin uses the expression, τελείῳ γενομένῳ, Dial. p. 225 D Man is called πλάσμα καὶ εἰκὼν Θεοῦ, L. i. p. 72 A.

[3] p. 102 A. The Benedictine Editors employ a chapter of their Preface in proving that Theophilus, when he calls Adam an infant, speaks metaphorically.

was evil in itself; and, therefore, productive of death. This Theophilus denies, and says, that knowledge is in itself good. "It was not, therefore, the fruit of the tree which brought pain, and sorrow, and death into the world; but Adam's disobedience. God, however, when he cast our first parents out of Paradise, determined in his mercy that they should not continue for ever in sin; but having been punished by banishment, and disciplined for an appointed time, should be restored to Paradise. This restoration will take place after the resurrection. For as an earthen vessel which has a flaw is broken up and formed anew by the potter, that it may be sound and perfect, so man is broken to pieces by the power of death, that he may be rendered *sound* in the resurrection; that is to say, without spot, just and immortal." In conformity to this view of Adam's original state and fall, Theophilus [1] states that God created him free.

Though I find nothing in the three books of Theophilus which has a direct bearing on the question of Justification; there is in the first book a passage, p. 74 D. deserving notice, in which he describes faith as the moving principle of human

---

[1] ἐλεύθερον γὰρ καὶ αὐτεξούσιον ἐποίησεν ὁ Θεὸς τὸν ἄνθρωπον, p 103 D. So also τὸν ἄνθρωπον κύριον ὄντα ἁμαρτῆσαι, L. 2. p 96 B.

conduct. With respect to the Divine Providence, Theophilus [1] says, that it may be traced in the provision made, that every kind of flesh should have its appropriate food. "The care of God," he says in [2] another place, "extends to the dead, as well as to the living."

Page 87. note 1. The expression διὰ τοῦ παρ' αὐτοῦ (τοῦ Θεοῦ) λόγου occurs repeatedly in Athenagoras, p. 5 C. 11 A. 12 D. 17 D. 34 D. In all these instances it is to be understood of the λόγος.

Page 90. Justin speaks of the renunciation of all worldly things, but not with any direct reference to the profession made in Baptism, p. 348 A. I find in Tatian no express reference either to Baptism or the Eucharist. A [3] passage has already been cited, in which he speaks of himself as "born anew according to the imitation of the Word."

Athenagoras is also silent respecting the Christian Sacraments. In defending the Christians against

---

[1] τήν τε πρόνοιαν ἣν ποιεῖται ὁ Θεὸς, ἑτοιμάζων τροφὴν πάσῃ σαρκί. L i. p 73 A. See also L. iii. p. 122 D. καὶ προνοίᾳ τὰ πάντα διοικεῖσθαι ἐπιστάμεθα.

[2] L. ii. p. 116 B.

[3] κἀγὼ κατὰ τὴν τοῦ λόγου μίμησιν ἀναγεννηθείς, p. 145 C. See note 28.

the charge of not offering sacrifices to the gods, he says, that [1] the best sacrifice is to know the true God, and to approach him with pure uplifted hands. He requires only a bloodless sacrifice, and a reasonable worship.

[2] Theophilus, on one occasion, says, that Christians are so called, because they are anointed with the oil of God; but whether he meant to allude to the practice of anointing as a part of the ceremony of Baptism, or, figuratively, to the unction of the Holy Spirit, is uncertain. [3] On another occasion he says, that God, in the work of creation, blessed the creatures inhabiting the waters, to show that hereafter all who come to the truth, and are re-

---

[1] ἀλλὰ θυσία αὐτῷ μεγίστη, ἢν γιγνώσκωμεν τίς ἐξέτεινε καὶ συνεσφαίρωσε τοὺς οὐρανοὺς—ὅταν—ἐπαίρωμεν ὁσίους χεῖρας αὐτῷ, ποίας ἔτι χρείαν ἑκατόμβης ἔχει ;——καίτοι προσφέρειν δέον ἀναίμακτον θυσίαν, καὶ τὴν λογικὴν προσάγειν λατρείαν. Legatio, p. 13. B C D.

[2] τοιγαροῦν ἡμεῖς τούτου εἵνεκεν καλούμεθα Χριστιανοί· ὅτι χριόμεθα ἔλαιον Θεοῦ, L. i. p. 77 C.

[3] ἔτι μὲν καὶ εὐλογήθη ὑπὸ τοῦ Θεοῦ τὰ ἐκ τῶν ὑδάτων γενόμενα, ὅπως ᾖ καὶ τοῦτο εἰς δεῖγμα τοῦ μέλλειν λαμβάνειν τοὺς ἀνθρώπους μετάνοιαν καὶ ἄφεσιν ἁμαρτιῶν διὰ ὕδατος καὶ λουτροῦ παλιγγενεσίας πάντας τοὺς προσιόντας τῇ ἀληθείᾳ καὶ ἀναγεννωμένους καὶ λαμβάνοντας εὐλογίαν παρὰ τοῦ Θεοῦ, L. ii. p. 95 B. Tertullian calls Christians Pisciculi : De Baptismo, c. 1. See my work on that Author, c. I. note 73. Theophilus has been supposed to allude to Baptism in the concluding words of the Third Book, ὅπως σχῇς σύμβολον καὶ ἀρραβῶνα τῆς ἀληθείας.

generated and receive a blessing from God, shall obtain repentance and remission of sins through water and the laver of regeneration. Theophilus [1] twice uses the word ἐξομολόγησις to express that confession of sin which originates in genuine repentance; but not with any reference to ecclesiastical discipline.

Page 97. note 1. In l. 2. p. 91 D. Theophilus says, ἔτι μὴν καὶ περὶ τῆς ἑβδόμης ἡμέρας, ἣν πάντες μὲν ἄνθρωποι ὀνομάζουσιν, οἱ δὲ πλείους ἀγνοοῦσιν ὅτι παρ' Ἑβραίοις ὃ καλεῖται σάββατον Ἑλληνιστὶ ἑρμηνεύεται ἑβδομάς· ἥτις εἰς πᾶν γένος ἀνθρώπων ὀνομάζεται μὲν, δι' ἣν δὲ αἰτίαν καλοῦσιν αὐτὴν οὐκ ἐπίστανται.

Page 100. Tatian, as we have seen, agrees with his master, Justin, in affirming that the soul is not immortal. "[2] The soul, O Grecians, is not immortal in itself, but mortal. It may, however, escape death. For, being ignorant of the truth, it dies and is dissolved together with the body; and rises again together with the body at the consummation of all things, suffering death by a punishment of eternal duration. On the other hand, having obtained the knowledge of God, it dies not, though it is dis-

---

[1] L. ii. p. 103 B. 105 C.
[2] p. 152 B. quoted in p. 184.

solved for a time. For in itself it is darkness, and there is no light in it." In a [1] subsequent passage he says, that " the soul is not simple, but complex,—being compound, so as to be visible through the body. For neither can it appear without the body; nor does the flesh rise again without the soul. Man is not, as some babblers affirm, a rational animal, capable of intelligence and knowledge. For irrational creatures will be shown to be, according to them, capable of intelligence and knowledge." On [2] another occasion he says, that the soul is the bond of (that which keeps together) the flesh; and that the flesh holds in the soul.

Viewing these passages in connexion with [3] others already quoted in this Chapter, we find that Tatian conceived man to consist of a body and soul. The soul is a portion of the Spirit pervading matter, and, consequently, not in itself immortal; and the union between the soul and body is dissolved by death. But [4] after the consummation of all things

---

[1] p. 153 D.
[2] δεσμὸς δὲ τῆς σαρκὸς ψυχὴ, σχετικὴ δὲ τῆς ψυχῆς ἡ σάρξ, p. 154 B. quoted in p. 187.
[3] p. 184—189.
[4] p. 145 D. We find ἐν ἡμέρᾳ συντελείας πυρὸς αἰωνίου βορᾷ παραδοθήσεται, p. 155 D. Tatian affirms that above the visible heavens exist the better ages, αἰῶνες οἱ κρείττονες, having no change of seasons, from which various diseases take their origin; but blessed with an uniform goodness of temperature, they enjoy

the body will rise again, and the soul be reunited to it; and the general judgment will take place. They who have during this life endeavoured to unite their souls to the Divine Spirit, will attain to an eternity of happiness; they who have allowed their souls to sink downwards, and to be occupied entirely with material things, will be doomed to an eternity of misery.

According [1] to Athenagoras, God made man of an immortal soul and a body; and gave him intelligence, and a law implanted in his nature. If, [2] however, the soul unites itself to the Spirit pervading matter, and looks not upwards to the heavens and to their Creator, but downwards to the earth, as if it was mere flesh and blood, it ceases to be a pure Spirit. The opinions of [3] Athenagoras,

perpetual day, and light inaccessible to men who dwell here below. p. 159 A. In contradistinction from those better ages, he calls the present state of things τοὺς καθ' ἡμᾶς αἰῶνας, p. 145 D.

[1] καθ' ἣν ἐποίησεν ἄνθρωπον ἐκ ψυχῆς ἀθανάτου καὶ σώματος, νοῦν τε συγκατεσκεύασεν αὐτῷ καὶ νόμον ἔμφυτον, κ. τ. ἑ. De Mort. Res. p. 54 A. Compare Legatio, p. 31 A.

[2] πάσχει δὲ τοῦτο ψυχὴ μάλιστα τοῦ ὑλικοῦ προσλαβοῦσα καὶ ἐπισυγκραθεῖσα πνεύματος, οὐ πρὸς τὰ οὐράνια καὶ τὸν τούτων ποιητὴν, ἀλλὰ κάτω πρὸς τὰ ἐπίγεια βλέπουσα καθολικῶς (εἰς γῆν f. om.) ὡς μόνον αἷμα καὶ σὰρξ, οὐκέτι πνεῦμα καθαρὸν γιγνομένη. Legatio, p. 30 C.

[3] In the Legatio, Athenagoras says, that after death the good will remain with God, exempt from change and suffering as to their soul; not as flesh, though they will have flesh, but as an

respecting the resurrection of the body, are detailed in the Tract, which he wrote expressly on that subject. In it may be found nearly all the arguments which human reason has been able to advance in support of the doctrine.

We have [1] seen that Theophilus describes Adam as neither mortal nor immortal, when created; but capable of either condition. In order [2] to obtain immortality, man must believe in God and fear him. For God will raise up his flesh in a state of immortality together with his soul; and, being made immortal, he will see God perfectly. [3] Theophilus speaks of the punishment to be undergone by the wicked hereafter as eternal. We [4] have remarked that, according to Theophilus, man will after the resurrection be restored to Paradise, which [5] he describes as situated on this earth, in the eastern

---

heavenly Spirit, p. 35 D. See also p 39 B. C. where he intimates an intention of writing expressly on the Resurrection of the Body.

[1] p. 193. He says also, that the majority concluded the soul to be immortal, because God is said in Scripture to have breathed into Adam's nostrils the breath of life, and thus to have made him a living soul, L. ii. p. 97 C.

[2] L. i. p. 74 C. In p. 77 D. Theophilus urges some of the common arguments, in order to show that the resurrection of the body is probable. See also L. ii. p. 93 B. 94 D.

[3] L. i. p. 79 A. C. L. ii. p. 110 D.

[4] p. 192.

[5] Compare p. 97 D. with p. 101 B.

parts, refulgent with light, and abounding in beautiful plants.

Page 105. In stating Tatian's notions respecting the fall of man, we [1] quoted a passage in which it is said, that, before the creation of man, the Λόγος created Angels, who were endowed with freedom; that one of these Angels, to whom Tatian applies the epithet πρωτόγονος, being more [2] subtle than the rest, rebelled against the Divine Law, and persuaded others to join him in his revolt, and to proclaim him as a God. That, in consequence of this revolt, he and his followers were excluded from the Divine intercourse, and became a host of Dæmons, he being their chief. They [3] taught men to believe that all events happened by a fatal necessity, being dependent upon the position of the stars, of which they drew schemes. For, when expelled from heaven, they sojourned among the

---

[1] p. 182.
[2] The Greek word is φρονιμώτερος (φρονιμώτατος, in the Septuagint). The serpent is described in Genesis, c. iii. as more subtle than any beast of the field.
[3] διάγραμμα γὰρ αὐτοῖς ἀστροθεσίας ἀναδείξαντες, ὥσπερ οἱ τοῖς κύβοις παίζοντες, τὴν εἱμαρμένην εἰσηγήσαντο λίαν ἄδικον, p. 147 A. So p 148 B. τοιοῦτοί τινες εἰσὶν οἱ δαίμονες, οὗτοι οἳ τὴν εἱμαρμένην ὥρισαν· στοιχείωσις δὲ αὐτοῖς ἡ ζώωσις ἦν, κ. τ. ἑ. The word στοιχείωσις is used with reference to the artifices of the Dæmons, first in producing diseases, and afterwards in removing them, p. 156 B Saturn and the other planets and stars are called τῆς εἱμαρμένης οἰκονόμοι, p. 149 B. 150 A.

different animals which either creep on the earth, or swim in the waters, or range the mountains; and in order that they might be thought still to dwell in heaven, and might give a specious appearance to their irrational life, they raised the creatures among which they lived, to heaven, and named the constellations after them. Hence, the names of the signs of the Zodiack.

In a [1] subsequent passage Tatian says, " The Dæmons (so you call them), taking their composition from matter, and having the Spirit which is in it, became intemperate and luxurious; some of them turning to the purer, some to the inferior portions of matter, and framing their conduct accordingly. These, O Greeks, you worship, though formed out of matter, and having deviated far from their appointed and regular course. For the above-mentioned (Dæmons) turning aside through their folly to vain-glory, and casting off all control, desired to steal the honours of Divinity—and the Lord of the universe has permitted them to revel

---

[1] p. 151 C Tatian, as we have seen, held that the ἄγγελος πρωτόγονος and his followers, after their revolt, became Dæmons. He now appears to be speaking of their subsequent condition. when they had departed still further from their allegiance to God. The Paris Editors are careful to guard the readers of Tatian against what they term his error, in supposing that Dæmons are material. Tatian applies the name δαίμονες to the Heathen Gods, p. 165 A.

(in their rebellion) until the world shall come to an end, and be dissolved, and the Judge shall appear, and all men, who, notwithstanding the opposition of the Dæmons, aspire to the knowledge of the perfect God, shall receive through their trials a more perfect testimony in the day of judgment."

But though [1] the Dæmons are material, they have not flesh. Their composition is spiritual, like that of fire or air. Their bodies, consequently, cannot be seen, excepting by those who are guarded by the Spirit of God: those who are only animal (οἱ ψυχικοί) cannot see them.—On this account, also, the substance of Dæmons has no place of repentance; for they are the brightness (ἀπαυγάσματα) of matter and evil—and the design of matter is always to bring the soul within its power. Hence, the sole object of the Dæmons is to lead men away from the truth. With this view they [2] invented

---

[1] p. 154 C. Tatian afterwards says, that the Dæmons occasionally exhibited themselves to the ψυχικοί, p. 155 B.

[2] p. 152 B Compare p. 153 B. where Tatian, after he has observed that the Dæmons deceive solitary (deserted by the diviner Spirit) souls by visions, adds that, "as they have not flesh, they do not easily die; but even while living they work the works of death, themselves dying as often as they discipline their followers in sin; so that what is peculiar to them at present, viz. that they do not die like men will, when they come to be punished, be the cause of their dying through all eternity. The shortness of man's existence curtails his power of transgression; whereas, the Dæmons, whose existence is infinite, contract an

the Arts of Divination, and set up the Oracles. They [1] employ every artifice to prevent the soul from rising upwards, and pursuing its way to Heaven. If [2] they possessed the power, they would drag down the Heavens together with the rest of the creation; but, as they cannot effect this, they are continually—by means of the inferior matter—warring against the matter which is similar to themselves. Successfully to resist them, we must put on the breast-plate of the Heavenly Spirit. [3] One great object of the Dæmons is, to persuade man that whatever happens to him, either of good or evil, whether he falls sick or recovers from sickness, is owing to their agency. To this end they invented amulets, philters, and charms, in order that man might be induced to trust to them, or, at least, to the properties of matter, rather than to his Creator.

On [4] one occasion Tatian combats the notion that the Dæmons are the souls of dead men. "For how," he asks, "can souls become efficient agents

---

infinite guilt." I am not sure that I understand the author's meaning in this passage, in which he seems strangely to confound natural with spiritual death: but I conceive it to be, that no change can take place in the condition of Dæmons, because they are not subject to death, as men are; they go on sinning to eternity—a state which he calls eternal death.

[1] p. 155 A.   [2] p. 155 C.   [3] p. 155 C.
[4] p. 154 D. The passage is corrupt, but the meaning clear.

after death? unless we suppose that man, after death, can acquire greater powers of action than he possessed while living."

We have [1] seen that Athenagoras speaks of Angels to whom God assigned the office of watching over the well-being of the Universe. In a subsequent [2] passage, having recited the opinions of the Gentile Philosophers respecting Dæmons, he goes on to explain his own views of the subject. He says, that " Christians, in addition to the Father, the Son his Word, and the Holy Spirit, acknowledge other powers, conversant about matter and pervading it, one of whom is opposed to God; not as strife is to friendship in the system of Empedocles, or night to day in the phænomena of nature (since any thing actually opposed to God must cease to exist, its very composition being dissolved by the power and force of God); but because to the goodness of God, which is his inseparable attribute, is opposed the Spirit conversant with matter; created indeed by God, as the other Angels were created by him, and entrusted with the administration of matter and its forms. For the Angels were created

---

[1] p. 190. See p. 11 A.
[2] Legatio, p. 27 A. I have given the sense rather than a literal translation of the passage.

by God with reference to his various works; that, as God exercised a *general* Providence over the Universe, they might exercise a *particular* Providence over the different parts assigned them. But, as in the case of men who are free to choose virtue and vice (since you would neither honour the good nor punish the bad, unless virtue and vice were in their own power) some are found faithful, some unfaithful, in that with which they are entrusted; so of the Angels, some continued such as they were created by God, fulfilling the ends for which he created and designed them; but others abused both their nature and the power committed to them; among them the Ruler of matter and its forms, and others who were placed immediately around this first firmament; *they* smitten with the desire of women, and yielding to carnal lusts; *he* becoming negligent and faithless about the administration of that with which he was entrusted. From the intercourse of the Angels with women sprang those who are called giants. The Angels, therefore, who were expelled from Heaven, hovering about the air and earth, and no longer able to elevate themselves to heavenly things; and the souls of the giants, who are the Dæmons, wandering about the world, excite motions corresponding, some to the substances which the Dæmons assumed, others to the desires which the Angels felt. But the Ruler of matter, as may be seen from the events which happen, opposes himself in his whole conduct to the goodness of God. So much were even the Gentiles struck with the confusion apparent throughout the world, that they doubted whether it was under the direction of Providence; and Aristotle determined that the parts below the Heavens were not. Whereas the general Providence of God extends alike to all things; and each particular thing follows its own particular law; but the motions and influences of the Dæmons introduce these disorders, impelling individuals and nations, in part and generally, from within and from without, according to the proportion subsisting between matter and the affection to divine things. On which account, some men of no small repute thought that the Universe was not constituted with any order, but was driven about by irrational chance; being ignorant that, with reference to the composition of the Universe, nothing is without its fixed object, or is neglected, and that there is a reason for the creation of each part; so that it never transgresses its appointed order." Then follows a passage [1] already quoted, relating to the original constitution of man: after which, Athenagoras adds, " The powers which draw men towards idols are the abovementioned Dæmons, who settle upon the victims,

[1] p. 190.

and suck the blood; but the gods, in whom the multitude delights, and whose names are given to the statues, were [1] men; as we may know from their respective histories." He [2] then states that the Dæmons in reality exert the powers which are ascribed by the vulgar to the idols; and goes on to explain the mode in which men are perverted to the worship of idols. His notion is, that, "the irrational and visionary movements of the soul with respect to opinions, call up different idols; sometimes extracting them out of matter; sometimes framing and begetting them to themselves. And the soul is principally subject to this affection, when it lays hold of, and is mixed up with, the material spirit; not looking upwards to heavenly things and to their Maker, but downwards entirely to the earth, as if it were only flesh and blood, and no longer a pure spirit. These irrational and visionary movements of the soul beget imaginations leading to a mad desire of idols. But when the tender and flexible soul, untaught, and unacquainted with

---

[1] Athenagoras proves this at great length, p. 31 A.

[2] p. 30 C. Athenagoras seems in this passage to use the word εἴδωλον ambiguously; either to signify an image presented to the mind, or a material object of worship. Concerning the powers exerted by the idols, τὰς εἰδώλων ἐνεργείας, see p. 17 C. 25 A. where Athenagoras admits that some wonders are wrought by the idols; but says that they ought not to be ascribed to the gods whose names the idols bear.

sound reasonings, having never contemplated the truth, or comprehended in its thought the Father and Maker of the Universe, receives the impression of these false opinions; the Dæmons, who hover about matter, sucking up the steam and blood of the victims, laying hold, in order to deceive man, of these movements of the souls of the multitude which lead to falsehood, cause images to flow into them, as if proceeding from the idols and images, the names of which they have appropriated to themselves. Thus, too, the Dæmons obtain the credit of those rational movements of the soul, which belong to it as immortal, when it either foretells the future, or remedies the present."

[1] Theophilus appears to have written a work, in which he had said much respecting Satan, whom he describes as still working in men, and calls a Dæmon and Dragon; assigning as the reason for this latter name, that he [2] was a fugitive from God; for he was originally an Angel. Speaking of the Heathen poets, Theophilus says, [3] that they were inspired by Dæmons: and in proof of this assertion states that, when men under the influence of a Dæmoniacal possession were exorcised in the name of the true

---

[1] L. ii. p. 104 D.
[2] διὰ τὸ ἀποδεδρακέναι αὐτὸν ἀπὸ τοῦ Θεοῦ, p. 104 D.
[3] L. ii. p. 87 C.

God, the Spirits which seduced them confessed themselves to be Dæmons.

With respect to the gods of the Heathen, Theophilus [1] affirms repeatedly, that they were dead men. He calls them [2] also Dæmons, impure Dæmons; whence we may infer, that he agreed with Athenagoras in thinking, though he does not expressly say so, that the Dæmons were the instigators of idolatry, and reaped the advantage of the worship which they caused to be paid to the statues of dead men.

P. 114. Tatian, speaking in his own person, [3] thus describes the moral character of the Christians of his day: "I wish not to reign; I wish not to be rich; I avoid military office; I abhor fornication; I will not make long voyages through the insatiate desire of gain; I contend not at games in order to obtain a crown; I am far removed from the mad love of glory; I despise death; I am superior to every kind of disease; my soul is not consumed by grief. If I am a slave, I submit to my servitude; if I am free, I pride not myself in

---

[1] L. i. p. 75 A 76 A.   L. ii. p. 80 D.   86 B.   110 A.
[2] L. i. p. 76 C.   L. iii p. 118 A.
[3] p. 150 B.   Compare p. 162 D.

my noble birth. I see one sun common to all; I see one death common to all, whether they live in pleasure or in want."

In a [1] subsequent passage Tatian says, "With us there is no desire of vain-glory, and we consequently affect not a variety of doctrines; but separated from the vulgar and earthly sentiment, and obeying the precepts of God, and following the law of the father of incorruption, we renounce all that rests on human opinion. Not only do the rich learn philosophy, but the [2] poor also enjoy instruction gratis; for that which comes from God cannot be paid for by any worldly compensation. Thus we receive all who wish to hear, even though they are old women or children. In a word, all ages receive honour with us; but all lasciviousness is far removed from us." Speaking of his own conversion to Christianity, Tatian [3] says, that "observing the trifling questions on which the Gentiles, who affected the character of wisdom, employed themselves; their ignorance of all that really deserved to be known; their presumption; their pride; the variety of opinions which prevailed among them even on the nature of virtue and vice, some holding that to be

---

[1] p. 167 A.
[2] See p. 168 C. Compare p. 14, Note 2.
[3] p. 163 C. to 165 C.

honorable which others deemed infamous—whereas the nature of virtue must be always the same;—observing all these things, and having been initiated into their mysteries, and ascertained the flagitious character of their rites, he considered with himself in what manner he could arrive at the truth. While he was thus considering, he met with certain barbarous writings, ancient in comparison with the dogmas of the Greeks; divine in comparison with their error. To these he gave his assent, moved by the unpretending character of the diction; the simplicity of the speakers; the mode in which the work of creation was rendered easy of comprehension; the prediction of future events; the excellence of the precepts; and the doctrine of the subjection of the Universe to one God."

As Tatian [1] exposes at some length what he deems the abominations of the theatrical exhibitions, and of the public games, we may conclude that he did not deem it consistent with the profession of Christianity to attend them.

Athenagoras, having recited some of the moral precepts delivered by our Saviour, in order to explain to the emperors the real character of Christ-

---

[1] p. 160 D. to 162 B.

ianity, ¹ asks, "Who among those, who analyze syllogisms, and resolve ambiguities, and explain etymologies, and define homonymes and synonymes, and categories, and axioms, and the subject, and the predicate, and profess that by such instructions they can make their hearers happy—who among them are so purified in their souls, as, instead of hating, to love their enemies; as, instead of doing that which is even deemed a mark of the greatest moderation—of retorting evil language—to bless their calumniators, and even to pray for those who are laying snares against their life? The Heathen teachers of knowledge, on the contrary, are ever forming some forbidden scheme against their adversaries, and desiring to do them injury; ² making their profession a mere flourish of words, and not a rule of practice. But among us you may find illiterate persons, and artisans, and old women, who, if they cannot show the benefits resulting from their profession by their words, show it by practice. For they do not commit words to

¹ Legatio, p. 11 C.
² τέχνην λόγων, καὶ οὐκ ἐπίδειξιν ἔργων, τὸ πρᾶγμα πεποιημένοι. So p. 37 A. οὐ γὰρ μελέτῃ λόγων, ἀλλ' ἐπιδείξει καὶ διδασκαλίᾳ ἔργων, τὰ ἡμέτερα. Quotus enim quisque Philosophorum invenitur, qui sit ita moratus, ita animo ac vita constitutus, ut ratio postulat? qui disciplinam suam, non ostentationem scientiæ, sed legem vitæ putet? qui obtemperet ipse sibi, ac decretis suis pareat? Cicero Tusc II. c. 4 or 12.

memory, but show forth good deeds:—when struck, they strike not again—when robbed, they have not recourse to the law—they give to those who ask—and love their neighbours as themselves. Is it likely that we should thus purify ourselves, unless we believed that God presided over the human race? No one can say so. [1] But because we are persuaded that we shall render an account of our present life to the God who made both us and the world, we choose the moderate and benevolent, and (in human estimation) despised course of life; thinking that even if we lose our lives, we cannot suffer any evil *here*, to be compared with the reward which we shall receive *hereafter* from the great Judge, on account of our gentle and benevolent and temperate behaviour." In a subsequent [2] passage, Athenagoras states that, agreeably to the injunctions of their blessed Master, Christians are pure, not only in their actions and their words, but even in their thoughts; knowing that the eye of God is ever over them, and that being himself wholly light, he looks into the very heart.

He alleges [3] as a proof that the Christians were not guilty of the crimes imputed to them, that no

---

[1] The same argument is again urged, p. 35 C.
[2] p. 35 C 36 A.
[3] p. 38 B.

one of their slaves, who must have been privy to the fact, had ever been brought forward to give evidence against them; or had even laid such crimes falsely to their charge. "For how," he says, "can any one accuse of homicide, or of eating human flesh, those who cannot bear to be present even at the execution of a person justly condemned? While others rush with eagerness to behold the combats of the gladiators, and the conflicts with wild beasts, we renounce such sights; thinking that there is little difference between witnessing and committing homicide. Can we then commit murder, who will not even look upon it, lest we should bring upon ourselves guilt and pollution?" Athenagoras then goes on to say, that the Christians would neither use medicines in order to procure abortions, nor expose their offspring.

Having stated [1] that the purity of the Christians extended not only to their actions, but also to their desires and thoughts, he adds, that they regarded the younger members of the community as their children; those of their own age as brothers and sisters; those advanced in years as their parents. "Having then," he proceeds, "the hope of eternal life, we despise the things of this life, and all in

[1] p. 36 A.

which the soul takes pleasure. Each of us confines himself to his own wife; and marries not to satisfy desire, but to beget children. Many among us, both men and women, have grown old in a state of celibacy, through the hope that they shall thereby be more closely united to God. But if the condition of virgins and eunuchs is more acceptable to God; and even thoughts and desires exclude us from his presence: surely we shall renounce the act, when we shun the very wish. For our profession consists not in well-composed sentences, but in practice. Either we remain as we were born, or we contract one marriage; for a second marriage is a decorous adultery. *For whoever,* he (Christ) says, *puts away his wife and marries another, commits adultery;* neither allowing us to put away our wives, nor to marry again. For he who cuts himself off from his first wife, even though she be dead, is a concealed adulterer; transgressing the hand (work) of God in the creation (for God in the beginning created one man and one woman), and dissolving the union of the flesh." [1] M. Barbeyrac has animadverted, and not without reason, upon the preference ascribed to a life of celibacy in the above passage; upon the restriction of the use of marriage to the sole object of having children; and

---

[1] Traité de la Morale des Pères, c. 4. § 6

upon the condemnation pronounced against second marriages. Nothing indeed can be more forced than the application of the texts of Scripture, or more inconclusive than the reasoning.

Theophilus pursues the same course of argument as Athenagoras, in defending the Christians against the calumnious accusations of their adversaries. Having recited the precepts of the Gospel, respecting purity of thought and wish, universal benevolence, humility, obedience to magistrates, he [1] asks, " Can they who learn such precepts live like brute beasts, or indulge in unnatural lusts, or eat human flesh? they who are not permitted even to behold the combats of the gladiators, lest they should become, as it were, accessaries to murder; they who are not permitted to frequent the theatres, lest their eyes and ears should be polluted by the horrible and vicious stories which form the subjects of the dramatic exhibitions? Far be the thought of doing such acts from Christians, who are chaste, temperate, who confine themselves to one wife—among whom purity is cultivated, injustice and sin are extirpated, justice and law are observed, piety is practised, God is confessed, truth sits in judgment, grace and peace act as guardians and pro-

[1] L. III. p. 126 D.

tectors, the Holy Word is the guide, Wisdom the teacher, ¹ the true life the director, God the king."

Theophilus does not appear to have entertained the exaggerated notion of the merit of celibacy which we have remarked in Athenagoras. ² Speaking of what he terms the prophecy of Adam, in Genesis ii. *Therefore shall a man leave his father and his mother, and shall cleave unto his wife; and they shall be one flesh,* he says, that it was accomplished in the conduct of the Christians. " For who," he asks, " being lawfully married, does not (comparatively) despise his father, and mother, and kindred, and relations—cleaving and united to his wife, and concentrating his affections in her? so that many have not refused to encounter death for the sake of their wives." ³ Theophilus describes himself as originally a Gentile; and converted to Christianity by reading the Sacred Writings of the Prophets, and observing how events corresponded to their predictions.

P. 121. On the subject of the subsistence of miraculous powers in the Church, most of my readers will

---

¹ I entertain doubts about the words ζωὴ βραβεύει in the Text; if they are not an interpolation, ζωὴ must refer to the title which our Saviour gives himself, John xi. 25 xiv. 6.
² L ii. p. 104 C
³ L i. p. 78 D. L. ii. p. 88 A.

remember the remarks of [1] Gibbon on the reply made by Theophilus, when challenged by Autolycus to point out a single person who had been raised from the dead. Theophilus answers, that there is no great merit in believing what we see; that Autolycus, who believed that Hercules, who was burned, and Æsculapius, who was killed by a thunder-bolt, still lived, was not very consistent in doubting the assertions of God himself in Scripture, respecting the resurrection of the dead; that perhaps, if his demand was satisfied, he would still remain incredulous; that the natural world supplies many analogies from which we may infer that the dead will rise. But Theophilus certainly does not accept the challenge of Autolycus; he does not even say that he himself knew an instance in which a dead man had been raised. Having [2] elsewhere stated my opinion respecting the date of the cessation of miraculous powers in the Church, I shall now say nothing further on the subject.

P. 125. Theophilus opposes ἐκκλησίας ἁγίας to αἱρέσεις, L. 2. p. 94 A.

---

[1] Chapter xv. p. 476 Quarto Ed. Autolycus does not promise, on the production of a person so raised, *to embrace Christianity*, but to believe in the resurrection of the dead, L. ii. p. 77 C.

[2] In my Work on Tertullian, p. 100

P. 129. Justin speaks of Damascus and Rama as situated in Arabia, Dial. p. 305 A. 304 D.

Page 130. Tatian [1] speaks as if Moses was considered by some to be contemporary with Inachus; and says, that in that case he lived 400 years before the Trojan war. The Sibyl is also [2] mentioned as more ancient than Homer.

The verses of the Sibyl are [3] once quoted by Athenagoras, who says, that Plato had mentioned her. Theophilus gives long [4] extracts from the verses of the Sibyl, and names [5] her together with the Prophets.

According to Theophilus, [6] Moses lived 900 or 1000 years before the Trojan war. He says [7] also

[1] p. 172 C.   [2] p. 173 C.
[3] Legatio, p. 33 D. See the Hortatory Address to the Greeks, p 16 D.
[4] L. ii. p. 81 B. 88 A. 107 C. 112 A.
[5] τοίνυν Σίβυλλα καὶ οἱ λοιποὶ προφῆται, p. 116 A.
[6] L. iii. p. 131 C.
[7] L. ii. p. 106 D. In L. iii. p. 129 B. he assigns the reason why Noah was so called, ὡς Νῶε, καταγγέλλων τοῖς τότε ἀνθρώποις μέλλειν κατακλυσμὸν ἔσεσθαι, προεφήτευσεν αὐτοῖς λέγων, δεῦτε, καλεῖ ὑμᾶς ὁ Θεὸς εἰς μετάνοιαν, διὸ οἰκείως Δευκαλίων ἐκλήθη. He had previously said, ὑπὸ τοῦ Νῶε Ἑβραιστὶ, ὃς διερμηνεύεται τῇ Ἑλλάδι γλώσσῃ ἀνάπαυσις In l. 2, p. 108, C. we find the following derivation of the word Ἰερουσαλήμ. κατὰ δὲ τὸν αὐτὸν καιρὸν ἐγένετο βασιλεὺς δίκαιος, ὀνόματι Μελχισεδὲχ,

that, according to some, Deucalion was the same as Noah. We have seen that he [1] speaks of the prophecy of Adam.

The author of the Hortatory Address to the Greeks [2] speaks of Moses as the first Prophet and legislator, Ἄρξομαι τοίνυν ἀπὸ τοῦ πρώτου παρ' ἡμῖν προφήτου τε καὶ νομοθέτου Μωσέως.

Page 147. We find in Athenagoras [3] a passage, which appears to be meant for a quotation from the New Testament, but is not found in our present books. [4] Lardner says, that " there is no necessity of supposing that Athenagoras ascribes them (the words) to Christ, or that he took them out of any

---

ἐν πόλει Σαλὴμ, τῇ νῦν Ἱεροσόλυμα. (f. Ἱερουσαλήμ.) οὗτος ἱερεὺς ἐγένετο πρῶτος πάντων ἱερέων τοῦ Θεοῦ τοῦ ὑψίστου· ἀπὸ τούτου ἡ πόλις ὠνομάσθη Ἱερουσαλὴμ, ἡ προειρημένη Ἱεροσόλυμα.

[1] p. 217. [2] p. 9

[3] πάλιν ἡμῖν λέγοντος τοῦ λόγου, ἐάν τις διὰ τοῦτο ἐκ δευτέρου καταφιλήσῃ ὅτι ἤρεσεν αὐτῷ· καὶ ἐπιφέροντος, οὕτως οὖν ἀκριβώσασθαι τὸ φίλημα, μᾶλλον δὲ τὸ προσκύνημα, δεῖ· ὡς, εἴ που μικρὸν τῇ διανοίᾳ παραθολωθείη, ἔξω ἡμᾶς τῆς αἰωνίου τιθέντος ζωῆς, Legatio, p. 36 C. The Benedictine Editors refer to Clemens Alexandrinus, Pæd, L iii p. 301. Ed. Potter

[4] Credibility, c. 18. §. 20   Lardner refers to Jones on the Canon, vol. i. p. 551. Le Nourry doubts whether Athenagoras quoted the Nazarene Gospel; or gave the sense, instead of the precise words of Scripture, p. 487. Tatian speaks of αἱ θειότεραι ἑρμήνειαι, p. 151 C.; and of himself as θειοτέρας τινὸς ἐκφωνήσεως λόγῳ καταχρωμένου, p. 152 A

copies of our Gospels, or from any Apocryphal Gospel. They may be as well cited from some Christian writer, whom Athenagoras thought to have expressed himself upon this subject agreeably to the strict doctrine of Christ delivered in the Gospels." I must confess, that I am not satisfied with this solution,—though I cannot suggest a better.

THE END